p99
Bellr not
present at
torture of two
elves Emilia's
absence in
araucana

M Ferguson

very
rich references
in Ital German
yes English, Spanish
French [F? ? - 126
199 vic transform
p 84 a problem

Kallendorf
edited Virgil
the classical
Heritage'
see 105

105 takes someone's
view, then undermines
it - cf P 45 + 71
assumes sh'
read V w/o
intermediaries
117

critical
ambition - k
'solve' problem
in detering
poems ideology
by 'a new kind
of allusion'

"pessimism"
oddly tied
to "realism"
adaptive &
even progress (184
/85)

CLASSICAL PRESENCES

General Editors

Lorna Hardwick   James I. Porter

CLASSICAL PRESENCES

The texts, ideas, images, and material culture of ancient Greece and Rome have always been crucial to attempts to appropriate the past in order to authenticate the present. They underlie the mapping of change and the assertion and challenging of values and identities, old and new. Classical Presences brings the latest scholarship to bear on the contexts, theory, and practice of such use, and abuse, of the classical past.

The Other Virgil

'Pessimistic' Readings of the Aeneid *in Early Modern Culture*

CRAIG KALLENDORF

OXFORD

UNIVERSITY PRESS

OXFORD
UNIVERSITY PRESS

Great Clarendon Street, Oxford OX2 6DP

Oxford University Press is a department of the University of Oxford.
It furthers the University's objective of excellence in research, scholarship,
and education by publishing worldwide in

Oxford New York

Auckland Cape Town Dar es Salaam Hong Kong Karachi
Kuala Lumpur Madrid Melbourne Mexico City Nairobi
New Delhi Shanghai Taipei Toronto

With offices in

Argentina Austria Brazil Chile Czech Republic France Greece
Guatemala Hungary Italy Japan Poland Portugal Singapore
South Korea Switzerland Thailand Turkey Ukraine Vietnam

Oxford is a registered trade mark of Oxford University Press
in the UK and in certain other countries

Published in the United States
by Oxford University Press Inc., New York

British Library Cataloguing in Publication Data

Data available

Library of Congress Cataloging in Publication Data

Data available

Typeset by SPI Publisher Services, Pondicherry, India
Printed in Great Britain
on acid-free paper by
Biddles Ltd., King's Lynn, Norfolk

ISBN 978–0–19–921236–1

1 3 5 7 9 10 8 6 4 2

Preface

This book, like all other scholarly projects, is a participant in a larger conversation, and I think it would be helpful to place what I have written into the particular dialogue that generated it right away. The focus of the book is Virgil's *Aeneid*, the epic poem about the establishment of Rome that served as a foundation for Roman civilization and for the succession of cultures that defined themselves in relation to their classical origins. After the fall of Troy, Aeneas leads a group of survivors across the Mediterranean to Italy, where he founds the city that will eventually rule the world. Along the way he overcomes a series of obstacles and in the process learns a good deal about what it means to be a leader. As Aeneas lands in Italy and conquers its indigenous inhabitants, he articulates more and more successfully the values that would come to be associated with imperial Rome, until in the final scene of the poem he slays Turnus, the enemy leader, and removes the last obstacle to Roman power and glory. By this point he has overcome the forces of *furor* ('rage') and *ira* ('anger'), both within himself and as represented by the people who oppose him, so that he successfully embodies *pietas*, that particularly Roman virtue that embraces one's duties to God, country, and family. This approach is fundamentally optimistic, with Aeneas serving as the ideal hero of ancient Rome, the *Aeneid* celebrating the achievements of Augustus and his age, and the poem enduring as a monument to the values of order and civilization.

This is the basic interpretation of the poem that predominated through the middle of the last century, as it was set forth by Heinze, nuanced by Pöschl, and disseminated in the English-speaking world by Eliot.[1] But after the Second World War, a group of Anglophone

---

[1] R. Heinze, *Vergils epische Technik* (Leipzig: B. G. Teubner, 1903), tr. *Virgil's Epic Technique*, tr. Hazel and David Harvey and Fred Robertson (Berkeley-Los Angeles: Univ. of California Press, 1993); T. S. Eliot, *What Is a Classic?* (London: Faber & Faber, 1945); V. Pöschl, *Die Dichtkunst Vergils: Bild und Symbol in der Aeneis* (Innsbruck: Margareta Friedrich Rohrer, 1950); *The Art of Vergil*, tr. G. Seligson (Ann Arbor: Univ. of Michigan Press, 1962); see also A. Wlosok, 'Vergil in der neueren Forschung', *Gymnasium*, 80 (1973), 129–51; and S. J. Harrison, 'Some Views of the *Aeneid* in the

Preface

scholars centred at Harvard and Oxford began listening more sympathetically to what have come to be called the 'further voices' in the
Aeneid—not the voice of Aeneas as the prototype of Roman imperialism, but the voices of those who stand in opposition to him: Dido,
the Carthaginian queen whose love is sacrificed to Aeneas's higher
mission; Turnus, the Italian prince who falls before Aeneas while
trying to defend his country against the Trojan invaders; and so
forth. These scholars also pointed out that in the course of the
poem, Aeneas himself sometimes speaks in one of these further
voices. That is, Aeneas himself is often inconsistent in the set of values
he articulates, especially in the last scene of the poem, which was
reinterpreted as a key failure in which Aeneas surrenders to the very
voices of barbarism and fury within himself that he had struggled
throughout the poem to suppress. Within the narrative structure of
the poem, these other voices also project worthy values, and this new
school of criticism, which has challenged the robust optimism of the
traditional approach, has helped us see what was sacrificed in pursuit
of Rome and the civilization it engendered.[2]

Twentieth Century', in Harrison (ed.), *Oxford Readings in Vergil's Aeneid* (Oxford:
Clarendon Press, 1990), 1–20. 20th-cent. German scholarship that retains the key
features of the traditional approach may be exemplified by K. Büchner, *Der Schicksal-
gedanke bei Vergil* (Freiburg im Breisgau: Novalis-Verlag, 1946), P. *Vergilius Maro, der
Dichter der Römer* (Stuttgart: A. Druckenmüller, 1955), and *Humanitas Romana*
(Heidelberg: C. Winter, 1957), 147–75; the essays of F. Klingner collected in *Römische
Geisteswelt* (Munich: H. Rinn, 1961), 239–311, 600–30, and his *Virgil: Bucolica,
Georgica, Aeneis* (Zurich and Stuttgart: Artemis Verlag, 1967); and V. Buchheit, *Vergil
über die Sendung Roms. Untersuchungen zum Bellum Poenicum und zur Aeneis, Gym-
nasium* Beiheft, 3 (Heidelberg, 1963). Influential English-language studies from a
similar perspective include Brooks Otis, *Virgil: A Study in Civilized Poetry* (Norman,
Okla.: Univ. of Oklahoma Press, 1995; repr. of Oxford, 1964 edn.); and P. Hardie,
Virgil's Aeneid: Cosmos and Imperium (Oxford: Clarendon Press, 1986).

   [2] The generally cited, seminal works are Robert A. Brooks, '*Discolor Aura*: Reflec-
tions on the Golden Bough', *American Journal of Philology*, 74 (1953), 260–80; Adam
Parry, 'The Two Voices of Virgil's *Aeneid*', *Arion*, 2 (1963), 66–80, repr. in *The
Language of Achilles and Other Papers* (Oxford: Clarendon Press, 1989), 78–96;
Wendell Clausen, 'An Interpretation of the *Aeneid*', *Harvard Studies in Classical
Philology*, 68 (1964), 139–47 (written in 1949); and Michael C. J. Putnam, *The Poetry
of the Aeneid: Four Studies in Imaginative Unity and Design* (Cambridge, Mass.:
Harvard Univ. Press, 1965). This approach has been surveyed by F. Serpa, *Il punto
su Virgilio* (Bari: Laterza, 1987), 76–88, and given an elegant recasting by Steven
Shankman, 'The Ambivalence of the *Aeneid* and the Ecumenic Age', in *In Search of
the Classic: Reconsidering the Greco-Roman Tradition, Homer to Valéry and Beyond*
(University Park, Penn.: Pennsylvania State Univ. Press, 1994), 217–45.

In the last decades of the twentieth century, the adherents of the traditional approach came to be called 'optimists' and those of the second approach 'pessimists' or 'members of the Harvard school'.[3] As scholars like Karl Galinsky have been pointing out recently, there are dangers to easy dichotomies like this.[4] For one thing, no responsible 'optimist' would deny that Aeneas makes mistakes in at least the early parts of the poem, and no responsible 'pessimist' would argue that what was lost in founding Rome exceeds what was gained. That said, I would suggest that there is still a very real difference in emphasis, even if the difference is more a matter of shades of grey than black versus white. I shall therefore retain the terms but place them within quotation marks to remind the reader that caution must be exercised in using them.

A more fundamental problem has arisen from the claim that the second approach, the 'pessimistic' one, is ahistorical. It entered modern classical scholarship in its fully articulated form after the Second World War, and this has led Karl Galinsky, again, to argue that ancient criticism lacks the kind of hesitation about Aeneas and his actions that the 'pessimists' believe they see,[5] with the assumption being that they are reading their own concerns back into Virgil's text. As S. J. Harrison puts it, 'For an outside observer, it is difficult to separate such an interpretation from the characteristic concerns of U.S. (and other) intellectuals in these years: the doubt of the traditional view of the

---

[3] The 'Harvard school' label appears to have been coined by W. R. Johnson, *Darkness Visible: A Study of Vergil's Aeneid* (Berkeley, Calif.: Univ. of California Press, 1976), 11 n. 10, who notes that pessimistic readings of the *Aeneid* 'were written by critics who have been associated with classics at Harvard from the late forties to the present at some time or other'. Richard Thomas notes that the Harvard connection is tenuous at best, with the major works often having been produced when their authors were elsewhere: Parry was at Yale, Clausen at Amherst, and Putnam at Brown ('Ideology, Influence, and Future Studies in the *Georgics*', *Vergilius*, 36 (1990), 64 n. 1). Thomas suggests that the term implies a closer collaboration than there actually was, and Clausen makes the same point, noting that while he and Parry were colleagues at Amherst in the mid-1950s and talked often about the *Aeneid*, he did not meet Putnam until 1957 and met Brooks socially only once in 1959 or 1960 ('Appendix', in Nicholas Horsfall (ed.), *A Companion to the Study of Virgil* (Leiden: Brill, 1995), 313–14). I shall therefore use the label 'pessimist' in the discussion that follows.

[4] Karl Galinsky, 'Clothes for the Emperor', *Arion*, 10 (2003), 143–69, an extended review of Richard Thomas's *Virgil and the Augustan Reception* (Cambridge: CUP, 2001).

[5] Karl Galinsky, 'The Anger of Aeneas', *American Journal of Philology*, 109 (1988), 322.

Aeneid has at least some connection with the 1960s' questioning of all institutions, political, religious, and intellectual, and in particular with attitudes towards America's own imperialism.'[6] This is a serious charge. It is one thing to say that contemporary concerns have made contemporary readers more attuned to some things in Virgil's text than others. But if it indeed took readers almost two thousand years to get any idea that these concerns are in Virgil's poem, one has to wonder how important they really are.

The discussion took a dramatic turn in 2001, when Richard Thomas published a groundbreaking book, *Virgil and the Augustan Reception*, that shows that the ancient *Aeneiskritik* does indeed contain a clearly 'pessimistic' strain.[7] Thomas's concern was primarily with ancient readers and with their successors in the twentieth century who have shaped the scholarly understanding of the poem in our day, but he did begin to say something about the centuries in between, with a focus on the influential translation of John Dryden. My book is designed to bridge this gap, to show in some detail that there is a continuous tradition of 'pessimistic' readings that extends through the early modern period in Europe and the western hemisphere, in works written in English, French, Italian, Latin, and Spanish. What is more, Thomas's story focuses on suppression, on how the 'optimists' worked to occlude any 'pessimistic' reading of the poem that would threaten the traditional values on which such a reading rested. My book stresses the liberating power of the 'pessimistic' readings. I have focused more on poetic imitations of the *Aeneid*, although scholarship from the early modern period certainly receives its due, and tried to show how reading Virgil 'against the grain', so to speak, helped unleash artistic creativity in some totally unexpected ways.

The works treated in the pages that follow contain allusions to many classical authors, but in each case the connection to the 'pessimistic' *Aeneid* is unusually close. Some of these works, like Filelfo's *Sphortias* and Le Plat's *Virgile en France*, never achieved

---

[6] Harrison, 'Some Views', 5. Clausen, however, clarifies the chronology: 'The mild-minded pessimism of the Harvard school—the so-called Harvard school—reflects the mood of the fifties: it had little or nothing to do with the dissent and anguish of the sixties...' ('Appendix', 313).

[7] See n. 4 above.

much popularity, as befits the efforts of writers whose allusive strategies rested on an interpretation that most of their contemporaries did not accept or really even understand. Others, like Ercilla's *La Araucana*, Barlow's *Columbiad*, and Sor Juana's lyrics, were widely read in their own day and are still known at least to scholars specializing in this period. And others, like Shakespeare's *The Tempest* and Milton's *Paradise Lost*, have been familiar to educated readers everywhere for hundreds of years, although the interpretation I present is not. Thus my discussion will introduce the reader to some new poems and, I think, suggest some very different insights into some of the basic canonical works of the western literary tradition. I have made a special effort to link these insights to the broader concerns of literary theory and cultural studies at the beginning of the twenty-first century, because I believe that the 'pessimistic' reading of the *Aeneid* allows Virgil's poetry to speak to those concerns in some surprising ways. The linkages, however, are not arbitrary: each of the theories applied here is logically associated with an approach to the *Aeneid* itself that today's classicists are developing.

As I have been saying, books like this are not born in a scholarly vacuum, and it is a particular pleasure to thank those who have helped me articulate and develop my ideas. The Tanner Humanities Center at the University of Utah (Gene Fitzgerald, Director) and the Faculty Development Leave Program at Texas A&M University (coordinated by Karan Watson, Dean of Faculties) provided sabbatical time for research and writing, and it is no exaggeration to say that, without their support, this book might never have been completed. Parts of my argument were first presented at meetings hosted by the American Philological Association, the Renaissance Society of America, the Classical Association of Great Britain, the Association of Literary Scholars and Critics, and the international congresses on humanistic studies that take place in Sassoferrato, Italy, and as invited lectures at the University of Warsaw, Brigham Young University, the University of Copenhagen, Cambridge University, the University of Warwick, Bristol University, the University of Texas, the University of Utah, the Istituto Orientale Universitario, Naples, the Università degli Studi, Naples, and the Università di Roma II 'Tor Vergata'. The approach developed in these talks remains especially controversial in continental Europe—I have a distinct recollection of a young woman in Naples who reacted furiously to my paper because she saw it as an attack on the traditional values that she believed ran in an unbroken line from Augustan Rome to modern Italy—and my gratitude to these audiences for listening patiently and engaging with my arguments therefore transcends what is customary. Virginia Brown (Toronto), Reinhold Glei (Bochum), Heinz Hofmann (Tübingen), Maggie Kilgour (McGill), David Lupher (University of Puget Sound), the late Peter K. Marshall (Amherst), David Mickelsen (Utah), Letizia Panizza (London), Diana Robin (New Mexico), and Richard Thomas (Harvard) provided advice and material for me to use. Steve Ferguson, Curator of Rare Books at Princeton University, offered me ready access to the incomparable riches of the Junius Morgan Virgil Collection, for which I am especially grateful. I would also like to thank Richard J. Golsan, Christoph Konrad, Hilaire Kallendorf, and Filipe Vieira de Castro for helping me with translations of some of the passages cited in the text. Earlier versions of parts of this book have been published in *Harvard Studies in Classical Philology, Comparative Literature Studies*, and *Classics and the Uses of Reception* (edited by Charles Martindale and Richard Thomas),[8] and I appreciate the opportunity to refine this material and integrate it into the larger argument here. Quotations from the *Aeneid* are taken from *P. Vergili Maronis opera*, ed. R. A. B. Mynors, Oxford Classical Texts (Oxford: Clarendon Press, 1969), with translations by Allen Mandelbaum, from *The Aeneid of Virgil* (New York: Bantam Books, 1971). Unattributed translations of other works are my own. Finally, I would like to dedicate this book to my wife, Hilaire—always my first, and best, reader—who has lived with the project from the beginning and made it better in innumerable ways.

C.K.

---

    [8] 'Historicizing the "Harvard School": Pessimistic Readings of the *Aeneid* in Italian Renaissance Scholarship', *Harvard Studies in Classical Philology*, 99 (1999), 391–403; 'Representing the Other: Ercilla's *La Araucana*, Virgil's *Aeneid*, and the "New" World Encounter', *Comparative Literature Studies*, 40 (2003), 394–414; and 'Allusion as Reception: Virgil, Milton, and the Modern Reader', in Charles Martindale and Richard Thomas (eds.), *Classics and the Uses of Reception* (Oxford: Blackwell, 2006).

Contents

List of Figures

Introduction

> 'Classicizing' can be formally defined as a mode of action in
> which present interests act on the symbolic resources of
> antiquity to produce 'classics.' It is thus analogous to 'oriental-
> izing,' producing exemplars of Self rather than Other.
>
> (Christopher Stray, *Classics Transformed*[1])

Our story begins in the second quarter of the fifteenth century, when a
group of scholars and teachers in northern and central Italy launched
a systematic assault on the educational system of their day, which they
found to be too narrow, too focused on technicalities at the expense of
larger questions about human nature and about how the student can
be prepared to take a meaningful place in society. The *quadrivium*, the
mathematical part of the liberal arts system, was de-emphasized and
the *trivium*, the language-based part, was transformed. Grammar was
retained, but the focus shifted from speculative theory to usage as
determined by the best classical authors. Rhetoric was also retained,
but again, the focus shifted, from the rigidities of medieval *dictamen* to
a more flexible system based on Ciceronian theory and practice. Logic
was replaced by moral philosophy, and history and poetry, both
sources for appropriate moral choice, were added, along with the
study of Greek, which had languished for centuries. The point of
reference was consistently classical, as the source of models for how
to live well and how to express one's self appropriately. The break with
the past was not always as clear as the polemics of the time suggest—
the grammar books actually used in classrooms, for example, retained
much from the Middle Ages, and Greek was always marginal in

---

[1] Christopher Stray, *Classics Transformed: Schools, Universities, and Society in
England, 1830–1960* (Oxford: Clarendon Press, 1998), 10 n. 8.

relation to Latin—but the new 'humanism' did succeed in effecting a true revolution in education.[2]

By 1500, the humanist model prevailed throughout Italy, and by 1600 it dominated in the rest of Europe as well, initiating a remarkable period in which the schools of Europe and its colonies shared the same basic curriculum, teaching methods, and canon of authors for over three hundred years. The focus of this system was Latin. To be sure, the vast majority of students stopped their education after primary school, but even here Latin was supposed to have been the language of instruction. And to be sure, university education complemented what went before, but was more focused on the professional disciplines of law, medicine, and theology. Thus for the upper-class students who attended a French *lycée*, an Italian *liceo*, a German *Gymnasium*, or an English public school, secondary education was tied to the same language that dominated the church (at least in Catholic countries) and governmental and administrative affairs (at least to the beginning of the nineteenth century). Challenges to this system began in earnest towards the end of the eighteenth century, when control of Latin was no longer so obviously necessary, especially in the new world; but until then, the education that the upper classes shared in both the old world and the new was a Latin education.[3]

[2] The standard treatment of the humanist educational reform, with full references to relevant secondary bibliography, may be found in Paul F. Grendler, *Schooling in Renaissance Italy: Literacy and Learning, 1300–1600* (Baltimore, Md., and London: Johns Hopkins Univ. Press, 1989), esp. 111–41, updated slightly and given a somewhat more theoretical perspective in Craig Kallendorf, 'Humanism', in Randall Curran (ed.), *A Companion to the Philosophy of Education* (Oxford: Blackwell, 2003), 62–72. Relevant primary sources may be found in Eugenio Garin (ed.), *L'educazione in Europa (1499–1600)* (Bari: Laterza, 1957); and Craig Kallendorf (ed.), *Humanist Educational Treatises* (Cambridge, Mass., and London: Harvard Univ. Press, 2002). Robert Black, *Humanism and Education in Medieval and Renaissance Italy: Tradition and Innovation in Latin Schools from the Twelfth to the Fifteenth Century* (Cambridge: CUP, 2001), has recently warned that the success of the humanists was somewhat less thorough and rapid than earlier scholars have claimed.

[3] On the Latin school in Europe, see now Françoise Waquet, *Latin or the Empire of a Sign: From the Sixteenth to the Twentieth Centuries*, tr. John Howe (London and New York: Verso, 2001), which supersedes all previous considerations of this topic. Thoughtful discussions of the challenges presented to the traditional system of education and the arguments marshalled in its defence may be found in Stray, *Classics Transformed*, 105–6, 110–13; Waquet, *Latin*, 178–206; and (in the US) Caroline Winterer, *The Culture of Classicism: Ancient Greece and Rome in American Intellectual Life, 1780–1910* (Baltimore, Md., and London: Johns Hopkins Univ. Press, 2002).

Some model schools like St Paul's in London or the Boston Latin School, whose curriculum was modelled on its English predecessors, presented curricula that are impressive in their range and breadth,[4] but when we look at what was actually accomplished in the typical secondary school, the narrow range of reading is striking. Throughout most of this period, reading was intensive rather than extensive— that is, reading focused not on rapid absorption of large numbers of books, but rather on careful, meticulous study of a small number of texts that were held in great esteem.[5] Classroom work privileged repetition and memorization, so that diligent students often ended up committing large blocks of these texts to memory at an age when they were likely not to forget them for many years, if ever. Most commonly, the Latin schools focused on Cicero for rhetoric and moral philosophy, Virgil, Terence, Horace, and Ovid for poetry, and Valerius Maximus, Caesar, and Sallust for history, with Cicero dominating in prose and Virgil in poetry.[6]

Thus for several hundred years, Virgil's poetry formed an integral part of the common educational experience of almost every educated person wherever the Latin secondary education of Europe took hold. Somewhere in Europe or the Americas, four or five editions of Virgil

---

[4] The Latin curriculum at St Paul's at the end of the 17th cent. began with Erasmus, Ovid, and Justin, then proceeded to Martial, Sallust, Virgil, Cicero's speeches, Horace, Juvenal, and Persius. Greek began in the fifth form (there were eight), and involved readings first from the New Testament, Winterton's *Poetae minores Graeci*, and Apollodorus's handbook on mythology, then from Homer, Arrian, and 'Dionysius' (M. L. Clarke, *Classical Education in Britain 1500–1900* (Cambridge: CUP, 1959), 41–2).

[5] The traditional account is that of Rolf Engelsing, *Der Bürger als Leser: Lesergeschichte in Deutschland, 1500–1800* (Stuttgart: Metzler, 1974), who has argued that the intensive reading and rereading of a small number of books of great cultural significance was replaced at the end of the 18th cent. by a new, extensive form of reading predicated on the rapid consumption of large numbers of books. Reinhard Wittmann, 'Was There a Reading Revolution at the End of the Eighteenth Century?', in Guglielmo Cavallo and Roger Chartier (eds.), *A History of Reading in the West*, tr. Lydia G. Cochrane (Amherst, Mass.: Univ. of Massachusetts Press, 1999), 284–312, provides some necessary nuances to this argument, but it is clear that a major change took place at the end of the 18th cent., and that Virgil was one of the handful of culturally significant texts that had been read intensively across Europe before this.

[6] Grendler, *Schooling*, 111–271. Charles Martindale also notes that Virgil occupied the central place in the European literary canon for longer than any other writer ('Introduction: "The Classic of All Europe"', in Charles Martindale (ed.), *The Cambridge Companion to Virgil* (Cambridge: CUP, 1997), 3).

were published every year for centuries,[7] and an examination of these editions confirms how closely connected they were to the schools. Their title-pages and prefaces confirm that they were published for 'the use of public and private schools of this kingdom', for 'the use of students in the colleges, academies, and other seminaries in the United States', even specifically 'for the use of students at the École Royale Militaire in Paris'.[8] The pages of these books often contain handwritten commentaries, presented initially by the teacher in class and copied diligently by generations of students between the lines and in the margins of their texts.[9] Indeed, a copy of Virgil often served as a tangible symbol of success in school, bound with the school crest on the covers and given to the students who achieved the highest marks on their examinations. Such 'prize bindings' can thus be used to track a student's progress through the system, from preparatory to secondary school, then from secondary school to university (see Figure 1).[10]

---

[7] Howard Jones, *Printing the Classical Text* ('t Goy-Houten: Hes & De Graaf, 2004), 118–19, shows that in the first decades of printing, Virgil was second only to Cicero in the number of edns. that had been printed. My statement about the number of edns. published each year through the early modern period is based on the material provided by Giuliano Mambelli, *Gli annali delle edizioni virgiliane* (Florence: Leo S. Olschki, 1954), but my experience suggests that Mambelli may have missed as many as half of the relevant edns., a good many of which are not identified in any other printed source either. In one ten-day period recently, I was able to obtain copies of three 18th-cent. edns. that seem to be unattested in any of the secondary literature (all French, an *opera omnia* printed by Antoine Delcros in Clermont Ferrand in 1787 and two small edns. printed in Grenoble by André Faure, of book 1 of the *Aeneid* (1734) and book 1 of the *Georgics* (undated)). I suspect that bibliographical completeness will forever elude Virgilian scholarship, but my point should stand anyway.

[8] The edns. cited here were published in Oxford by W. Baxter in 1827, in New York, by N. and J. White in 1832, and in Paris by Nyon l'aîne in 1778, respectively.

[9] A group of representative commentaries entered in 15th- and 16th-cent. edns. by students in Venice and the surroundings are analyzed in Craig Kallendorf, *Virgil and the Myth of Venice: Books and Readers in Renaissance Italy* (Oxford: Clarendon Press, 1999), 55–61. As Waquet, *Latin*, 129–51, notes, the type of pedagogical activity reflected in these early commentaries remained essentially unchanged for generations afterwards.

[10] Prize bindings have been studied at length by Chris Coppens, first in the catalogue to an exhibition held at the University Library in Leuven, *De prijs is het bewijs: Vier eeuwen prijsboeken* (Leuven: Centrale Bibliotheek K. U. Leuven, 1991), then in a long essay, 'The Prize is the Proof: Four Centuries of Prize Books', in Mirjam M. Foot (ed.), *Eloquent Witnesses: Bookbindings and Their History* (London and New Castle, Del.: Bibliographical Society, British Library, and Oak Knoll Press, 2004), 53–105. A large collection of prize books was formed by William Burton Todd and left recently to the Harry Ransom Humanities Research Center at the University of Texas.

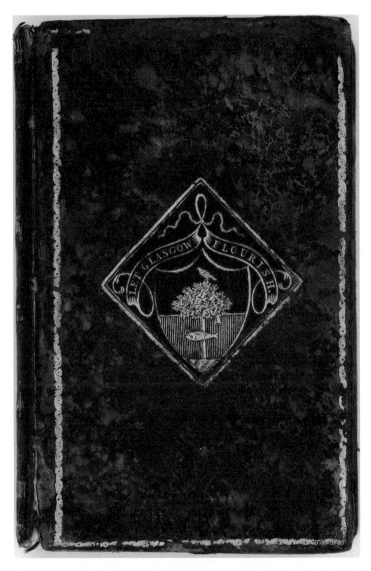

Figure 1. Prize binding for Glasgow Grammar School. Virgil, *Bucolica, Georgica, et Aeneis* (Glasgow: In aedibus Academicis, 1800)

From the vantage point of the present, however, after the student revolts of the 1960s marked the final exile of Latin from the centre to the periphery of the educational system, it is by no means apparent what function poetry about pastoral life (the *Eclogues*) or farming (the *Georgics*), or even about the founding of a long-dead empire (the *Aeneid*), was supposed to serve in the curriculum. First, as Christopher Stray put it, Virgil's poetry was used 'in maintaining the solidarity of élite social groups and the exclusion of outsiders'.[11] In other words, to enter the world of power and privilege, one had to learn to speak the language of that world and to manipulate the social codes by which its members validated their right to belong. The language was Latin, which was not the native language even of the privileged in early modern Europe, so that entering the world of the schools marked an initiation of sorts.[12] What one emerged with, the ability to speak extemporaneously on any subject and to write formal letters in Ciceronian Latin, could lead to appropriate employment, in law, the church, or government service.[13] More importantly, however, the educational system remained largely unchanged well past the point where career advancement in these areas really depended on facility in the Latin language. This confirms the assertion that fundamentally, a Latin education 'imparted class'—that is, it identified a gentleman as someone who could 'waste' time, money, and effort to learn and then display something that had little practical use. Those who did not have it, like the hero of Thomas Hardy's *Jude the Obscure*, recognized that they needed a Latin education to move up in society,[14] while those who did, like the *arbitristas* in seventeenth-century Spain, restricted it as a means of keeping the lower

[11] Stray, *Classics Transformed*, 1.

[12] As Walter Ong put it, 'the Renaissance teaching of Latin involves . . . a survival of what anthropologists, treating of more primitive peoples, call puberty rites' ('Latin Language Study as a Renaissance Puberty Rite', *Studies in Philology*, 56 (1959), 104).

[13] As Anthony Grafton and Lisa Jardine note, a humanist education was intended in theory to be non-vocational, to train students to take their places as citizens, but it also opened up career paths in the late 15th and 16th centuries in particular (*From Humanism to the Humanities* (Cambridge, Mass.: Harvard Univ. Press, 1986), 23–4).

[14] The phrase 'imparted class' is from Waquet, *Latin*, 212, who notes as well that 'what counted was not so much knowing Latin as having learned it' (211) since, as Zola noted, the person who does not recognize a quotation from Homer or Virgil 'is a condemned man' (215).

classes from abandoning 'productive' careers in agriculture, commerce, or artisanry in favour of 'unproductive' ones in the church and government.[15] To be sure, the goal was not to retain a detailed grasp of the language or the literature written in it, especially after the end of the eighteenth century, but rather to make an appropriate reference to Virgil when speaking in Parliament and to smile in recognition when someone else did the same.[16] Once one knew the source of 'una salus uictis, nullam sperare salutem' ('the lost have only this one deliverance: to hope for none'; *Aen.* 2. 354), success could follow naturally.

The ruling classes ruled because they felt they deserved to, of course, and their right to expand their hegemony rested as much in the classics as their fundamental right to rule itself. Indeed, as Richard Waswo has noted, European civilization distinguishes itself by tracing its origins to a *translatio imperii*, a transferral of political power through conquest. Here Virgil plays a prominent role directly, for one European ruler after another traced his or her line back to Aeneas and his followers, who had moved from Troy to Rome and conquered the indigenous inhabitants, sweeping them up forcibly into a new civilization. When Columbus, Magellan, and Vasco da Gama sailed off to explore, they simply continued the pattern, viewing their travels and conquests through the filter of the *Aeneid*.[17] And the same pattern continued for centuries. When the East India College was set up in Haileybury, Hertfordshire, to train administrators in India, the curriculum still rested on Caesar, Virgil, and Xenophon, and the exams given to the Oxford and Cambridge graduates in the 1830s who aspired to colonial service were still

[15] Richard Kagan, 'Il latino nella Castiglia del XVII e del XVIII secolo', *Rivista storica italiana*, 85 (1973), 299–307. Waquet cites a similar example, that of Jeronimo Lopez, who complained in 1545 that the Indians who had been taught Latin in a *colegio* established in Mexico City by the Augustinian friars became insolent and refused to be treated like slaves any more (*Latin*, 222–3). Many Latin schools throughout Europe set aside a few places for scholarship recipients from the lower classes, but the numbers of such places were generally quite limited.

[16] Stray, *Classics Transformed*, 65–6, who notes that for many alumni of English public schools, all that remained at the end of their classical education were a few half-remembered tags that they had learnt in their progress from one form to another.

[17] Richard Waswo, *The Founding Legend of Western Civilization: From Virgil to Vietnam* (Hanover, NH, and London: Univ. Press of New England, for Wesleyan Univ. Press, 1997), 60–1, 82–94.

based heavily in the classics.[18] As Sir Richard Livingstone noted in his *A Defence of Classical Education* (1917), in a Ciceronian sentence that would have made his public school teacher proud,

We must go to Rome for our lessons. To govern peoples who differ in race, language, temper, and civilization; to raise and distribute armies for their defence or subjection; to meet expences civil and military; to allow generals and governors sufficient independence without losing control at the centre; to know and supply the needs of provinces two thousand miles from the seat of government... Latin then stands in our education partly on linguistic grounds, partly on the heroic characters in its history, or the interest of its political and imperial problems, and on the capacities of its peoples for government.[19]

The *Aeneid* served as a particularly appropriate source for 'heroic characters' who could shed light on 'political and imperial problems', as the first Brazilian edition of the poem shows. Published in 1818–19, this edition contains the translation of Josè de Lima Leitão, which was presented to King João VI as a 'Monumento à elevaçao da colònia do Brazil a reino, e ao estabelecimento do trìplice impèrio luso' ('Monument to the elevation of the colony of Brazil to kingdom, and the establishment of the triple Portuguese empire'). As the dedicatory letter notes, from the *Aeneid* 'appontarà em Vossa Majestade um nunca visto nùmero de pontos de contacto Moraes, e Polìticos com o Heroe desta Epopeia, o qual lançou os cimentos à mais primorosa Naçção do Glôbo, e que em filial piedade, e em Reaes virtudes passarà sempre por modêlo' ('your majesty will point out a never-before-seen number of moral and political points of contact with the hero of this story, who has laid the foundations of the most perfect nation on the globe, and who in filial piety and in royal virtues will always be held as a model').[20] The Portuguese empire, in other words, is connected to the Roman one, with the points of contact being political and public as well as private and moral.

[18] Stray, *Classics Transformed*, 53–4.

[19] Qtd. in F. Campbell, 'Latin and the Elite Tradition in Education', in P. W. Musgrave (ed.), *Sociology, History and Education: A Reader* (London: Methuen & Co., 1970), 255.

[20] *As obras de Pùblio Virgìlio Maro, traduzidas em verso portuguez, e annotadas pêlo doutor Antònio Josè de Lima Leitão*, 2 vols. (Rio de Janeiro: Na Impressão Régia, 1819), fos. A2ʳ (title-page), A3ʳ (dedicatory letter) (my copy). I am grateful to Filipe Vieira de Castro for translating these two quotations.

A particular kind of person was required to preserve, and then expand, the values and institutions on which privilege depended, and the Latin school produced just such a person. Instruction rested on the paraphrase/commentary, in which the teacher proceeded through a text word by word, parsing and explaining syntax, then providing historical, mythological, and geographical background, with moral observations thrown in along the way, much as his predecessors had done in ancient Rome.[21] The system rested on identifying short passages worth remembering for their style (*methodice*) or content (*historice*), as Battista Guarino explained in one of the earliest educational treatises of the period, with the student putting an indexing note next to the passage in the text, then copying out the relevant passages into commonplace books under the headings indexed in the margins of the text.[22] The commonplace books in turn served as sources for maxims and examples that were used in 'original' speeches and compositions, initially for the classroom, but in response to speaking and writing obligations later in life as well.[23]

This system had two results. First, it shattered antiquity into shards of morality and eloquence that could easily be made compatible with a much later culture founded on a value system that modern scholars find different in many ways from that of antiquity. In the Latin school experience, in other words, 'Virgil' meant 'quondam etiam uictis redit in precordia uirtus' ('at times new courage comes to beaten hearts'; *Aen.* 2. 367), or 'audentis Fortuna iuuat' ('fortune helps those who dare'; *Aen.* 10. 284), or 'optima quaeque dies miseris mortalibus aeui | prima fugit' ('life's fairest days are ever the first to flee for hapless mortals'; *Georg.* 3. 66–7). The tone in these

[21] Grendler, *Schooling*, 222–9; and Kallendorf, *Virgil and the Myth of Venice*, 55–61.

[22] *A Program of Teaching and Learning*, in Kallendorf, *Humanist Educational Treatises*, 268–9. Battista Guarino cites the example of Pliny the Elder from antiquity, who prepared 160 notebooks filled with citations from other writers, which he could have sold to Larcius Licinus for 400,000 sesterces (ibid. 294–7).

[23] The *ars excerpendi* is described in more detail by Jean-Marc Chatelain, 'Humanisme et culture de la note', *Revue de la Bibliothèque nationale de France*, 2 (1999), *Le livre annoté*, 27–30. The standard study of commonplace books is Ann Moss, *Printed Commonplace Books and the Structuring of Renaissance Thought* (Oxford: Clarendon Press, 1996), to be supplemented by the valuable exhibition catalogue of Earle Havens, *Commonplace Books: A History of Manuscripts and Printed Books from Antiquity to the Twentieth Century* (New Haven, Conn.: Beinecke Rare Book and Manuscript Library, Yale Univ., 2001).

commonplace
books

passages is typical of the one that characterizes what many other readers of the period took from their reading of Virgil: hortatory and optimistic whenever possible, marked by a certain resignation in the face of what cannot be changed. The classics, in other words, spoke with one voice in the schools, urging the student to respect authority, to work for the good within existing institutions, and to adhere to the conservative values of discipline, fortitude, and hard work.[24]

The Latin educational system also moulded a certain kind of character, one that learnt to succeed at court or in the ecclesiastical hierarchy by learning to succeed in the schoolroom. The school day consisted of copying, memorizing, repeating, and imitating, with a premium placed on taking orders from an authority whose basic principles were neither articulated nor questioned.[25] Corporal punishment was the norm: although there were exceptions, schools of this period generally strike modern observers as brutal places.[26] One did not get ahead by questioning but by doing as he was told and, as Anthony Grafton and Lisa Jardine have noted, obedience and docility were traits that would have appealed to any governor or bishop of the day. The graduate of the Latin school thus tended to be conservative politically, to resist change, and to rest in the often banal wisdom of his commonplace book.[27] Louis MacNeice described the system well, although it was almost dead by the time he was writing:

We learned that a gentleman never misplaced his accents,
  That nobody knows how to speak, much less how to write
English who has not hob-nobbed with the great-grandparents of English,
  That the boy on the Modern Side is merely a parasite
But the classical student is bred to the purple, his training in syntax
  Is also training in thought
And even in morals; if called to the bar or the barracks
  He will always do what he ought.[28]

The Ancien Régime, in other words, rested on the classical education of its privileged classes, as the texts that provided that education

[24] Kagan, 'Il latino nella Castiglia', 317–19; Grendler, *Schooling*, 264; and Kallendorf, *Virgil and the Myth of Venice*, 31–5.

[25] Grafton and Jardine, *From Humanism to the Humanities*, 24; Waquet, *Latin*, 178–9.

[26] Ong, 'Latin Language Study', 103–25; Waquet, *Latin*, 138–45.

[27] Grafton and Jardine, *From Humanism to the Humanities*, pp. xiii–xiv, 23–4.

[28] The extract is from *Autumn Journal* (1938), qtd. in Stray, *Classics Transformed*, 286.

attest. That Virgil's patron was the emperor Augustus was well known to early modern readers, as the title-page to an early sixteenth-century Venetian edition shows (see Figure 2),[29] and the popular commentary of Jodocus Badius Ascensius from the same period states that Virgil endowed Aeneas with wisdom, courage, justice, and temperance as models for Augustus.[30] On this analogy, Virgil and his poetry were drawn explicitly into the service of the nation-states that emerged in early modern Europe, as shown by the dedication of Pierre Perrin's translation to Cardinal Mazarin, the influential cleric and diplomat who played an important role in shaping the foreign policy of several French monarchs:

En effet, Monseigneur, le siecle fameux de ce grand Autheur ne semble t'il pas revolu dans le present? Qu'est-ce maintenant que Paris, qu'une Rome triomphante, comme elle, immense dans son peuple & dans ses limites, comme elle, Reine des Citez, maistresse des Nations, capitale du Monde? nostre Monarque qu'un Auguste naissant, dans ses premieres années déja le plus victorieux, déja le plus auguste des Roys? & V. Eminence, Monseigneur, qu'un fidele Moecene; comme luy Romain, comme luy son plus grande & plus cher Ministre, & le sacré Depositaire de ses secrets & de sa puissance? Pour achever ces illustres rapports, le Ciel ne devoit il pas à la France un Virgile François?[31]

In effect, Sir, the famous century of this grand author, does it not seem to have come around again in the present? Is Paris not now a Rome triumphant, like her enormous in population and territory, like her queen of cities, mistress of nations, capital of the world? Is our monarch not a nascent Augustus, in his first years already the most victorious, already the most august of kings? And your eminence, sir, are you not a faithful Maecenas, like him a Roman, like him the most grand and the most cherished minister, and the sacred depository of his secrets and his power? To complete these illustrious connections, does not Heaven require for France a French Virgil?

[29] The edn. was published in Venice by Bartolomeus de Zannis de Portesio in 1508, with a full description available in Bernd Schneider, *Vergil: Handschriften und Drucke der Herzog August Bibliothek* (Wolfenbüttel: Herzog August Bibliothek, 1982), 67.

[30] I have used Ascensius's commentary in *Publii Virgilii Maronis poetae Mantuani universum poema...* (Venice: Joannes Maria Bonellus, 1558), fos. 123ᵛ–4ʳ. See Craig Kallendorf, 'Ascensius, Landino, and Virgil: Continuity and Transformation in Renaissance Commentary', in J. F. Alcina *et al.* (eds.), *Acta Conventus Neo-Latini Bariensis*, Proceedings of the Ninth International Congress of Neo-Latin Studies (Tempe, Ariz.: Medieval and Renaissance Texts and Studies, 1998), 353–60.

[31] *Leneide de Virgile fidellement traduitte en vers heroiques avec le latin a costé... par M. P. Perrin...* (Paris: Estienne Loyson, 1664), fos. 31ʳ⁻ᵛ.

P.V.M. Omnia opera:diligenti caftigatione exculta:aptiffimifcg ornata figu ris:
comentantibus Seruio:Donato:Probo:Domitio:Landino:Antonioq; Man
cinello uiris clariffimis.Additis infuper in Seruium multis:quæ dee
rant:græcifcg dictioibus:& uerfibus qplurimis:qui paffim cor
rupte legebantur: in priftinum decorem reftitutis.

Cum Gratia z Priuilegio.

Figure 2. Virgil presenting his poetry to the Emperor Octavian. Virgil, *Omnia opera* (Venice: Bartolomeus de Zannis de Portesio, 1508), title-page (Herzog August Bibliothek, Wolfenbüttel)

Perrin, of course, is presenting himself as the French Virgil, but in doing so he transfers the entire ideological framework of Virgil's Rome to seventeenth-century France. In one sense this is simply one more in a centuries-long series of attempts to use the *translatio imperii* gesture to legitimate national consciousness and governmental authority. But it is worth noting that Perrin's version, like most of its predecessors, is straightforward and unproblematic: as Virgil served and supported Augustus, so the new Virgil will also serve and support his political successor.[32]

This, then, is the Virgil that emerges from the schools as part of the common classical heritage of the ruling élites of the early modern West, a Virgil whose language and sentiments encoded power and privilege, who provided the model for the imperial expansion that projected the power of Europe onto every continent of the newly expanded world, and who served to defend the Ancien Régime against any threat to its political, economic, and cultural hegemony. This Virgil is well enough known, for by now several generations of researchers have uncovered the lines of influence linking his poetry to the high culture of the early modern period and the institutions that supported it.[33] To be sure, the language and perspective of

[32] A fuller discussion of this edition and the issues it raises for the later understanding of Virgil may be found in my 'The *Aeneid* Transformed: Illustration as Interpretation from the Renaissance to the Present', in Sarah Spence (ed.), *Poets and Critics Read Virgil* (New Haven and London: Yale Univ. Press, 2001), 133–5.

[33] A complete bibliography on this topic is obviously impossible, but exemplary recent studies include Annabel Patterson, *Pastoral and Ideology: Virgil to Valéry* (Berkeley-Los Angeles.: Univ. of California Press, 1987); Theodore Ziolkowsi, *Virgil and the Moderns* (Princeton: Princeton Univ. Press, 1993); Marie Tanner, *The Last Descendant of Aeneas: The Hapsburgs and the Mythic Image of the Emperor* (New Haven and London: Yale Univ. Press, 1993); John Watkins, *The Specter of Dido: Spenser and Virgilian Epic* (New Haven and London: Yale Univ. Press, 1995); Waswo, *Founding Legend*; and John C. Shields, *The American Aeneas: Classical Origins of the American Self* (Knoxville, Tenn.: Univ. of Tennessee Press, 2001). Much useful information can be found in a number of publications that appeared to mark the bimillennium of Virgil's death in 1981–2, e.g. R. D. Williams and T. S. Pattie, *Virgil: His Poetry through the Ages* (London: British Library, 1982); Charles Martindale (ed.), *Virgil and His Influence: Bimillennial Studies* (Bristol: Bristol Classical Press, 1984); and the invaluable catalogue that accompanied the exhibition of Virgilian material at Rome's Biblioteca Nazionale Centrale, Marcello Fagiolo (ed.), *Virgilio nell'arte e nella cultura europea* (Rome: De Luca Editore, 1981). Additional references can be found in the annual bibliographies prepared by Alexander G. McKay and published in the journal *Vergilius*; more specialized studies will be cited in the notes to the chapters that follow.

scholarship change from generation to generation, so that connections that once seemed positive are now being questioned by those who find the classics complicit with sexism, racism, and class oppression.[34] But in general, more innovative scholarship is challenging its more traditional predecessors on the merits of the picture that has emerged, not on the configurations of the picture itself.

I am not prepared to argue that generations of scholars are wrong, and that the picture that has been sketched out thus far must be abandoned. But while what has been said so far may well be true, it is not the whole truth, for there is another Virgil, one that coexisted alongside this one during the early modern period—not the dominant paradigm, to be sure, but an alternative one that was available to those who had reason later in life to question the unquestioned verities they had learnt in school and to use Virgil's poetry, more specifically the *Aeneid*, as a way to envision a society that was different in one or more ways from the one in which they lived.

In the chapters that follow, I shall work to recover this other Virgil, who served in turn as a filter through which a series of highly original thinkers could construct a series of meditations on marginalization, colonization, and revolution. I shall begin with Francesco Filelfo, a humanist scholar who was well known in the fifteenth century and whose mastery of Latin scholarship should have positioned him at the centre of power and privilege. Not surprisingly, he chose to advertise his skill by imitating the *Aeneid*, but the *Aeneid* he saw was not the straightforward one that was being presented by the first generations of humanist schoolmasters. As we shall see, his efforts to play Virgil to the Augustus of Quattrocento Milan, Francesco Sforza, are fraught with all the ambiguities that Michel Foucault has identified in the definition and exercise of power, so that Filelfo's Virgilian imitation collapses in failure along with his position at Sforza's court.

The second chapter develops the connection between the *Aeneid* and the imperial projects of the fifteenth and sixteenth centuries.

[34] See e.g. the special issue of *Arethusa*, 8/1 (1975), J. P. Sullivan (ed.), *Marxism and the Classics*; Phyllis Culham, Lowell Edmunds, and Alden Smith (eds.), *Classics: A Discipline and Profession in Crisis* (Lanham, Md.: Univ. Press of America, 1989); and Peter W. Rose, *Sons of the Gods, Children of Earth: Ideology and Literary Form in Ancient Greece* (Ithaca, NY: Cornell Univ. Press, 1992), 1–42 ('Marxism and the Classics').

It was easy for the colonizers to cast themselves in the role of Aeneas and the conquering Trojans, as we have seen, and this approach accorded well with the demands of the schools, which tended then, as now, to eschew moral complexity. But then as now, again, more mature readers in different environments were able to see that Virgil presented both what is lost as well as what is gained in conquest, so that as early as Bartolomé de Las Casas, some Europeans were able, like Virgil, to see imperialism from the other side. Some of them, like Alonso de Ercilla and Sor Juana Inés de la Cruz, are still known to specialists and to educated people in their own countries; and others, like William Shakespeare, are known wherever Western culture has penetrated. All of them, however, turned the model text of the colonizers against them, focusing on the 'other voices' in the *Aeneid* in a series of protests that became more insistent as the Virgilian imitations moved from epic to drama to lyric.

This line of argument suggests in turn that Virgil's place in the ideology of the Ancien Régime is also more complicated than traditional historiography suggests. Generations of students were taught that literature can reflect reality, but that history is made by powerful individuals who, when they succeed, remake society and its institutions in accordance with their will. The so-called 'new historicists', however, have turned this traditional paradigm inside out, suggesting that literature can also provide the belief systems through which historical reality is made. In the final chapter, I turn to three key assaults on the Ancien Régime, those of Oliver Cromwell in the seventeenth century, the American colonies at the end of the eighteenth, and the French citizenry from the assault on the Bastille to the rise of Napoleon. In each case, an imitation of the *Aeneid* develops into an effort to come to terms with rapid political and social change. In the case of *Paradise Lost*, John Milton produced a poem that reveals all the complexities of the Restoration and his efforts to find a place within it, while in the case of the *Columbiad*, the production and revision of the poem show how Joel Barlow succeeded in creating an epic that articulates the values of a new revolutionary society. The third poem, the little-known *Virgile en France* of Victor Alexandre Chrétien Le Plat du Temple, makes the *Aeneid*, traditionally seen as a pro-imperial poem, into an allegory of the establishment of the French republic. That all three poems are deeply rooted in Virgil

confirms the richness and depth of the model, which shows itself
fully capable of being appropriated by readers working for a broad
range of political objectives.

In the discussion that follows, I shall read primary source material
from the middle of the fifteenth to the first decade of the nineteenth
centuries through a series of theoretical positions that are very much
anchored in the culture of my day. I suspect that most, if not all, of
the theorists I cite knew the *Aeneid*, but my argument does not
depend on this. The issues raised by these theorists are the same
ones raised by some early modern readers of the *Aeneid*, so I take
refuge in the practice of the poets on whom I shall focus, who also
viewed Virgil and the other classical texts they knew from the perspective of their own values and concerns.[35]

[35] Here, as elsewhere in this study, I am strongly influenced by the arguments of
Charles Martindale, whose *Redeeming the Text: Latin Poetry and the Hermeneutics of
Reception* (Cambridge: CUP, 1993), addresses this point at greater length. Martindale
posits 'two theses, one "weak" and the other "strong." The "weak" thesis is that
numerous unexplored insights into ancient literature are locked up in imitations,
translations, and so forth (this thesis may be uncontroversial, but it is more honoured
in the breach than the observance). The "strong" thesis is that our current interpretations of ancient texts, whether or not we are aware of it, are, in complex ways,
constructed by the chain of receptions through which their continued readability has
been effected. As a result we cannot get back to any originary meaning wholly free of
subsequent accretions' (7). I believe the argument to be presented in this book
inclines more towards support of the 'strong' than the 'weak' thesis, but the material
presented here should also be of interest to those who are not prepared to go this far.

1

Marginalization

[P]ower is exercised rather than possessed; it is not the 'privilege' acquired or preserved of the dominant class, but the overall effect of its strategic positions—an effect that is manifested and sometimes extended by the position of those who are dominated. Furthermore, this power is not exercised simply as an obligation or a prohibition on those 'who do not have it'; it invests them, is transmitted by them and through them; it exerts pressure upon them, just as they themselves, in their struggle against it, resist the grip it has on them.

(Michel Foucault, *Discipline and Punish*[1])

1. LAUDATORY EPIC AND THE NATURE OF POWER IN THE EARLY RENAISSANCE

Time has not been kind to the *Sphortias*, the epic poem recounting how the *condottiere* Francesco Sforza won control of Milan in the months after the death of Filippo Maria Visconti in 1447. The poem has never been printed and survives in only a handful of manuscripts,[2] a clear sign that it never found the audience its author felt it deserved. Some of those who received copies from the author responded politely enough, but over the centuries those who have read the poem have been more eager to criticize than to praise.

---

[1] Michel Foucault, *Discipline and Punish: The Birth of the Prison*, tr. Alan Sheridan (New York: Random House/Vintage Books, 1991), 26–7.

[2] See Appendix 1.

Galeotto Marzio (1424–97), for example, condemned the poem almost immediately for what he considered its lack of invention, its pedestrian style, and its errors in prosody and metrics[3]—errors that have been diligently marked in the margins of an autograph manuscript by an eighteenth-century reader.[4] Francesco Filelfo's nineteenth-century biographer, Carlo De' Rosmini, balanced his criticisms against the recognition that one finds in the *Sphortias* 'a happy disposition toward poetry, not always found in literature of the period',[5] but John Addington Symonds, whose judgement has been especially influential in the English-speaking world, concluded that '[o]f deep thought, true taste, penetrative criticism, or delicate fancy he [Filelfo] knew nothing. The unimaginable bloom of style is nowhere to be found upon his work.'[6] The denunciations peaked at the beginning of the twentieth century in the article of A. Novara, who disliked almost everything about the poem: its characterizations are impoverished and its hero odious, he wrote; its depiction of love is vulgar and its gods are little more than evanescent shadows; the style of the poem is prosaic and the

[3] Galeottus Martius, *Invectivae in Franciscum Philelphum*, ed. L. Juhàsz (Leipzig: B. G. Teubner, 1932); see Guglielmo Bottari, 'La "Sphortias"', in *Francesco Filelfo nel quinto centenario della morte* (Padua: Antenore, 1986), 460. I have been unable to locate a copy of F. Lo Parco, *La Sforziade di Francesco Filelfo* (Tripani, 1902). Not all Quattrocento references to the poem were negative, however. In his efforts to win the commission to sculpt an equestrian statue of Francesco Sforza, Leonardo da Vinci turned to an associate of Filelfo's, the humanist Piattino Piatti, who gave him three poems, one of which compared the statue to the *Sphortias*: 'Si tam magna fores animus fuit in duce quantus, | Sfortiada cuius corpus et ora refers, | Tanta si stares virtutis ut aemula formae, | Vertice pulsares astra polumque tuo.' ('If you [i.e. the statue] have as much spirit as was in the duke, such as his body and speech referred to in the *Sfortiade*, if you could be as prominent in form as he was in virtue, with your achievement you could reach the stars and the ends of the earth'; qtd. in Evelyn S. Welch, *Art and Authority in Renaissance Milan* (New Haven and London: Yale Univ. Press, 1995), 201 (tr.) and 313 n. 103 (Latin text)).

[4] G. Giri, 'Il codice autografo della Sforziade di Francesco Filelfo,' in G. Benaducci (ed.), *Atti e memorie della Reale deputazione di storia patria per le provincie delle Marche*, 5 (1901), 435–41 attributed the notes and corrections in Rome, Biblioteca Casanatense, 415, to Filelfo himself, but as Vladimiro Zabughin, *Vergilio nel Rinascimento italiano da Dante a Torquato Tasso*, 2 vols. (Bologna: Nicola Zanichelli, 1921–3), i. 335 n. 174 points out, the hand is 18th cent.

[5] Carlo De' Rosmini, *Vita di Francesco Filelfo da Tolentino*, 3 vols. (Milan: Muigi Mussi, 1808), ii. 156.

[6] John Addington Symonds, *The Renaissance in Italy*, ii. *The Revival of Learning* (Gloucester, Mass.: Peter Smith, 1967; repr. of London, 1877 edn.), 197. Later references are no more sympathetic: 'Without plan, a mere versified chronicle, encumbered with foolish mythological machinery, and loaded with fulsome flatteries, this leaden *Sforziad* crawled on until 12,000 lines had been written' (206).

author's love of rhetoric causes him to say everything twice, once in a speech and once in narration; in short, the author lacks the spirit of a poet, in every sense.[7] Vladimiro Zabughin noted several years later that some lovely similes can be found in the poem along with a realistic depiction of the military life of the day,[8] but the most comprehensive recent study of the milieu in which the poem was produced concludes, with a twinge of British understatement, that the *Sphortias* is not the incomparable treasure its author would have us believe it is.[9]

No one would argue that this poem, clearly modelled (*inter alia*) on the *Aeneid*, is as good as its source. Nevertheless most poetry with far greater shortcomings is spared criticism of this duration and intensity, so that it is worth exploring why the *Sphortias* has drawn such scathing denunciations. One reason, I believe, is that its author was not very likable, to say the least. A contemporary described Francesco Filelfo (1398–1481) as 'calumnious, envious, vain and so greedy of gold that he metes out praise or blame according to the gifts he gets,'[10] while one influential modern observer describes him as litigious, vain, and combative,[11] another as having 'developed an exaggerated sense of self-assurance which frequently bordered on narcissism and aggressive arrogance'.[12] Notwithstanding the warnings of late twentieth-century criticism, it has often proved difficult to separate works from their authors, so that some of the hostility felt towards Filelfo himself has spilt over into the evaluation of his

---

[7] A. Novara, 'Un poema latino del Quattrocento: *La Sforziade* di Francesco Filelfo', *Rivista ligura di scienze, lettere ed arti*, 28 (1906), 4–5, 7, 15, 17–18, 23–4, 27. Novara's comments only extend to book 4; presumably if the MS he had used had contained the rest of the poem, he would have found ways to extend his criticisms in new directions.

[8] Zabughin, *Vergilio*, 299; even here, however, there are complaints about lack of stylistic purity; i.e. the poem abounds in Italianisms, prosaic word choice, and linguistic irregularities (ibid.).

[9] Rudolf Georg Adam, 'Francesco Filelfo at the Court of Milan (1439–1481): A Contribution to the Study of Humanism in Northern Italy', Ph.D. thesis (Oxford, 1974), 77; although it is difficult to imagine how this could be confirmed, Adam also claims that Filelfo 'was always inebriated with the sound of his own voice' (38).

[10] The criticism is from a letter of Gregorio Lollio to the Cardinal of Pavia, printed in Rosmini, *Vita*, ii. 147 and quoted with relish in Symonds, *Revival*, 205, who continues, 'Not only Francesco Sforza, but all the patrons upon whom Filelfo thought he had a claim, were assailed with reptile lamentations and more reptile menaces' (ibid.).

[11] Eugenio Garin, 'L'opera di Francesco Filelfo', in *Storia di Milano*, vii. *L' età Sforzesca dal 1450 al 1500* (Milan: Fondazione Treccani degli Alfieri, 1956), 543.

[12] Adam, 'Francesco Filelfo', 13.

writing. Thus the same modern observer who described Filelfo as litigious, vain, and combative simply continues his acerbic commentary when he evaluates Filelfo's works: his orations are tissues of commonplaces, his treatises lack all originality, his translations are devoid of real sympathy for the original, his philology is dry erudition, his satires and invectives are often crude and vulgar, and his verses (predictably by this point) are pastiches woven together from other poetry, made without inspiration or art.[13]

There is, however, another, more important issue blocking a fair assessment of the *Sphortias*. At the beginning of this century, Novara began his denunciation by stating what he believed to be obvious: 'The *Sphortias* of Francesco Filelfo is an encomiastic poem.'[14] By this he meant, as another critic put it, that the *Sphortias* is a poem begun to praise its hero.[15] This approach is now a given in what little criticism of the poem one can find,[16] and the explanation of how the process is said to work leaves the *Sphortias* open to criticism on several fronts. The encomiastic process begins with a great and powerful person, who acts in pursuit of glory. Glory is manufactured by poets, who attend the powerful and write the verses that confer immortality on their deeds. These verses, however, are not available without cost; in one way or another, the poet must be paid for his efforts. As Eugenio Garin puts it, 'Filelfo always proposes to the powerful the same bargain: in exchange for writings in verse or prose, a certain number of zecchini, or florins, or ducats.'[17] It is easy to see how this general understanding of panegyrical epic leaves

---

[13] Garin, 'L'opera', 549. Garin's dislike of Filelfo was ultimately so strong that he concluded: 'he placed himself outside the great humanistic tradition. . . . In the end, only the faintest traces of genuine humanism can be detected in Filelfo' (*Italian Humanism: Philosophy and Civic Life in the Renaissance*, tr. Peter Munz (New York: Harper & Row, 1965), 48), even though Filelfo was one of the greatest classical scholars of his day. This point is made by Christopher S. Celenza, *The Lost Italian Renaissance: Humanists, Historians, and Latin's Legacy* (Baltimore, Md., and London: Johns Hopkins Univ. Press, 2004), 172 n. 58.

[14] Novara, 'Un poema', 3.

[15] Georg Voigt, *Die Wiederbelebung des classischen Alterthums, oder das erste Jahrhundert des Humanismus*, 2 vols., 3rd edn., ed. Max Lehnerdt (Berlin: Georg Reimer, 1893; repr. of Berlin, 1859 edn.), i. 524.

[16] See e.g. Rosmini, *Vita*, ii. 156; Bottari, 'La "Sphortias"', 468–9, 476, 478–89; Adam, 'Francesco Filelfo', 36, 46–7.

[17] Garin, 'L'opera', 545.

poems in the genre open to criticism. For one thing, the process seldom worked as it was supposed to, for in fact few powerful people owe their fame to this kind of poem.[18] What is worse, the encomiastic motive distorts the truth—that is, the need to praise the powerful makes the poet at least to some degree into a liar.[19] But what is worst of all, the panegyrical poet is a paid liar, for when it is distorted like this, poetry is transferred from the sphere of disinterested aesthetics to a mercantile world where art and truth alike are tainted by wealth and power. Seen in this way, the *Sphortias* ends up looking like a failure in several ways: largely unread, it could not confer glory on its central character; it attempts to present a perfect hero far removed from the historical Sforza, whose pursuit of power made him appear less than perfect to many of his contemporaries; but worst of all, the *Sphortias* becomes a literary sell-out—perhaps the greatest literary sell-out in recorded history, as one influential evaluation put it.[20]

This approach to the poem has the merit of focusing our attention on Filelfo's position in relation to the various economic and political power networks of fifteenth-century Italy. This is even more of an issue in his case than with many other humanists of his day, for unlike many of his contemporaries, Filelfo was a self-made man without an independent income. As a result, he needed the support of those richer and more powerful than himself to meet his basic daily needs. In theory he was entitled to good salaries through much of his career, but the evidence suggests that he was seldom paid everything that was promised to him, and in the end he was reported to have died in poverty.[21] While he was working on the *Sphortias*, his

---

[18] Jacob Burckhardt, *The Civilization of the Renaissance in Italy*, tr. S. G. C. Middlemore, rev. and ed. Irene Gordon (New York: Mentor Books, 1960), 196.

[19] Bottari, 'La "Sphortias"', 478–9.

[20] Garin, 'L'opera', 555. Writing some twenty-five years later, Garin seems to have moderated his stance somewhat, repeating his criticisms of Filelfo's character but now stressing more clearly that Filelfo was 'unequalled in Milan as a disseminator of the new culture' and that he 'contributed not a little in facilitating access to the ancient world' ('La cultura a Milano alla fine del Quattrocento', in *Milano nell'età di Ludovico il Moro*, Atti del convegno internazionale 28 febbraio–4 marzo 1983, 2 vols. (Milan: Comune di Milano, 1983) i. 27).

[21] Adam, 'Francesco Filelfo', 62–77, works carefully through the evidence and shows that there are reasons why Filelfo often seems to have been concerned about money. He was clearly treated well and satisfied under Filippo Maria Visconti, whose death left him feeling nervous and vulnerable. A shaky start under Sforza was followed by several good years (1454–9), a time when the *Sphortias* was well under

Epistolario shows him in constant search of patronage, complaining of his position in Milan and exploring other options either directly with the rulers of his day or through friends and supporters as intermediaries.[22] Thus Filelfo found himself throughout his life in a curious position: he was intimate with those in power, yet often powerless to secure the basic necessities of life for himself and his family. Added to these day-to-day worries were several more momentous events that reminded this proud, yet insecure, man of his impotence. In May of 1433, for example, his former patron Cosimo de' Medici had him physically attacked for his political indiscretions, leaving him with a scar on his face. Some years later, Filelfo was trapped in Milan when Sforza besieged the city, a time when many around him died of hunger. Then in 1464–5, his posthumous attacks on one of his former patrons, Pope Pius II, led Sforza, another of his patrons, to imprison him for five months.[23] Thus Filelfo was no ivory-tower academic, isolated from the flow of events around him, but rather an active participant in the economic and political life of his day.

Nevertheless the approach to panegyrical epic outlined above, I believe, has seriously impeded our ability to see all that the *Sphortias* has to teach us. For one thing, it seems to assume that an epic poem on Sforza's ascent to power should be held to the same standards of accuracy as a history of these events, and that what 'actually happened' during that ascent can be observed from a position of objectivity against which departures from truth can be measured. Both of these assumptions, however, are open to challenge.

When Filelfo began work on the *Sphortias*, Sforza himself was particularly eager to have a history of his rise to power that would confer a sense of legitimacy on a conquest that many felt lacked any legal justification. In a letter to his son Xenophon, dated 9 October

way. Filelfo never managed money well, however, and seems to have earned next to nothing from 1460 to 1467. With the succession of Sforza's son, Filelfo's debts were settled, but he got little of his promised stipend, which in any event was fixed at half of what it had been (at least in theory) under Francesco Sforza. Little financial information survives from Filelfo's later years, but he was widely reported to have left only his books at his death.

[22] See below, pp. 25–8.
[23] Diana Robin, *Filelfo in Milan, Writings 1451–1477* (Princeton: Princeton University Press), 7, 17–18.

1452, Filelfo explains that he was working on this history, which he tentatively titled 'De vita et rebus gestibus Francisci Sphortiae', but there is no evidence that the project ever got beyond the planning stage. When it became clear that Filelfo was more interested in writing poetry than history, Sforza turned to Leodrisio Crivelli (1420–76), a protégé and former student of Filelfo's, who produced the desired *De vita Francisci Sphortiae*.[24] It would be reasonable to conclude here that Filelfo relinquished the unfinished project voluntarily to a friend because he preferred to treat the events in poetry rather than in historical narrative. It would also be reasonable to conclude that he must have been motivated at least in part by a desire to have more freedom in treating the material than history would allow.

That is not to say, of course, that the *Sphortias* is not bound to the events of its day, for Filelfo was not free, for example, to make Sforza the victor in a battle everyone knew he had lost. Indeed, readers from Filelfo's day to our own have acknowledged that the poem stays close to history—too close, if anything.[25] This should not surprise us, given that he was an eyewitness to some of the events he depicts and had documents from Sforza's chancery to help fill in some of the others. These documents, of course, were preselected to cast Sforza in

[24] Gary Ianziti, *Humanistic Historiography under the Sforzas: Politics and Propaganda in Fifteenth-Century Milan* (Oxford: Clarendon Press, 1988), 61–80.

[25] In Filelfo's own day, Galeotto Marzio complained that 'differunt, differunt, inquam, poemata et commentarii' ('they are not the same, I say, they are not the same, poems and commentaries', quoted in Bottari, 'La "Sphortias"', 472), with 'commentaries' here being a technical term referring to a new type of humanist historical writing organized around the deeds of a single, contemporary figure (Ianziti, *Humanist Historiography*, 7). The same basic point can be followed through a succession of later critics: Rosmini complains that the poem is 'an historical description in verse…rather than a true poem' (*Vita*, 174), Symonds calls the *Sphortias* 'a mere versified chronicle' (*Revival*, 206), and Garin quotes Rosmini ('L'opera', 555). Bottari refers to the *Sphortias* as 'a long chronicle in hexameters' ('La "Sphortias"', 473), but for him this observation has positive overtones, for he points out that the poem was in fact the first effort to systematize the historical events of the change of power in Milan, and that as such it influenced later treatments of the same material, including Giovanni Simonetta's *De rebus gestis Francisci Sfortiae commentarii* (ibid. 469–70, 473). A good modern account of the events described in the *Sphortias* may be found in F. Cognasso, 'La lotta tra Filippo Maria e Francesco Sforza', 346–83, and idem, 'La repubblica di S. Ambrogio', 387–448, in *Storia di Milano*, vi. *Il ducato visconteo e la repubblica ambrosiana (1392–1450)* (Milan: Fondazione Treccani degli Alfieri, 1955).

the most favourable light possible, but we should be careful not to be too critical here. Humanists of Filelfo's day understood that what happens in human affairs is not an 'absolute, pre-existing entity', but instead 'an essentially socially constructed value'[26] that is bound to the interests and values of the society in which it emerges. Thus both the poet and the historian selected among competing perspectives, so that writing became the effort to make one position that was open to debate more acceptable than the alternatives.[27] Michel Foucault has understood with unusual clarity what anyone writing about Sforza's rise to power in mid-Quattrocento Milan understood, that all perspectives are compromised and that 'truth' is inseparable from the constraints of power operating on those who attempt to see and present it.[28] In other words, condemning the *Sphortias* for praising Sforza assumes that some other option was available to Filelfo and distorts the connection between knowledge and power at the moment the poem was produced.

There are other ways as well in which labelling the poem 'encomiastic' and then dismissing it as simple flattery of Sforza distorts the power relationships governing its production. The *Sphortias* was not 'commissioned' by Sforza in the same way as Crivelli's history, although Filelfo did offer Sforza a presentation copy of the poem (now Paris, Bibliothèque nationale de France, Lat. 8126) that contains the arms of both donor and recipient to symbolize the relationship Sforza was seeking (see Figure 3). Sforza, however, was but

[26] Ianziti, *Humanist Historiography*, 64–5, with the quotation coming from 13–14. Richard Waswo, *Language and Meaning in the Renaissance* (Princeton: Princeton Univ. Press, 1987), shows in general how, for some humanists at least, language constructs reality.

[27] Ibid. See also Victoria Kahn, *Rhetoric, Prudence, and Skepticism in the Renaissance* (Ithaca, NY: Cornell Univ. Press, 1985), which shows how the much-discussed love of rhetoric among humanists of the period derives from this proposition.

[28] '...truth isn't outside power, or lacking in power: contrary to a myth whose history and functions would repay further study, truth isn't the reward of free spirits, the child of protracted solitude, nor the privilege of those who have succeeded in liberating themselves. Truth is a thing of this world: it is produced only by virtue of multiple forms of constraint.... Truth is linked in a circular relation with systems of power which produce and sustain it, and to effects of power which it induces and which extend it' (Michel Foucault, 'Truth and Power', in *Power/Knowledge: Selected Interviews and Other Writings 1972–1977*, ed. Colin Gordon, tr. Colin Gordon, Leo Marshall, John Mepham, and Kate Soper (New York: Pantheon Books, 1980), 131, 133; see also 119).

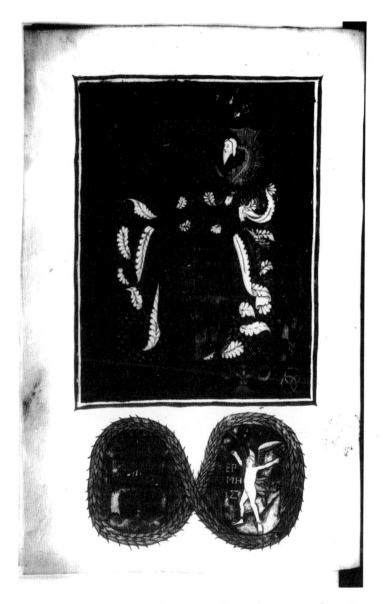

Figure 3. Filelfo's *Sphortias* with arms of author and Francesco Sforza. Francesco Filelfo, *Sphortias*, Paris, Bibliothèque nationale de France, Ms. lat. 8126, fo. IIᵛ (Bibliothèque nationale de France)

one of a good number of potential patrons whose attention Filelfo tried to draw to the poem. Of special interest is the group of *condottiere*-princes to whom Filelfo sent copies of the *Sphortias* between 1453 and 1456: Ludovico Gonzaga of Mantua, Sigismondo Malatesta of Rimini, Federigo Montefeltro of Urbino, Borso d'Este of Ferrara, and Alfonso of Naples, in particular.[29] By sending the poem to men like these, Filelfo was clearly suggesting that he could help confer legitimacy on other *novi homines* ('new men') as well. In 1455 he disseminated the first four books more widely, with one copy going to Piero de' Medici; the accompanying letter (dated 17 May) indicates that Filelfo was interested in changing his professional situation, and since there is a suggestion that Piero already had a copy of part of the poem, it appears that Filelfo had been working for some time to repair the damage done by his earlier anti-Medicean political activity.[30] On 13 January 1460 he sent the beginning of book 11 to Pius II so the pope could see Filelfo's version of the speech he had given as Emperor Frederick III's ambassador to the Ambrosian Republic and, Filelfo hoped, arrange to have his annual pension paid. In February 1460 extracts from book 8 went to Lodovico Gonzaga, and on 20 May of the same year Filelfo was again communicating with Piero de' Medici about the progress of the poem. Several letters of 1463 suggest a well-thought-out strategy for spreading the work, with Nicodemo Tranchedini, Sforza's ambassador to Florence, playing a pivotal role. On 1 August 1465 Filelfo wrote to Leodrisio Crivelli that the first books 'aediti sunt' ('have been published'), and on 1 August 1467 he sent this much of the poem to Federico di Urbino. On 11 August 1472 Filelfo sent book 9 to Lorenzo de' Medici and suggested that the next two books were under way; book 9 was also sent around this time to Giacomo Cardinale di Pavia, to be added to the eight books he already had, and extracts from the same

---

[29] Robin, *Filelfo in Milan*, 59–60. The MS sent to Alfonso of Naples is now in Paris, Bibliothèque nationale de France, lat. 8125. As Kristen Lippincott notes, such princes were being approached by other humanists who wanted to write epics about their exploits in Latin as well; see 'The Neo-Latin Historical Epics of the North Italian Courts: An Examination of "Courtly Culture" in the Fifteenth Century', *Renaissance Studies*, 3 (1989), 415–28.

[30] Bottari, 'La "Sphortias"', 465. Giri, 'Il codice', 445 n. 1; and Ianziti, *Humanist Historiography*, 66 and n. 14, suggest that Florence, Biblioteca Laurenziana, Plut. 33,33 is the copy Filelfo sent to Piero de' Medici in 1455.

book went to Jacopo Piccolomini in September and October of 1473.[31] In his own way, each of these men was in a position potentially to do something for Filelfo, and his use of the *Sphortias* to cultivate all of them shows clearly that power in his world was not concentrated only in the hands of Francesco Sforza, but rather in the hands of the larger network whose operation Foucault, again, has understood so well:

> Power must be analysed as something which circulates, or rather as something which only functions in the form of a chain. It is never localised here or there, never in anybody's hands, never appropriated as a commodity or a piece of wealth. Power is employed and exercised through a net-like organisation. And not only do individuals circulate between its threads; they are always in the position of simultaneously undergoing and exercising this power. They are not only its inert or consenting target; they are always also the elements of its articulation.[32]

In the end, the relationship between Filelfo and Sforza cannot be reduced to the simplistic paradigm set out by Garin, in which the powerful prince purchases praise without qualification from the impotent poet. While Sforza was effecting his takeover of Milan, Filelfo was anything but a committed supporter: what he wrote during this period shows his allegiance wavering among the various factions until, during the last few weeks of the Ambrosian Republic, he cast his lot with Sforza as his best hope among the options that remained.[33] In one sense, the two were kindred spirits, since both were self-made men from comparatively humble backgrounds—one might say that Filelfo was attempting to achieve with his pen the success that had come to Sforza by his sword. Sforza, however, had little interest in humanistic culture and seems to have seen Filelfo as little more than a political asset that turned out in the end to be of dubious value. He certainly never showed any interest in his work,[34]

---

[31] Giri, 'Il codice', 423–4; and Bottari, 'La "Sphortias"', 464–8.

[32] Michel Foucault, 'Lecture Two: 14 Jan. 1976', in *Power/Knowledge*, 98.

[33] Adam, 'Francesco Filelfo', 23–4; Garin, 'L'opera', 554; and Bottari, 'La "Sphortias"', 462 and n. 16.

[34] Adam, 'Francesco Filelfo', 38, 46–7. As Colin Burrow has pointed out, English translations of the *Aeneid* in the early modern period were often written by authors who wanted to be closer to the centre of political power than they actually were ('Virgil in English Translation', in Charles Martindale (ed.), *The Cambridge Companion to Virgil* (Cambridge: CUP, 1997), 21–37).

which caused Filelfo to complain in a letter of 17 February 1477 to Ludovico Gonzaga that 'fuit sane Franciscus Sphortia...litteraturae urbanioris et Musarum ignarus' ('Francesco Sforza was certainly ignorant of the more elegant literature and of the arts in general').[35] Some periods were better than others, but through most of his time in Milan Filelfo's attitude towards his supposed patron was ambivalent at best. As Diana Robin has pointed out, the same pattern emerges throughout Filelfo's *œuvre*: in his *Odae* Filelfo vilifies Milan's republican governors but refuses to praise Sforza consistently, now drawing him in grandiose terms, now in diminished and jejune ones; the *Psychagogia* contains only one very short poem dedicated to Sforza, which seems insulting under the circumstances; the letter of 8 October 1438 praises Sforza, but also reproaches him in a passage couched in hypothetical subjunctives and framed between adulatory sections; and so forth.[36] Filelfo's frustrations seem to have peaked with the attacks on Pope Pius II that led ultimately to his imprisonment in 1464–5, for he complains of his treatment by Sforza in a series of letters sent all over Italy and in literary works like *De iocis et seriis*.[37] Sforza was

[35] Qtd. in Robin, *Filelfo in Milan*, 57 n. 6. Sforza may have had his rough edges, but he took care that the image he presented to the public hid them: e.g. the medal that Pisanello struck for him shortly after his marriage to Bianca Maria in 1441 indeed has a horse and sword symbolizing his role as a soldier on the obverse, but they are accompanied by a book that symbolizes learning (Kendall Curlee, *The Sforza Court: Milan in the Renaissance 1450–1535* (Austin, Tex.: Archer M. Huntington Art Gallery, Univ. of Texas, 1988), 8–9). Given the subject of this chapter, it is worth noting that Virgil was among a group of classical authors whose works Sforza had copied for his eldest son, Galeazzo Maria (ibid. 7).

[36] Robin, *Filelfo in Milan*, 8–9, 43, 45–7. It is worth noting that Filelfo's situation in Milan, and his response to it, were hardly unique. Antonio Averlino (il Filarete), the architect who was supposedly in charge of one of the major building projects undertaken by Francesco Sforza, the Ospedale Maggiore, found himself underappreciated as an artist and unpaid for the work he had done. Over the course of time, he reworked his *Trattato de architectura* (*c.*1461–5) and changed its dedicatee from Sforza to Piero de' Medici. This treatise, like the *Sphortias*, contains both praise of its original dedicatee and signs of its author's disillusionment; see Welch, *Art and Authority*, 148–9, 188.

[37] Adam, 'Francesco Filelfo', 39–45; Adam (44) provides a list of letters that show Filelfo's increasing frustration with his position in Milan: to Lodovico Trevisan (23 Aug. 1464), Giacomo Ammanati Piccolomini (15 Sept. 1464), Bernardo Giustinian (20 Sept. 1464), Lodovico Foscarini (24 Sept. 1464), Filippo Calandrini (25 Sept. 1464), Bartolomeo Rovarella (4 Oct. 1464), and Cardinal Bessarion (31 Oct. 1464). *De iocis et seriis* 7, as Adam points out, is but thinly veiled criticism of Sforza (ibid. 43).

certainly a powerful man—the most powerful single individual in Filelfo's world—but as Foucault has noted, power always stimulates resistance, and there are plenty of signs of resistance in Filelfo's work.[38]

Here and there, other critics have noted some of these signs in the *Sphortias*. Novara, who stresses the encomiastic character of the poem, nevertheless lodges repeated criticisms of Sforza as he is depicted in the poem: he is a traitor and an odious personality, totally unsympathetic to the suffering he inflicts on others; a man driven by greed rather than grand, selfless motives; and so forth.[39] Both Novara and Robin note that the reader's sympathies end up with the victims of the sack of Piacenza in book 3, not with Sforza as conqueror,[40] and Bottari observes that Filelfo has presented the Venetians, who are definitely the antagonists in the poem, with sympathy as well, praising some of the Venetian leaders and celebrating the values to which they adhered.[41] Observations like these offer the potential for reading the poem in a new way, but for the most part they simply lead to another negative evaluation within the usual critical parameters. Typical is the judgement of Bottari, who concludes that Filelfo simply failed to draw together the various strands of his material into a consistent line of propaganda.[42] Once again we are back where most previous criticism ends up sooner or later (usually sooner), at the effort to explain how a man so widely respected (if not liked) in his own day could have produced such a bad poem.

[38] Michel Foucault, 'Powers and Strategies', in *Power/Knowledge*, 142; and idem, *Discipline and Punish*, 27. Foucault makes the same point a bit differently elsewhere ('The Subject and Power', in *Power*, ed. James D. Faubion, tr. Robert Hurley *et al.* (New York: New Press, 2000), in terms that apply perfectly to the relationship between Filelfo and Sforza: 'At the heart of the power relationship, and constantly provoking it, are the recalcitrance of the will and the intransigence of freedom. Rather than speaking of an essential antagonism, it would be better to speak of an "agonism"—of a relationship that is at the same time mutual incitement and struggle' (342). Robin, *Filelfo in Milan*, is the only scholar to have applied insights like these to Filelfo: 'in his encomiastic and dedicatory writings, often the masks of collaborator and resister are curiously superimposed, the apparition of the one glinting confusingly through the fabric of the other' (4).

[39] Novara, 'Un poema', 3, 5, 8–9, 12.

[40] Ibid. 20; and Robin, *Filelfo in Milan*, 63–81.

[41] Bottari, 'La "Sphortias"', 481.

[42] Ibid. 480–3.

2. VIRGIL AND THE CHALLENGE
TO LAUDATORY EPIC

As I have tried to suggest, viewing the *Sphortias* as a univocal panegyric of its namesake has made it almost impossible for previous critics to see much in the poem that makes it worth our attention today. In the previous section, I have tried to show how a more sophisticated analysis of power might begin to open up a new reading of the *Sphortias*. In this section, I shall turn to Filelfo's principal source and suggest how a previously underexplored approach to that poem provides unexpected support for this new reading of the *Sphortias*.

As one of the most competent Hellenists of his day, Filelfo certainly had Homer in mind as he composed his *Sphortias*, and other epics ranging from Statius's *Thebaid* to Lucan's *Pharsalia* provided points of reference as well.[43] The scholarly culture of Quattrocento Italy, however, was primarily Latin, and a humanist looking back to ancient Rome for inspiration in writing epic would centre his attention on the *Aeneid*. This point has been made before in discussions of the *Sphortias*,[44] but many of the consequences that have been deduced from it strike me as wide of the mark. Novara, for example, argues that the *Aeneid* praises the achievements of Rome, especially

---

[43] In the introduction to the poem e.g. Filelfo claims that the deeds he is going to recount are more worth remembering than those preserved in past epics. One of the references to past epics is to Parthenopaeus, who appears in the catalogue of heroes in Statius's *Thebaid* 4. 246–344 as an ambitious but untested youth who is always described in langorous, erotic terms; he appears again in the footrace in *Thebaid* 6. 550–645, where his physical beauty is again stressed; finally, in *Thebaid* 9. 570–907, Diana gives him an *aristeia*, but he dies amid great pathos as a victim of overambitious inexperience (see David Vessey, *Statius and the Thebaid* (Cambridge: CUP, 1973), 201, 218, 298). On the surface, Filelfo is saying that Sforza's deeds are greater than these, but in light of the arguments being developed in this chapter, it is probably worth thinking about why Filelfo did not cite a greater hero like Achilles, and whether the comparison to a character like Parthenopaeus is wholly flattering to Sforza. Garin, 'L'opera', 554–5, proposes the *Iliad* as a model for the *Sphortias*, and Bottari, 'La "Sphortias"', has noted a few parallels to Statius (471–2), Lucan (486), and Silius Italicus (486, 491), but much more work needs to be done on Filelfo's allusions to classical literature.

[44] Zabughin, *Vergilio*, 297–9, 334–41, concentrates his attention on the love affair of Carlo Gonzaga and its connection to the Dido story in *Aeneid* 4. See also Robin, *Filelfo in Milan*, 61–2, 71–2, 75.

under the leadership of Augustus, who encouraged associations between himself and the mythical founder of the state. The *Sphortias* was written in imitation of the *Aeneid*, so it praises the achievements of Francesco Sforza; that is, the encomiastic character of the *Sphortias* derives at least in part from the encomiastic character of its model.[45]

As I have tried to show elsewhere, the *Aeneid* was generally read through precisely the kind of filter Novara describes in the first generations of Italian humanism.[46] Scholars in search of guidance on how to interpret the poem regularly turned to the commentary of Tiberius Claudius Donatus (late fourth century AD), who saw the poem as an 'artem dicendi plenissimam' ('a most thorough rhetorical treatise') whose 'materiae genus' ('genus of subject matter') is 'laudativum' ('encomiastic'): that is, the *Aeneid* is an epic poem, but this poetic genre was thoroughly contaminated by contact with epideictic, the rhetoric of praise and blame.[47] More specifically, the goal of epic poetry was to praise the virtue of its hero and condemn the vice of his enemies, so that (as Filelfo's contemporary Maffeo Vegio (1407–58) put it), Virgil presented Aeneas as a man 'omni virtute praeditus' ('endowed with every virtue'), someone by whom the reader 'ad virtutis studium magnopere incendatur' ('would be greatly aroused toward zealous pursuit of virtue').[48] This approach reached its peak in the work of Cristoforo Landino (1424–92), who taught the *Aeneid* from this perspective from his chair in the Florentine Studio and published his interpretation of the poem in both commentary and dialogue form in the later Quattrocento. As Landino put it,

Qua obsecro ille acrimonia, quo verborum fulmine metum, ignaviam, luxuriam, incontinentiam, impietatem, perfidiam ac omnia iniustitiae genera reliquaque vitia insectatur vexatque? Quibus contra laudibus, quibus

---

[45] Novara, 'Un poema', 3.

[46] Craig Kallendorf, *In Praise of Aeneas: Virgil and Epideictic Rhetoric in the Early Italian Renaissance* (Hanover, NH, and London: Univ. Press of New England, 1989).

[47] Tiberius Claudius Donatus, *Interpretationes Vergilianae*, ed. Henricus Georgii, 2 vols. (Leipzig: Teubner, 1905–6), i. 2. Later references to this edn. will be placed in the text. Although modern scholars have tended to question the value of Donatus's criticism, a more sympathetic approach may be found in Marisa Squillante Saccone, *Le Interpretationes Virgilianae di Tiberio Claudio Donato* (Naples: Società Editrice Napoletana, 1985).

[48] Maffeo Vegio, *De educatione liberorum et eorum claris moribus*, ed. M. W. Fanning and A. S. Sullivan, 2 vols. (Washington, DC: Catholic Univ. of America Press, 1933–6), i. 87–8 (s. 2.18); see also Kallendorf, *In Praise of Aeneas*, 100–28, esp. 102–3.

praemiis invictam animi magnitudinem, et pro patria, pro parentibus, pro cognatis amicisque consideratam periculorum susceptionem, religionem in Deum, pietatem in maiores, caritatem in omnes prosequitur!...Ita locum concludam, ut universum huius scriptoris poesim laudem esse virtutis atque omnia ad illam referri sine dubitatione affirmem.

With what sharpness, I ask you, with what verbal thunder does he rail at fear, sloth, dissipation, intemperance, impiety, treachery, and every kind of injustice along with the remaining vices? On the other hand, with what praises and rewards does he pursue invincible magnanimity and the well-considered undertaking of dangers on behalf of country and parents, relatives and friends, respect toward God, devotion toward elders, love toward all.... I conclude by declaring that without any doubt, this writer's entire poem praises virtue and that everything concerns that.[49]

Different critics took this approach in different directions—Landino, for instance, was a Neoplatonist, so he saw Aeneas passing from the active life to the contemplative one through a gradation of virtues[50]—but the general consensus was that Virgil's poem was encomiastic.

This approach had particular consequences for how Aeneas himself was viewed. Donatus had gone to remarkable lengths to show that Virgil had praised Aeneas's virtue on every possible occasion: he is a good leader (on *Aen.* 1. 159–79), pious toward the gods (on *Aen.* 1. 379), chaste (on *Aen.* 1. 310–20), handsome and brave (on *Aen.* 1. 594–5), etc. Indeed, according to Donatus, Aeneas never makes a mistake. It might appear, for example, that he displays cowardice in fleeing Carthage, but this is not the case: it is no crime to flee a city destined by fate to fall, and Aeneas's flight is justified by a visit from Hector, by one brave man appearing to another, and by a special vision of the gods that confers special merit on Aeneas by allowing him to see the divine with human eyes. Even in his dealings with women, Aeneas cannot be blamed: Creusa absolves him from losing her (on *Aen.* 2. 775 ff.), and Donatus

---

[49] Cristoforo Landino, 'In P. Vergilii interpretationes prohemium', in *Scritti critici e teorici*, ed. Roberto Cardini, 2 vols. (Rome: Bulzoni, 1974), i. 215–16. Landino's commentary to Virgil was reprinted many times in the 15th and 16th cent.; see Giuliano Mambelli, *Gli annali delle edizioni virgiliane* (Florence: Olschki, 1954). Many of the same points were developed in greater detail in his *Disputationes Camaldulenses*, ed. Peter Lohe (Florence: Sansoni, 1980).

[50] Kallendorf, *In Praise of Aeneas*, 129–65, esp. 136–7.

aeneas as perfectly virtuous (handwritten marginalia)

even outlines a defence that Aeneas could have given of his actions
with Dido had the narrative line of the poem allowed it (on *Aen.* 4. 271).
This approach in turn is also found in the writings of humanists like
Francesco Petrarca (1304–74), whose famous allegorization of the
Aeneid in *Seniles* 4. 5 interprets Aeneas sometimes as the 'vir fortis ac
perfectus' ('the brave and perfect man'), other times simply as 'virtus'
('virtue'). The final battle with Turnus therefore marks the final
victory of good over evil, in a simple, unambiguous way.[51]

This interpretation of the *Aeneid* presents the moral world of the
poem in stark, black-and-white terms, which are in turn carried over
into imitative epics of the period. As Ennius's speech about Scipio
in book 9 shows, for example, Petrarca's *Africa* rests on the same
understanding of epic as his interpretation of the *Aeneid* in *Seniles* 4. 5:

> Hoc igitur mecum indignans sub mente movebam,
> Precones meritos tua quod notissima virtus
> Non habitura foret....
>   ... Non parva profecto
> Est claris fortuna viris habuisse poetam
> Altisonis qui carminibus cumulare decorem
> Virtutis queat egregie monimentaque laudum.

> It was indeed this thought that moved my heart
> to indignation: that your peerless worth
> would find no proper eulogist....
>   ... Indeed
> it's no small thing for famous men to know
> a poet skilled in use of lofty verse
> to sing their virtues and proclaim their praise.

(*Africa* 9. 49–51, 54–7[52])

---

[51] The text of *Seniles* 4. 5 may be found in Francesco Petrarca, *Opera quae extant omnia* (Basle: Sebastianus Henricpetri, 1581), 786–9. Petrarca's understanding of Virgil has been treated by P. de Nolhac, *Pétrarque et l'humanisme*, 2nd edn. (Paris: H. Champion, 1907; repr. of Paris, 1892 edn.), 123–61; Zabughin, *Vergilio*, i. 25–8; P. de Nolhac, 'Virgile chez Pétrarque', *Studi medievali*, ns 5 (1932), 217–25; Don Cameron Allen, *Mysteriously Meant: The Rediscovery of Pagan Symbolism and Allegorical Interpretation in the Renaissance* (Baltimore, Md.: Johns Hopkins Univ. Press, 1970), 139–40; and Kallendorf, *In Praise of Aeneas*, 19–57.

[52] References to the *Africa*, which will be placed in the text, are to Nicola Festa (ed.), Edizione Nazionale delle Opere di Francesco Petrarca, 1 (Florence: Sansoni, 1926), with tr. from *Petrarch's Africa*, tr. and annotated by Thomas G. Bergin and Alice S. Wilson (New Haven and London: Yale Univ. Press, 1977). Aldo S. Bernardo,

of Satan
as Hannibal

Thus when Scipio's friend Laelius describes the Roman leader, he says he is harsh towards his enemies and mild towards his friends, equally unmoved by both good fortune and bad, the defender of the weak and powerless, *pius* to gods, country, and family, and so forth (*Africa* 4. 34–388). In book 6, by contrast, Petrarca presents an extended condemnation of Hannibal, Scipio's nemesis in the poem: a member of a treacherous race (l. 120), he is personally wicked as well (l. 264). Indeed, Hannibal is linked intertextually with two of the most clearly evil characters in the *Aeneid*, Pyrrhus (ll. 449–83; cf. *Aen.* 2. 526 ff.) and Mezentius, who like Hannibal is called 'dux ferus et celi contemptor maximus alti' ('this scorner of the heavens, this savage chief', l. 485; cf. *Aen.* 7. 648).

If, then, the great epic poem of ancient Rome had set out to praise the virtues of its hero, poems written in imitation of it should do the same. This is what Petrarca had done, and this is what Novara believes that Filelfo, who also knew the *Africa*,[53] designed the *Sphortias* to do. The problem, though, is that Filelfo did not read the *Aeneid* as most of his contemporaries did, as a straightforward eulogy of Aeneas. This point was first suggested with some hesitation by Diana Robin in her brilliant analysis of book 3 of the *Sphortias*.[54] At the time when she was writing, however, not enough was known

self-
praise

Petrarch, Scipio, and the 'Africa': The Birth of Humanism's Dream (Baltimore, Md.: Johns Hopkins Univ. Press, 1962), 199–200, noted that the *Africa* follows the same general lines of development as Petrarca's Virgilian allegory in *Seniles* 4. 5, and Armando Carlini, *Studio su l''Africa'* (Florence: Successori Le Monnier, 1902), 133–4, observes that Petrarca's Scipio is simply an exaggeration of *pius* Aeneas. The most thorough analysis of the connections between the two poems is R. W. A. Seagraves, 'The Influence of Vergil on Petrarch's *Africa*', Ph.D. thesis (Columbia, 1976); see also Kallendorf, *In Praise of Aeneas*, 22–4, 50–1.

[53] Robin, *Filelfo in Milan*, 77.

[54] Robin cites the 'Harvard' (i.e. 'pessimistic') school of Virgilian criticism (ibid. 75 n. 67) and notes, as these critics would, that the duplicity of Aeneas's expansionist rhetoric provides the model for Sforza in Filelfo's poem (71–2), and that 'Filelfo seems to have been troubled by the insane rage (*ira* and *furor*) that Aeneas evinces in Book 10' (75). It is difficult, however, to bring these observations into line with some of Filelfo's other comments on the *Aeneid*, and in the end Robin appears to back away from attributing to Filelfo a full-blown 'pessimistic' reading of Virgil: 'Nor should we assume that Filelfo saw buried in the *Aeneid* a subtle critique of Augustus and his policies' (ibid.). Her analysis was not focused primarily on the relationship between the *Sphortias* and the *Aeneid*, but it has nevertheless provided me with invaluable guidance throughout this chapter.

either about the development of Filelfo's Virgilian studies or about the range of interpretive options open to a scholar of his generation to allow her (or anyone else) to defend this position with confidence. In the remainder of this section, I shall revisit both of these areas to try to show that in fact Filelfo saw far more ambiguity in Virgil's moral world than most of his contemporaries did.

First, Filelfo's Virgilian studies. The first significant document here is a letter Filelfo wrote to Ciriaco d'Ancona (1391–1452), who had written to ask him to explain his understanding of the *Aeneid*. Filelfo's answer relies heavily on allegory, providing first an introduction to the poem, then an analysis of Aeolus and the winds in *Aen.* 1. 157 with reference to moral philosophy, then an analysis of the same scene with reference to natural philosophy, and finally a brief excursus on the rest of the poem. Most of this is traditional exegesis, based on the allegorization of the *Aeneid* according to the successive ages of man made by Fabius Planciades Fulgentius (fifth–sixth centuries AD)[55] but also including the commonly accepted association of epic with epideictic rhetoric: 'Quod Virgilius... Aenean laudans Augustum quoque laudarit, nequaquam inficior' ('I by no means deny that Virgil, in praising Aeneas, also praised Augustus', ll. 22–24). The basic principle that Landino would develop in detail several decades later, that the first six books of the *Aeneid* examine the contemplative life and the second half exalts the active life, appears here as well (ll. 66–8). *Fortitudo* in particular is praised in the last six books, which leads Filelfo to a standard, morally unambiguous analysis of the final scene in Virgil's poem: 'Turnus enim qui se iniustitiae fecerat ignaviaeque obnoxium, in obscuritate nominis moritur sempiterna, Aeneas vero vir iustus et fortis quasi numen in dies magis atque magis diuturnitate gloriae illustratur' ('For Turnus, who had made himself subject to injustice and faint-heartedness, dies

---

[55] Vito R. Giustiniani, 'Il Filelfo, l'interpretazione allegorica di Virgilio e la tripartizione platonica dell'anima', in *Umanesimo e Rinascimento, studi offerti a Paul Oskar Kristeller* (Florence: Olschki, 1980), 36; the text of Filelfo's letter is printed on 37–42 and will be cited in the text. Filelfo is relying on the *Expositio Virgilianae continentia secundum philosophos moralis*, which may be read in Fulgentius, *Opera*, ed. Rudolfus Helm (Leipzig: Teubner, 1898), 81–107; the best introduction to this work, which may strike a modern reader as bizarre in places, remains Domenico Comparetti, *Virgilio nel Medioevo*, ed. Giorgio Pasquali, 2 vols. (Florence: La Nuova Italia, 1981; repr. of Florence, 1867 edn.), 107–16.

with his reputation in everlasting obscurity, but Aeneas, a man both just and strong like a god, grows more and more distinguished every day in enduring glory', ll. 134–6). This analysis is for the most part indistinguishable from many others of its time,[56] which is what we should expect given the circumstances of its composition. The letter is dated 21 December 1427, when Filelfo was only 29 years old and had just returned to Venice after a long stay in Constantinople, where he had concentrated on his Greek studies, not Latin. The plague was raging and his future was uncertain, so we could hardly expect him to give much time or thought to Virgil right then. We therefore see him responding to Ciriaco's request with points that were considered obvious in his day.[57]

Seven years later, we find Filelfo in Siena, where he had just taken up a position lecturing on the classics at that city's Studio. During the academic year 1434–5, his lectures included the *Aeneid*, and some of what he said has been found in the *recordationes* of a notary named Antonius Michaelis. These notes are predominantly lexical, grammatical, and etymological, although there are also a few observations on literary history that occasionally take on a philosophical bent. The level of learning displayed here is not in general very high; indeed, much of what Filelfo appears to have said was readily available in the common sources of the medieval grammatical and rhetorical tradition.[58] One note, however, is of particular interest. In commenting on Virgil's reference to the violation of Cassandra by the lesser Ajax, Filelfo wrote, '*Aen.* 1,41 (*furias*) Furor in sapientem cadit, insania

---

[56] Robin argues that careful attention to phrasing reveals that, in a couple of places, Filelfo pulls back from assigning unequivocal praise to Aeneas: he does not actually attain the *summum bonum*, but the path by which he might approach it ('qua via summum bonum parari posset'); and at the end Aeneas is not actually made into a god, but is compared to one ('quasi numen'), so that even at the end of the poem he is still struggling to attain his goals ('indies magis atque magis diurnitate gloriae illustratur') (*Filelfo in Milan*, 54–5). In the end, though, Robin agrees that 'Filelfo's famous letter to Ciriaco d'Ancona about the *Aeneid* indicates, on the contrary [to the "Harvard school"], that he accepted Servius's and Fulgentius's reading of the *Aeneid* first as a moral allegory, and second as a panegyric of the emperor' (ibid. 75).

[57] Giustiniani, 'Il Filelfo', 36.

[58] Rossella Bianchi, 'Note di Francesco Filelfo al "De natura deorum," al "De oratore," e all' "Eneide" negli appunti di un notaio senese', in *Francesco Filelfo nel quinto centenario*, which contains an analysis of the lecture notes (325–44) followed by a transcription of them (345–68). See Appendix 2.

minime, quia furor est vehementissima ira quae contra aliquem malum exercetur...' (*'Aen.* 1. 41 (*furias*): rage suits a wise man, [but] insanity certainly does not, since rage is the most vehement form of anger which is exercised against any evil person...').[59] 'Furor' and 'ira' are key words in Virgil's moral vocabulary, and it is by no means certain that someone can succumb to them and remain wise. Here Filelfo suggests that one can. The notes in this manuscript break off at line 254 of book 1, so we can only speculate about what Filelfo would have said about the rest of the poem on the basis of his comment on *Aen.* 1. 41. In the final scene of the poem, for example, Aeneas is driven by anger, but according to what Filelfo said in the beginning of his Siena lectures, he could retain his status as a wise man and, by extension, a praiseworthy hero if he did not sink into insanity.

Almost forty years later, in 1473, we find Filelfo at work on *De morali disciplina*, one of several works of its day which explore the relationship between Plato and Aristotle. Filelfo believed that the two philosophical systems were compatible, but since he was not a professional philosopher, he developed his argument using literary examples as well as formal logic.[60] In his discussion of courage, he dismissed Aristotle's doctrine of just anger and defends the proposition that 'iracundia debet abesse a fortitudine' ('anger ought not to be associated with bravery') in this manner:

Irae fervor in magnis etiam viris, si quis apparet, reprehensione non vacat. Itaque non parum mirari Virgilium soleo, qui Aeneam, quem religiosum, quem pium, vel propter Caesarem Augustum laudare debebat plurimum, ostendit quandoque ira inferiorem, cum de illo ita reliquit scriptum: 'saevae iamque altius irae | Dardanio surgunt ductori' [*Aen.* 10. 813–14]. Et alio loco circa nobilissimi carminis consummationem ait: 'Ille oculis postquam saevi monumenta doloris | Exuviasque hausit, furiis accensus, et ira | Terribilis, tune hinc spoliis indute meorum, | Eripiere mihi? Pallas te hoc vulnere Pallas | Immolat, et poenam scelerato ex sanguine sumit, | Haec dicens, ferrum adverso sub pectore condit | Fervidus' [*Aen.* 12. 945–51].

If the heat of anger appears at all in great men, it should be condemned. I therefore stand in no small perplexity before Virgil, who depicts Aeneas,

---

[59] Bianchi, 'Note', 346.
[60] Robin, *Filelfo in Milan*, 138–53, situates *De morali disciplina* within the Plato–Aristotle controversy and the intellectual programme of its author.

whom he ought to have been praising as religious and pious, even on
account of Augustus, as giving in to his anger in a certain place, when he
wrote in this way about him: 'at this | harsh anger rises in the Dardan chief'
[*Aen.* 10. 813–14], and in another place at the end of his most noble of
poems, he says, 'And when his eyes drank in this plunder, this | memorial
of brutal grief, Aeneas, | aflame with rage—his wrath was terrible— | cried:
"How can you who wear the spoils of my | dear comrade now escape me? It
is Pallas | who strikes, who sacrifices you, who takes | this payment from
your shameless blood." Relentless, he sinks his sword into the chest of
Turnus.' [*Aen.* 12. 945–51][61]

Filelfo's Aeneas is 'pius', but not perfectly so, for at several points in
the poem, including the crucial last scene, he fails to control his
anger. In other words, the fragmentary records of his Siena lectures
only allow us to speculate about whether succumbing to anger
affected Aeneas's standing as the perfectly praiseworthy hero, but in
De morali disciplina Filelfo took a clear stand. In doing so, he left
behind the standard interpretation of the poem in his day.

   This is a big step, but it is not necessary to conclude that Filelfo was
a solitary genius who worked out a new interpretation of the *Aeneid*
all by himself. In fact, I have identified nine passages from eight other
Renaissance scholars that are also incompatible with the idea that the
Aeneid must be read as simple, straightforward praise of a morally
perfect hero.

   1*a*. In *De otio religioso* Petrarca uses the familiar opposition
between *negotium* ('business') and *otium* ('leisure') to contrast the
peaceful contemplation of the religious life to the endless, and
ultimately meaningless, activity of worldly affairs. Addressed to the
monks of the Carthusian monastery at Montrieux to which his

---

   [61] *Francisci Philelphi de morali disciplina libri quinque* (Venice: Gualterus Scottus,
1552), 71–2. The Aristotelian doctrine of just anger (*NE* 1106^{b}20–26^{b}10) has been
cited in Aeneas's defence by a number of critics, ranging from Angelo Poliziano, *De
ira in pueris*, in *Opera* (Lyon: Sebastianus Gryphius, 1537–9), iii. 63; to Karl Galinsky,
'The Anger of Aeneas', *American Journal of Philology*, 109 (1988), 330–5. Lactantius
had lodged a similar complaint many centuries earlier, arguing that no one who gave
into anger as Aeneas had could be considered *pius* (*Div. Inst.* 5. 10. 9). This criticism
has been discussed at length by A. Wlosok, 'Zwei Beispiele frühchristlicher "Vergil-
rezeption"?: Polemik (Lact. div. inst. 5,10) und Usurpation (Or. Const. 19–21)', in
V. Pöschl (ed.), *2000 Jahre Vergil: Ein Symposium* (Wiesbaden: In Kommission bei
O. Harrassowitz, 1983), 63–8; its importance to the present discussion has also been
noted by N. Horsfall (ed.), *A Companion to the Study of Virgil* (Leiden: Brill, 1995), 197.

brother Gherardo belonged, the treatise examines the actions of
Aeneas from this perspective and finds them wanting:

Quanto id rectius nobis ille pater celestis, quam apud Virgilium Eneas filio:
'Disce puer virtutem ex me' [*Aen.* 12. 435]: Quam queso, virtutem, Anchi-
siades? An patrie proditionem, quamvis utcunque hic virgiliana te excuset
eloquentia, quam secuti poete et historici quidam non citata domo Priami
sententiis absolutam dimiserunt? An sacrificia demonum amicorum cedibus
et sanguine peragenda? Cristus autem verus pater et dominus et magister et
Deus noster iure suo precipit ut ab eo non virtutes illas et nequaquam
imitabiles discamus, sed, quod est hominis maxime proprium, esse mites
et corde humiles, qui ad hoc discendum alio equidem nos misisset, si
omnino ullum clarius exemplar mansuetudinis invenisset.

How much more correctly does that heavenly father [say] to us than Aeneas
in Virgil [says] to his son, 'From me, my son, learn virtue and true labor'
[*Aen.* 12. 435]. What virtue, I ask, o son of Anchises? The betrayal of your
country, although here the eloquence of Virgil excuses you as much as
possible—an eloquence which certain poets and historians have followed
and dismissed with a vote of acquittal, without summoning the dependents
of Priam as witnesses? Or sacrifices carried out with the bloody slaughter of
friendly demons? Christ, however, our true father and lord and master and
God, teaches through his law not that we learn from him virtues like these,
which are not to be imitated, but that we be gentle and humble in heart,
which is especially appropriate to a human being. He indeed would have
sent us to learn this from another, if he could have found any other clearer
example of meekness in any circumstances.[62]

First a traitor, then a worshipper of false gods, Aeneas is ultimately
culpable for not being *pius*, here understood as 'mitis et corde
humilis' ('gentle and humble in heart'). The comparison of Aeneas
to Christ may well appear to be a decidedly unhumanistic manœuvre,
but it is important to note that Petrarca's procedure is more in line
with emerging philological practice than it might at first seem. Many
scholars of the early Renaissance believed that pagan authors sometimes saw 'through the glass darkly' (1 Cor. 13: 12) into shadowy
adumbrations of Christian truth, so Petrarca could have approached

---

62 Francesco Petrarca, *Opere latine*, ed. Antonietta Bufano (Turin: UTET, 1975), i.
740. Mandelbaum translates 'virtutem' in this quotation as 'valor', which makes sense
in the original Virgilian context but would seriously distort Petrarca's point, which
rests in the broader matrix of values that developed later and are captured in the
English word 'virtue'.

Virgil as a prophet of Christ.[63] In this passage, however, he did not: Augustan culture was different from that of his own day, and the 'otherness' of the *Aeneid* is acknowledged at the same time as its values are called into question.

1*b*. Book 5 of the *Africa* functions as Petrarca's rewriting of the Dido-and-Aeneas story in the *Aeneid*. Scipio's ally Massinissa enters a North African city ruled temporarily by Sophonisba. Massinissa plays Aeneas to Sophonisba's Dido, falling in love in Virgilian terms ('insolitis ardebant viscera flammis', 'within him all ablaze with flame unwonted', l. 109) and then entering an irregular 'marriage' that provided grist for the mill of *Fama* ('rumor'). Instead of Mercury, however, it is Scipio who reminds Massinissa of his duty, and after Massinissa finally decides to do what is right, Sophonisba takes her life, cursing Scipio as Dido had cursed Aeneas. The key change here, of course, is that the new Aeneas, Scipio, is not the lover but a moral hero whose self-control, as Massinissa notes, is godlike (ll. 555–6). Indeed, Scipio can say what Aeneas cannot:

> Certe ego, si proprio michi non sordescit in ore
> Gloria, non alia tantum virtute superbum
> Me fateor, quam quod blande michi firma tenere
> Frena voluptatis videor.

> For my part I avow—if my words seem
> not too ignoble, coming from my lips,
> no other virtue that I may possess
> makes me as proud as this: that in my hands
> I firmly hold the reins of pleasure's lures.   (ll. 395–8)

Our suspicions that this amounts to a criticism of Aeneas are confirmed when we look at *Seniles* 4. 5, Petrarca's allegorization of the *Aeneid*. Here we read that, in loving Dido, Aeneas is temporarily deflected from the path of righteousness, for it is difficult for even the best of men ('perfectis') not to be deceived by appearances.[64] For

[63] On the relationship between poetry and theological truth in the Renaissance, see Ronald Witt, 'Coluccio Salutati and the Conception of the *Poeta Theologus* in the Fourteenth Century', *Renaissance Quarterly*, 30 (1977), 538–63; and Craig Kallendorf, 'From Virgil to Vida: The *Poeta Theologus* in Italian Renaissance Commentary', *Journal of the History of Ideas*, 56 (1995), 43–9.

[64] In Petrarca, *Opera*, i. 786–9.

Petrarca, book 4 of the *Aeneid* is a condemnation of sexual indiscretion, a vice that is strong enough to ensnare temporarily even a hero of Aeneas's moral strength.

2. One of the more curious contributions to the *fortuna* of Virgil is the *Supplement*, or *Book 13*, to the *Aeneid* written by Maffeo Vegio (1407–58). Though largely unknown in our day, Vegio's *Supplement* was widely read to the beginning of the sixteenth century and even won praise for its author from the hypercritical Julius Caesar Scaliger (Vegio was a 'grandis profecto poeta', 'a truly great poet', in whom 'Virgilianae lucis vestigia invenias', 'traces of Virgil's brilliance might be found').[65] The plot of the *Supplement* picks up where Virgil left off, with the Rutulians acknowledging their defeat and Aeneas accepting their surrender. With the end of hostilities, Turnus's body is returned home and Latinus dispatches an embassy to Aeneas. Aeneas then leads his men to Laurentum, where Lavinia is betrothed amid speeches and an exchange of gifts. Aeneas establishes his new city, and after three years of rule in peace and prosperity, Jupiter agrees to translate Aeneas's spirit to the stars in recognition of his meritorious deeds. Initially at least, the *Supplement* appears to support a straightforward, optimistic interpretation of the *Aeneid*: Turnus is clearly labelled 'improbus' ('villain', l. 354) and roundly condemned for the destruction caused by his 'dementia' ('madness', l. 24) and 'furor' ('madness', l. 31), while Aeneas, the hero 'quo nec pietate nec armis | maior in orbe fuit' ('unsurpassed in the world for loyalty and courage', ll. 332–3), is apotheosized because 'iam . . . optat matura polos Aeneia virtus' ('Already Aeneas's virtue in its fullness lays claim to the celestial pole', l. 605). Indeed, Vegio's Aeneas is never overcome by *ira* ('anger'), and neither *fortitudo* ('bravery') nor any other virtue is ever attributed to his Turnus. Yet the very relentlessness

---

[65] *Julius Caesar Scaliger poetices libri septem*, ed. August Buck (Stuttgart-Bad Cannstatt: F. Frommann, 1964; facsimile of Lyon, 1561 edn.), 303. For diffusion of the *Supplement* in MS form, see Craig Kallendorf and Virginia Brown, 'Maffeo Vegio's *Book XIII* to Virgil's *Aeneid*: A Checklist of Manuscripts', *Scriptorium*, 44 (1990), 107–25; for its diffusion in printed edns., see Mambelli, *Gli annali*. A modern edn. has been edited by Bernd Schneider, *Das Aeneissupplement des Maffeo Vegio* (Weinheim: VCH Verlagsgesellschaft, 1985), from which the citations that follow have been taken; trs. are from Maffeo Vegio, *Short Epics*, ed. and tr. Michael C. J. Putnam, with James Hankins (Cambridge, Mass., and London: Harvard Univ. Press, 2004).

with which Vegio seeks to impose such a black-and-white interpretation on the reader suggests that, on some level, he might well have
seen something else in Virgil and been disturbed by it. Vegio undoubtedly felt that he was only clarifying what Virgil intended, but
the decision that something needs clarifying is on some level a
recognition of ambiguity and complexity. We cannot say for sure
how much of Virgil's pessimism Vegio saw, but the decision to
complete the *Aeneid* in this way draws Vegio's supplement at least
peripherally into this discussion.[66]

3. As Sonja Eckmann has pointed out, Vegio's *Supplement* was not
the only attempt to complete the *Aeneid* in fifteenth-century Italy.
The supplement of Pier Candido Decembrio (1399–1477) consists of
only eighty-nine verses and survives in only one manuscript (Milan,
Biblioteca Ambrosiana, D112 Inf., fos. 173^v–5^r), but its interest and
importance are disproportionate to its length and obscurity. Decembrio manages only to have order restored and Turnus's corpse
returned to Ardea before the fragment breaks off, but what is noteworthy here is that everything is presented from the perspective of
the Rutulians. Turnus is described as 'magnanimus' ('noble in spirit',
l. 1), an epithet that Virgil generally applies to Aeneas, and the
Rutulians are presented as patriots whose 'patriae … amor' ('love of
country', ll. 9–10) led them to take up their swords and defend their
country when its fate was uncertain ('Quis proprios animus dabat
ense penates | tutari et dubiam patriae defendere sortem', ll. 11–12).
This makes Turnus into a sort of national hero and suggests that he is
not just the incarnation of vice who serves as a foil to the virtuous
Aeneas, but a character who is praiseworthy in his own right. This

[66] Among the few substantive modern discussions of the *Supplement* are Anna
Cox Brinton, *Maphaeus Vegius and His Thirteenth Book of the Aeneid: A Chapter on
Vergil in the Renaissance* (Stanford, Calif.: Stanford Univ. Press, 1930); D. V. Blandford,
'Virgil and Vegio', *Vergilius*, 5 (1959), 29–30; W. S. Maguinness, 'Maffeo Vegio
continuatore dell'Eneide', *Aevum*, 42 (1968), 478–85; George Duckworth, 'Maphaeus
Vegius and Vergil's *Aeneid*: A Metrical Comparison', *Classical Philology*, 64 (1969),
1–6; B. J. Hijmans, 'Aeneia virtus: Vegio's *Supplementum* to the *Aeneid*', *Classical
Journal*, 62 (1971), 144–55; Kallendorf, *In Praise of Aeneas*, 100–28; and Michael
C. J. Putnam, 'Introduction', in Maffeo Vegio, *Short Epics*, tr. Putnam, esp.
pp. vii–xxiii. Richard Thomas also believes that Vegio wrote the *Supplement* as a
response to a disquiet aroused by some perception of 'pessimism' in the *Aeneid*
(*Virgil and the Augustan Reception* (Cambridge, Mass.: Harvard Univ. Press, 2001),
279–84), as I suggested very tentatively some years ago (*In Praise of Aeneas*, 127–8).

complicates the black-and-white encomiastic reading of the poem. It is difficult to imagine how this perspective could have been maintained without qualification for very long, and given that Decembrio was only 20 years old when he began his supplement it is not surprising that no more than eighty-nine lines were written.[67]

4. *De fortitudine*, one of a series of treatises on the virtues by Giovanni Pontano (1426–1503), works towards a definition of courage and its various manifestations, as the title suggests. Like Filelfo, Pontano was not a professional philosopher, so he also chose to illustrate his arguments with examples from the literature he knew best. Several key examples come from the *Aeneid*, and they are notable because they focus not on Aeneas, but on his opponents. In arguing that an honourable death is preferable to a base life, Pontano turns to Mezentius and cites his speech in *Aen*. 10. 862–6 as 'verba . . . viro forti digna' ('words worthy of a brave man').[68] What is more, Pontano leaves no doubt that Turnus, too, is a 'vir fortis' endowed with several unambiguously positive attributes: 'Idem ille Turnus, de quo supra est dictum, docet fortem virum, nihil dolo agere, nihil fraude moliri, sed sola niti virtute, eamque unam sequi.' ('That same Turnus who was spoken about above teaches that a brave man does nothing through guile and labors at nothing through deceit, but puts his faith in virtue alone and follows this alone.')[69] In an especially interesting passage, Pontano argues along with Filelfo in *De morali disciplina* that courage cannot be joined to anger, and that Turnus shows how *fortitudo* ('bravery') can be preserved by controlling *ira* ('anger'):

Unde Virgilius ut fuit egregius pictor fortitudinis ait, 'Olli surridens sedacto pectore Turnus, | Incipe si qua animo virtus, et consere dextram' [*Aen*. 9. 740–1]. . . . [I]ram quoque abjecit illam, quae mentem atque consilium, rationem denique ipsam a vero rectoque detorquet, atque ubi vehementior

---

[67] Sonja Eckmann, 'Das Aeneis-Supplement der Pier Candido Decembrio: Die pessimistische "Stimme" der Aeneis', *Neulateinisches Jahrbuch*, 4 (2002), 55–88; the quotation appears on p. 71. I am grateful to Reinhold Glei for bringing this article to my attention.

[68] I have cited from *De fortitudine*, in *Ioannis Ioviani Pontani opera omnia soluta oratione composita*, 3 vols. (Venice: Aldus Manutius, 1518–19), i. 54^r–v.

[69] Ibid. i. 65^v, discussing *Aen*. 9. 150–3.

fuerit, prope ad insaniam impellit. Quamobrem iratus aliquis, aut furoris stimulis percitus, virum fortem praestare nequit.[70]

From which Virgil, as he was renowned in the depiction of bravery, says, 'Untroubled, Turnus smiles at him and says: "Throw first, if there is courage in your heart, | then try my right hand"' [*Aen.* 9. 740–1]. . . . He also cast away that anger which deflects the mind and good judgement, and finally reason itself from what is true and right, and where it has been more vehement, propels it almost toward insanity. For this reason anyone who is angered or aroused by the goads of rage is unable to excel among brave man.

Pontano does not discuss the last scene of the *Aeneid*, but the points he does make suggest clearly that he sees Turnus as a carrier of positive values and a worthy challenger to Aeneas within the Virgilian moral world.

5. The next passage is from one of the best-known poems of early modern Italy, the *Orlando furioso* of Lodovico Ariosto (1474–1533). As Sir John Harington, who translated the *Orlando furioso* in the sixteenth century, noted, Ariosto, 'to shew himself a perfect imitator of Virgill, endeth just as Virgil ends his Aeneads with the death of Turnus':

> E due e tre volte ne l'orribil fronte,
> alzando, più ch'alzar si possa, il braccio,
> il ferro del pugnale a Rodomonte
> tutto nascose, e si levò d'impaccio.
> Alle squalide ripe d'Acheronte,
> sciolta dal corpo più freddo che giaccio,
> bestemmiando fuggì l'alma sdegnosa,
> che fu sì altiera al mondo e sì orgogliosa.
>
> Raising his arm as high as would suffice,
> He plunged his dagger in that awesome brow,
> Retrieving it not once, but more than twice.
> To Acheron's sad shores, that spirit now,
> Freed from its body, colder far than ice,
> Fled cursing from the world, to disavow
> The right which all his life he had defied
> With insolence and arrogance and pride.
>
> (*Orlando furioso* 46. 140. 1–8)

[70] Ibid., i. 64^v–5^r.

... ferrum adverso sub pectore condit
feruidus. ast illi soluuntur frigore membra
uitaque cum gemitu fugit indignata sub umbras.

      Relentless,
he sinks his sword into the chest of Turnus.
His limbs fell slack with chill; and with a moan
his life, resentful, fled to Shades below.

                (*Aen.* 12. 950–2)

[Not very persuasive]

Harington assumed that Ariosto had simply followed Virgil in prais- *[sie]* ing Aeneas, Augustus, and the empire they founded: 'Virgil extolleth Aeneas to please Augustus, of whose race he was thought to come. Ariosto prayseth Rogero to the honour of the house of Este.' Joseph C. Sitterson, Jr., however, has argued that Ariosto saw the mixed feelings about human nature and its political institutions that emerge from a complex, nuanced interpretation of the *Aeneid* and embedded those same mixed feelings in his *Orlando furioso*. Given the prob- lematic nature of Virgil's ending, which in a non-encomiastic reading looks like a surrender to the very forces of anger and lack of self- control against which Aeneas has been struggling throughout the poem, this interpretation makes sense. If Ariosto had in fact wanted to stress Aeneas's failure to become the person he wanted to be, there would be no better scene to imitate than the concluding lines of the *Aeneid*.[71] *[weak argument]*

6. Lionardo Salviati (1540–87) did not qualify as a major scholar even in his own day, but he did participate over a period of years in an important literary quarrel focused on Lodovico Ariosto's *Orlando furioso* and its relationship to ancient epic. Salviati was a 'modern', a critic who rejected both the authority of the classics over *volgare* literature and the effort to evaluate the latter in relation to the

---

[71] Joseph C. Sitterson, Jr., 'Allusive and Elusive Meanings: Reading Ariosto's Vergilian Ending', *Renaissance Quarterly*, 45 (1992), 1–20; the stanza from the *Orlando furioso* is from the edn. of Emilio Bigi (Milan: Rusconi, 1982), and the tr. here, as elsewhere in this book, is that of Barbara Reynolds (New York: Penguin, 1977). The quotations from Harington are found on pp. 1 and 5, respectively, of Sitterson's article. Sitterson's essay relies rather heavily on speculation, but the author deserves credit for having intuited what Ariosto was up to before most of the background work that supports his position had been done. *[and what is this?]*

former.[72] In his efforts to defend Arioso in a letter to Giovanni de' Bardi da Vernio, Salviati levels a series of stinging objections at the *Aeneid*, objections which fall into two categories. The first is structural—'io direi imprima in prima [sic] che la favola di Vergilio non è tutta, come comanda Aristotile anzi non ha né principio né fine' ('I would say, first, that Virgil's plot is not whole, as Aristotle commands, having on the contrary neither a beginning nor an end')— and asserts that the action as Virgil presents it does not ultimately resolve anything: 'Fine oltr'a ciò, dico, che non ha quel poema, percioché se il fine d'Enea era di fondar la nuova città, e d'unire insieme i due popoli per mezzo del maritaggio, fino a quel termine doveva distendersi l'azione.' ('Besides, I say that that poem does not have an end, because if Aeneas's goal was to establish the new city and to unite together the two people by means of marriage, the action ought to have been extended to that limit.') Salviati's second objection is moral:

Direi oltr'a questo, che Virgilio havesse peccato nel costume d'Enea in due modi, contra 'l comandamento d'Aristotile prima dipignendolo coraggioso, contr'a quel, che gl'era prima stato descritto dagl'autori, di poi facendolo diseguale a se stesso, col fare a colui, che egli ci haveva preposto per esempio di pietà, e di virtù morale, fare una impietà, et una sceleratezza detestabile qual fu il violar la castità d'una donna reale, a cui egli doveva la vita stessa, a poi esserle traditore e spergiuro, e cagionarle morte di sempiterna infamia commettendo ancor qui un peccato gravissimo contro la storia.[73]

I would say, besides this, that Virgil erred in the character of Aeneas in two ways, against the precept of Aristotle, first in depicting him as courageous, contrary to the way he had first been described by the author, afterward making him inconsistent with himself, in making one whom he had set forth for us as an example of piety and of moral virtue do something impious and detestable in its wickedness, which was to violate the chastity of a queenly woman to whom he owed his very life, then to betray and perjure her and to be the cause of her eternally disgraceful death, also committing here a grave violation against history.

---

[72] The quarrel between the 'ancients' and the 'moderns' over Arioso's *Orlando furioso* can be followed in detail in Bernard Weinberg, *A History of Literary Criticism in the Italian Renaissance* (Chicago: Univ. of Chicago Press, 1961), 954–1073. Salviati's letter has been published and discussed by Peter Brown, 'In Defence of Arioso: Giovanni de' Bardi and Lionardo Salviati', *Studi seicenteschi*, 12 (1971), 3–27.

[73] Ibid. 7–8. This passage is discussed in Sitterson, 'Allusive and Elusive Meanings', 13.

These charges against Aeneas are serious: lack of courage, perjury, betrayal, and seduction. And it is important to note that Salviati does not mitigate them by suggesting moral growth or development on the part of Virgil's protagonist, who simply does not live up to the standard of *pietà* established for him.[74] What is more, Salviati questions Aeneas's achievements as well as his character by suggesting that the end of the *Aeneid* fails to propel him clearly into the new civilization he was supposed to establish.

7. During the sixteenth century, Marco Girolamo Vida's *Christiad*, a poem that is seldom read today, went through more than three dozen editions. Its status as a modern classic was confirmed by the massive commentary edition that appeared in Pavia in 1569. The author of this commentary was Bartolomeo Botta, who explains that Vida wrote his poem to provide an alternative to the seductive enticements of classical literature. In his preface, he explains that

> Virgilius semper in manibus habebatur, et quod in pueris videbatur permitti causa necessitatis, crimen in se faciebant voluptatis, ne igitur sub eruditionis figmento . . . ad impietatem idolarum, et perniciosam voluptatem libidinum, pueri et cuiusvis aetatis homines deducantur: mandatum fuit a Leone x. et Clemente vii. summis pontificibus, ut quaecumque ad litterariam eruditionem virgiliana lectio continebat, ea noster divinus vates colligeret, et in hoc piissimum opus transferret.

> Virgil has always been held in the hands, and because it seemed for the sake of necessity to be allowed in boys, they brought about the sin of passion in themselves. Therefore, lest under the power of the image of erudition . . . boys and men of any age should be drawn down toward the impiety of idols and the pernicious passion of lust, it was mandated by Leo X and Clement VII, supreme pontificates, that whatever the reading of Vergil has preserved for the learning of letters, it should be collected by our divine poet and conveyed in this most pious work.

According to Botta, in a passage that recalls both the errant Augustine of the *Confessions* and the passage from Petrarca's *De otio religioso* quoted above (1*a*), reading the *Aeneid* can easily lead to

---

[74] James D. Garrison, *Pietas from Vergil to Dryden* (University Park, Penn.: Pennsylvania State University Press, 1992), 117–26 offers some interesting observations on the semantic shifts that sometimes occur as *pietas* mutates into postclassical derivatives like *pietà*.

idolatry and the incitement of lust.[75] We should note, as I have shown elsewhere, that the *Christiad* in fact is heavily indebted to Virgil,[76] and that Botta himself is inconsistent in his criticism. In his lemma on 'angustum per iter' ('along the narrow path'), for example, he repeats the Fulgentian scheme that explicates the *Aeneid* as a pilgrimage through the stages of intellectual and moral development.[77] But the passage from the preface is clearly incompatible with the idea that Aeneas is a praiseworthy hero.

8. In the *Dialogo dell'honore* by Antonio Possevino (1533/4–1611), the discussion returns to the final scene of the *Aeneid*. In book 3, one of the main speakers, Giberto di Correggio, asks the other, Giovanni Battista Possevino, whether it is ever right for a man to kill another man in a duel. Giberto reminds his companion that they had already agreed that a duel should be fought to recover lost honour, not to kill one's adversary. Possevino replies that it would indeed be dishonourable to kill one's opponent, since Aristotle teaches that honour inheres in the victory itself. How, then, Giberto asks, can Aeneas have killed Turnus honourably? He cannot have, Possevino answers: Aeneas acted dishonourably at the end of the poem, violating his father's explicit instructions in the underworld to spare the humble and subdue the proud (*Aen.* 6. 833). Possevino suggests only one way in which Virgil's ending could be justified:

Io per me non veggio, come si possa difender Vergilio in questo luogo, senon allegando ch'egli non corresse l'Eneide; che se havesse havuto vita, haurebbe con molti altri mutato questo luogo.

For my part I do not see how Virgil can be defended in this passage, without pleading that he had not corrected the *Aeneid*; had he lived, he would have changed this passage, along with many others.

Here we are back with Decembrio and (perhaps) Vegio, to the belief that the slaying of Turnus signals such a threat to the 'optimistic' reading of the *Aeneid* that the scene in which it occurs cannot be allowed to stand as Virgil's last word.[78]

---

[75] J. Christopher Warner, *The Augustinian Epic* (Ann Arbor: Univ. of Michigan Press, 2005), 109–13.

[76] Kallendorf, 'From Virgil to Vida', 41–62.

[77] Warner, *Augustinian Epic*, 111.

[78] This passage is discussed by Lauren Scancarelli Seem, 'The Limits of Chivalry: Tasso and the End of the *Aeneid*', *Comparative Literature*, 42 (1990), 116–18, who is

Taken together, these passages undercut and complicate any straightforward reading of Virgilian accomplishment. Aeneas is a perjuror and a worshipper of false gods, a seducer and a traitor, a warrior who repeatedly gives in to an anger that is incompatible with true courage, especially in the crucial final scene of the poem. His opponents, on the other hand, show positive attributes; this is especially true of Turnus, who can also be seen as a patriotic defender of his country and whose courage is free from guile and able to dominate *ira* ('anger'). It is therefore no surprise to find that the end of the poem requires clarification, even completion, to direct the reader towards a proper appreciation of the moral values on which the Augustan achievement is supposed to rest.

These observations, I maintain, show a range of responses that lead us towards what would later come to be called a 'pessimistic' strain within the *Aeneid*. Some of them, like the lines from Petrarca's *De otio religioso* (1*a*), Salviati's letter (6), Botta's apology for the *Christiad* (7), and Possevino's dialogue on honour (8), are simple criticism of Aeneas and his actions, but this is already enough to move the writers away from the school-based belief that Virgil's hero was a flawless example of virtue. Pontano's willingness to see Mezentius and Turnus as carriers of positive values (4) goes a step further, giving us a poem in which moral choices are made in shades of grey. Decembrio's brief supplement (3) goes further yet, showing a writer who can see right and wrong quite literally from the perspective of Aeneas's adversaries. And when Ariosto imitates the ending of the *Aeneid* in all its complexity (5), he shows himself to be a reader who is able to respond to many, perhaps most, of the same Virgilian cues that would shape the interpretation of the poem almost five hundred years later. Taken together, these passages suggest that there was a second interpretive tradition within the criticism of early Italian humanism. This alternative tradition never challenged the straightforward encomiastic approach for supremacy—indeed, it is worth noting that it often existed in an uneasy tension along with the

fully aware of its importance in the history of Virgilian criticism. The quotation, which Seem cites, is from Giovanni Battista Possevino, *Dialogo dell'honore* (Venice: Gabriel Giolito de'Ferrara e fratelli, 1553), 137 (Antonio Possevino's dialogue is found at the end of the vol.). I am grateful to Francesca D'Alessandro Behr for bringing this dialogue to my attention.

very approach it challenged—but it was available in Renaissance Italy to those who found themselves attracted to it. Among them was Filelfo, who, as we have seen, knew Petrarca's *Africa* and was still working on the *Sphortias* when he penned the crucial passage in *De morali disciplina* that moved him definitively away from the idea that epic on the Virgilian model was limited to straightforward praise of its hero. Given the complexities of his relationships with rich and powerful men in general, and with Francesco Sforza in particular, it is not difficult to see why this alternative critical tradition would appeal to him as he sought a way to present Sforza's ascent to power in a poem that captures all the ambiguities of life as he saw it.

3. FILELFO'S *SPHORTIAS*: IMITATION AS RESISTANCE

As we have seen, imitating the *Aeneid* in the Quattrocento offered the opportunity to express reservations about a protagonist at the same time as the poet praised his accomplishments. In the hands of a talented writer, this formula could produce a work of literature that repays careful reading as a commentary on the nature of power as it is manifested in poetry. In this section I shall turn in some detail, finally, to the *Sphortias* and attempt to show that it is worth our attention today as an important document on conceptions of power and the relationship between literature and society in the early modern period.

In books 1 to 4, composed as a unit by 1455 and disseminated as the first instalment of the poem,[79] Filelfo uses the events immediately following the death of Filippo Maria Visconti as a background on which to paint his portrait of Sforza. A republic is established in Milan and peace prevails until Jupiter sends discord to create opportunities for Sforza to win glory. The Venetians attack, as do the French, whose claims on Milan are rebuffed by the citizens, who turn to Sforza to lead their army. In book 2, Parma, then San Columbano, then Pavia yield to Sforza; Piacenza remains loyal to

---

[79] Bottari, 'La "Sphortias"', 464–7, relying on various letters in Filelfo's *Epistolario*.

Venice, and Sforza directs his attention there as the city prepares to resist. Neptune sends aid to the Venetians by flooding the Po, but Sforza remains unmoved and is visited by the ghost of Visconti, who tells him he will prevail. The forty-four day siege of Piacenza occupies book 3. Sforza repeatedly attempts to minimize the suffering of the citizens, who defend their city bravely, but many atrocities are committed after the city falls until Sforza succeeds in restoring order. In book 4 Carlo Gonzaga, one of Sforza's chief lieutenants, falls in love with a married Piacenzan woman named Lyda, who first resists, then succumbs to his advances. The Milanese and Venetian leaders, meanwhile, attempt to seal a secret pact, but the people of Milan refuse to ratify it; next the Venetians consider allying themselves with Sforza, then reject this option, and battle is joined again.[80]

All of this plays out through constant reference to the *Aeneid*. As Robin notes, there is a significant connection between the two poems in terms of basic plot: like Aeneas, Sforza came as a foreigner to a new land, married the sovereign's daughter (Bianca Maria Visconti), conquered the people who were already there, and established a new dynasty.[81] The resemblances go regularly to individual scenes as well: Jupiter, for example, guarantees the future glory of Sforza (fos. 2^r–3^v) just as he did for Aeneas (*Aen.* 1. 223 ff).[82] The careful reader, however, notes that comparisons between the two poems quickly begin working to Sforza's disadvantage. For example, at a crucial point at the beginning of Aeneas's enterprise (*Aen.* 2. 776–89), his wife Creusa encourages him and directs his attention from Troy to the new project he is to undertake. Likewise Bianca Maria (or rather, Athena in the guise of Bianca Maria) encourages Sforza to establish his kingdom on the Po (fos. 3^v–4^r), but with one key difference: Sforza had withdrawn by himself deep within his home and was in despair, thereby appearing weaker than his Virgilian counterpart. Suitably emboldened by his wife, however, Sforza

---

[80] Fuller plot summaries, with somewhat different emphases, may be found in Rosmini, *Vita*, 158–68.

[81] Robin, *Filelfo in Milan*, 62.

[82] Bottari, 'La "Sphortias"', 486 n. 99. References are to the copy of the poem in Milan, Biblioteca Ambrosiana, H97 sup., no. 2 in the survey of MSS (Appendix 1, below), and will be placed in the text.

encourages his troops in an address (fos. 4^r–5^v) that is clearly modelled
on Aeneas's 'o socii...' speech (*Aen.* 1. 198–207, 'o comrades'), his
famous exhortation to his troops after they have been blown ashore
in Carthage. Verbal parallels link the speeches closely together until
Sforza begins expounding on the 'sedes... quietae' ('a peaceful settlement') that his troops can look forward to: 'Non vobis villae, non
rura, nec oppida vicis | Innumeris deerunt, non praedae, prata, nec
aurum.' ('You will not lack homes, nor lands, nor towns in countless
districts, nor booty, fields, nor gold.') It becomes clear that Sforza is
using material gain to motivate his troops, which undercuts the
reference to *pietas* in the first line of his speech and suggests that
Filelfo saw his protagonist here in relation to the hero of *Aeneid* 2,
who likewise oscillates between a *pietas* he does not understand and
adherence to the old Homeric value code that linked self-worth to
material possessions. This suspicion grows when we consider how
Filelfo describes Sforza in a simile found near the end of book 1:

> Sed lupus ut pecudes nunc has nunc opprimit illas,
> Quem stimulat vaesana fames praedaeque libido,
> Sic hostile furens agmen funditque necatque
> Tantus amor pugnae, tantum fervebat in armis.

But as a wolf who seizes now this livestock, now that, whom insane hunger
and passion for booty goads forth, thus a mad love for battle was so great
that the hostile army was routed and slain, so great was the fervor in
arms.   (fo. 14^v; cf. *Aen.* 9. 59 ff., 339 ff.)

Comparison to a wolf driven by insane lust for booty is hardly
flattering, especially when we recall that in *De morali disciplina*,
Filelfo criticizes Virgil's protagonist at the end of the *Aeneid* in
precisely these terms for being 'furiis accensus et irae' ('aflame with
rage—his wrath was terrible—', *Aen.* 12. 946). Thus Sforza is confronting the shortcomings of Aeneas, as they were understood by
those who could see them in early modern Italy.

Often, to be sure, Sforza takes on positive colouring from his
intertextual associations with Aeneas; indeed, he can even appear
more *pius* than Aeneas himself, as in the scene at the end of book 2
where Sforza is preparing to attack Piacenza. This scene has two
Virgilian subtexts: first, the prayer to Jupiter in *Aen.* 5. 687–92,
where Aeneas asks Jupiter to destroy his fleet if he deserves such a

punishment, and then Aeneas's encounter with the shade of his
father at the end of book 6, where Anchises encourages him with a
vision of all that will be accomplished through his actions. When
Sforza prays, he asks to take onto himself any necessary judgement so
that his comrades might be spared, which if anything makes Aeneas
look a little petulant in comparison. The shade Sforza encounters is
that of his father-in-law, Filippo Maria Visconti, whose encourage-
ment is similar to that of Anchises, but this vision is then compared
to a visit by the Virgin Mary, suggesting that the *pietas* of Sforza the
Christian is greater than that of the pagan Aeneas.

As we move through the capture of Piacenza, we continue to see
the positive side of Sforza, but Filelfo qualifies and nuances this
picture by raising a series of disturbing questions.[83] Within the first
few lines of book 3, we are told that Sforza is gentle by nature
('mitissimus') and reluctant ('invitus') to take the city, which seems
to leave him in a favourable light until we are told that the gods are
opposed to what he is doing ('superis damnantibus ipsis'). As he
sends his troops into battle, he tells them two things: all the booty
they might want will be theirs for the taking on this day ('Hic erit ille
dies qui vos opibusque bonisque omnibus accumulet', fo. 37ʳ), but
they should not loot indiscriminately ('in praeda nihil admiscere
profanum', fo. 37ʳ). This sounds like reasonable advice from a good
commander, until we hear from Sforza's Venetian counterpart:

> Odit enim deus ipse viros quicunque rapina
> Ducuntur, praedeque inhiant aliena petentes
> At iustisque probisque favet.

For God Himself hates whichever men are led by plunder and gasp in
pursuit of someone else's goods, but he looks favorably on those who are
just and upright. (fo. 39ʳ)

A short time later, Sforza's cavalry heads into battle with cries of
'praeda, praeda' ('booty, booty', fo. 40ᵛ), a motivation whose ironic
contrast with that of Aeneas and his men is obvious.[84] Our doubts

---

[83] My analysis of book 3 depends heavily on Robin, *Filelfo in Milan*, 56–81,
although I have chosen to emphasize some different aspects from those cited by Robin.
[84] As Lene Waage Petersen has observed, irony is an effective way to undercut
the encomiastic thrust of Renaissance epic ('Il poeta creatore del Principe: Ironia

grow when Carlo Gonzaga, Sforza's chief lieutenant, is restrained by Venus, who tells him 'Tantum parce nefas manibus patrare cruentis' ('refrain from carrying through so great a crime with bloody hands', fo. 41ʳ). The suggestion that the destruction of Piacenza is a 'crime' is made again less than twenty lines later by the omniscient narrator ('superi facinus prohibete nefandum', 'the gods forbid such an unspeakable crime', fo. 41ᵛ). When we compare the Piacenzans, fighting for their country and their families, to Sforza's troops, motivated by greed (fo. 45ᵛ), our hesitation grows, especially since 'furor' ('rage'), 'ira' ('anger'), and 'rabies' ('madness'), the negative value-words from the *Aeneid*, are associated with the Milanese (fo. 45ᵛ). After the city falls, Sforza's troops give in completely to their emotions, raping, defiling, and pillaging indiscriminately (fo. 46ʳ). This stimulates an outburst from the narrator, who twice refers to the sacking of the city as an 'impietas' ('impiety'), another pregnant word in Virgil's moral vocabulary. To be sure, Filelfo has taken pains to dissociate Sforza from all this, making him a force of *pietas* who grieves at what his men have done (fo. 46ᵛ). But we cannot help but wonder: is a commander not responsible for what those under him do? The book ends on a curious minor key, with Sforza insisting (in opposition to the omniscient narrator) that the Piacenzans are guilty ('nocentes', fo. 48ᵛ) and deserve what has happened to them, repeating that there is plenty of *praeda* for everyone, and pleading for restraint, not because it is right, but because the gods are stronger than people and do not allow us to indulge our desires freely:

> Non et enim vitam nostro deducere voto
> Arbitrioque datur, nam sunt humana perenni
> Curae cuncta deo, cuius ne nostra benignam
> Culpa repellat opem longe caveamus oportet.

---

e interpretazione in "Orlando Furioso"', in Marianne Pade, Lene Waage Petersen, and Daniela Quarta (eds.), *La corte di Ferrara e il suo mecenatismo 1441–1598* (Copenhagen: Museum Tusculanums Forlag, and Modena: ISR-Ferrara/Edizione Panini, 1990), 195–211, esp. 203–6. Colin Burrow notes perceptively that irony like this is heightened by the author's awareness that the *signorie* of northern Italy look small and insignificant next to the Roman Empire, in which Virgil's authority rested; see 'Virgils, from Dante to Milton', in Charles Martindale (ed.), *The Cambridge Companion to Virgil* (Cambridge: CUP, 1997), 85.

For it is not permitted to lead our life according to our own desire and will, for everything human is of constant concern to God. It is fitting that we take great care lest our guilt drive off His helpful aid.   (fo. 48ᵛ)

In this final speech, Sforza addresses his troops in the first person plural, making himself one with them. In the end, then, he is a flawed leader, bound to his troops and their 'impietas' at the same time as he grieves at their excesses; our sympathies in turn are not with him, but with the Piacenzans, victims of 'nefas' ('crime') and its unspeakable horrors.

A careful reading of book 4 finds it, too, resistant to the sort of oversimplistic analysis that has bedevilled much previous interpretation of the *Sphortias*. Here we find one of the most memorable sections of the poem, Carlo Gonzaga's love affair with a Piacenzan woman named Lyda, and this section is closely bound to book 4 of the *Aeneid* at every level.[85] Diana Robin, however, points out that Filelfo has departed from Virgil in one crucial way: the character who falls in love is not the protagonist, but his chief lieutenant.[86] As we saw earlier, Petrarca adopted the same strategy in his *Africa*, making not Scipio, but his right-hand man, the lover. Filelfo presumably followed Petrarca because he, too, did not want his new Aeneas to be tainted by association with what they both saw as a major flaw in the old one. This change reflects positively on Sforza, but when Filelfo returns to him in the poem, he does something that is a little more difficult to interpret. Sforza is a special object of concern to Athena, and when Filelfo wants to say that he fights bravely, he writes, 'nec enim metus opprimit ullus | Quem probitasque deusque nova pietate tuetur' ('for neither did any fear overwhelm the one whom both strength of character and God protect with a new piety', fo. 57ʳ). What does it mean to be infused with a new *pietas*? That after all that went wrong at the sack of Piacenza, Sforza will find new ways to do what he should? Or more generally, that *pietas* is not something that one possesses perfectly, but a quality that one can gain, lose, and then regain? Filelfo does not answer questions like these directly, but

---

[85] This section of the *Sphortias* has been analysed in some detail by Zabughin (*Vergilio*, 298–9), who has pointed out some parallels between this part of the *Sphortias* and *Aeneid* 4.

[86] Robin, *Filelfo in Milan*, 62.

one thing is clear: if Sforza were a perfect model of praiseworthy action, his *pietas* would not need to be renewed.

As we would expect in a Virgilian poem, *pietas* and its cognates play an important role in the moral structure of the poem, but they are intertwined with another value-word, *utilitas* ('usefulness'), which also requires discussion. In a letter to Piero de' Medici, Filelfo listed 'l'utilitate pecuniaria per la necessitate de la nostra vita' ('what is financially useful, for what is necessary for our life') as one of only three things that are really 'carissime e necessarie' ('dear to us, and necessary'),[87] and when the word first takes centre stage in the *Sphortias* (fos. 6ᵛ, 8ᵛ), it suggests by extension the material resources by which governments are preserved. At first blush it might seem that poetry should be made of grander stuff, and in fact passages like these have led some critics to complain that, in the *Sphortias*, everything is reduced to the mercantile level.[88] In fact, however, the first books of the poem function as an extended meditation on the true nature of *utilitas*. When Sforza is offered the city of Pavia, for example, he hesitates:

> Sed nec ita Franciscus adhuc se maximus heros
> Constituit facilem, pulchro ut praeferret honesto
> Utile sordidulum, nam non est utile factu
> Censendum, quidquid rationi pugnat honestae.

But Sforza, the greatest hero, still was not so readily disposed to prefer shabby utility to honourable virtue, for whatever is in conflict with virtuous reason should not in fact be considered useful.   (fo. 22ʳ)

Here it seems that what is truly 'useful' is what serves 'honourable virtue', not what is 'shabby', a judgement that is confirmed a little later by Athena; indeed, the oscillation between these two approaches gives intellectual drama to the first four books of the poem. This drama reaches its peak at the end of book 4, when two Venetian speakers give contradictory characterizations of Sforza. Francesco Foscaro speaks 'vocibus...piis' ('in pious words', fo. 62ʳ) to urge a peaceful, open alliance with Sforza, whom he presents as 'pius' ('pious'); he argues that since one's self interest is ultimately served

---

[87] Qtd. in Garin, 'L'opera', 545.
[88] See e.g. Zabughin, *Vergilio*, 297; and Garin, 'L'opera', 545.

by not appearing greedy and bellicose, true 'utilitas' merges with 'pietas' (fos. 62^r–3^r). Ermolao Donato counters these arguments (fos. 63^v–5^r): Sforza, he claims, is driven by greed and ambition and is totally untrustworthy; 'utilitas' and 'honestum' ('what is honorable') are different things, with the former being that which preserves power and the latter an artificial social construct ('Mos hominum tantum vel lex definit honestum | Utilitas urbes auget regnumque tuetur', 'Only human custom or law defines what is honourable; utility makes cities grow and preserves the state', fo. 64).[89] Which picture is accurate? Humanist rhetoricians loved to argue both sides of a question, and being able to see human affairs as debatable was one of the most tangible benefits of a humanist education in the early modern period.[90] But if the real-life Sforza was expecting unequivocal praise, this technique was not designed to give it to him, and it is worth noting as well that the last word here goes to the unflattering analysis of his character.

By 1463 Filelfo had finished and disseminated the next four books.[91] In book 5, Sforza recalls Carlo Gonzaga from his affair with Lyda, and in spite of the defection of Bartolommeo Colleone, he continues to prevail: Bianca Maria rallies his troops at Cremona, and he defeats the Venetian navy under Andrea Quirino. At the beginning of book 6, the Venetians consider what to do and decide to fight on until peace can be established on favourable terms. The battle is joined again, with Neptune and Pluto bringing aid to the Venetians and Jupiter sending Mars and Minerva to help Sforza. Giacomo and Francesco Piccinino withdraw their support at the crucial moment, which keeps Sforza from a definitive victory. In book 7 the Florentines attempt, unsuccessfully, to persuade the

---

[89] The *locus classicus* for the discussion of these points is book 2 of *De officiis*, where Cicero argues that expediency never conflicts with what is morally right and that one must keep one's word and deal honourably with everyone at all times. This conclusion was generally accepted until Machiavelli argued in *The Prince* that a wise ruler will be guided by expediency and will wish to appear honourable but not necessarily to be such. See Quentin Skinner and Russell Price's edn. and tr. of *The Prince* (Cambridge: CUP, 1988), 54–63 (chs. 15–18); and Quentin Skinner, *Machiavelli* (New York: Hill & Wang, 1981), 34–44. Filelfo, who also knew Cicero well, is thus anticipating some of the points that Machiavelli would develop some sixty years later. I am grateful to Letizia Panizza for bringing this point to my attention.

[90] Kahn, *Rhetoric, Prudence, and Skepticism.*

[91] Bottari, 'La "Sphortias"', 464–7.

Venetians to make peace. The book continues with a description of
the battle for Caravaggio, including the games held by Sforza's troops
during a lull in the fighting. Book 8 presents the Venetian games
and the debates that follow, which conclude with the decision to try
to placate the Florentines, sow enmity towards their leader among
the Milanese, and persuade Sforza himself to defect. The battle
resumes, with Sforza prevailing again but the reader who does not
know the history of the period left wondering whether the Venetian
treachery will succeed (it did).[92]

The general trajectory of books 5–8 raises Sforza above those
around him. He recalls Carlo Gonzaga by reminding him of the
proper relationship between reason and passion ('ratio dominetur
anhaelis | Motibus, imperio cedat malesana libido', 'let reason rule
over panting passions, let insane lust yield to authority', fo. 66^r), and
a short time later he succeeds in doing what he could not do at
Piacenza and extinguishes the flames of greed and blood-lust in his
soldiers before they do irrevocable damage (fo. 68^v). At the end of
book 5 Bianca Maria rallies the Milanese troops in a section that is
closely linked to the *aristeia* of Camilla in book 11 of the *Aeneid*, but
with one key difference: Camilla is defined by words with negative
value force in Virgil's world ('furens acrique accensa dolore', 'raging
and inflamed with keen indignation', l. 709) and destroyed by lust for
booty, but Bianca Maria speaks 'placido . . . ore' ('with calm counten-
ance', fo. 72^v) and reason retains control. The naval disaster with
which the book closes, in turn, is painted in starkly moralistic terms,
with 'arrogance' ('fastus') being assigned to the losing Venetians and
virtue ('pietas') linked to Sforza: 'Sic hominum fastus divina potentia
fuerit | Flectere. sola potest pietas placare tonantem' ('It was thus the
power of the gods to deflect human arrogance. Piety alone is able to
appease the most-high', fo. 81^r).

But just when we think that Filelfo is settling into the *laus Francisci*
that would bring his poem in line with the dominant literary theory
of his day, he moves again to complicate the moral picture. At the
beginning of book 6, Filelfo repeats a Virgilian technique from his
description of the sack of Piacenza and presents the action from the
perspective of the losers as he shows the Venetians debating on what

---

[92] Rosmini, *Vita*, 168–76, although again with slightly different emphases.

to do next. Our sympathies for the Venetians grow when it immediately becomes clear that the first speaker, Francesco Foscaro, is striving for *pietas* just as vigorously as Sforza, for it takes great moral courage indeed to stand up before one's countrymen as he does and argue that the gods have destroyed their fleet to punish them for their impiety and will continue to punish them until they act justly, which he feels means making peace (fos. 81^v–2^r). Ermolao Donato, on the other hand, begins from the same facts and urges precisely the opposite course: the fleet was destroyed through the human failure of Andrea Quirino, and the gods often inflict adversity to guide people to greater accomplishments, so the Venetians should stay the course and fight on (fos. 82^v–3^v). As the final speaker, Nicolaus Canalis, notes, 'Disceptando patres fas est reperire quid ipsa | Causa petit. verum argutis se premit elenchis' ('it is right for the leaders to find what the situation calls for by debating; the truth is expressed in eloquent inquiry'; fo. 84^r), but the truth that emerges from this process is always probable at best, and right remains difficult to distinguish from wrong. The difficulty grows when Filelfo adds to his description of Foscaro's *pietas* an account of how the Milanese, who are presumably the 'good guys' in this poem, use Canalis's rhetorical techniques to put the worst possible construction on everything Sforza does:

> At non Insubribus, quos dira cupido per omne
> Exagitat, raptatque nefas, mens ulla decori
> Ulla subest recti. nam quidquid fortiter actum
> A duce Francisco, quidquid sapienter et alto
> Consilio gestum praesentis nuncia veri
> Fama refert, fatis tribuunt, temptantque malignis
> Depravare dolis, vertentes omnia semper
> Peiorem in partem. tanta est vaesania gentis.

But among the Milanese, who are thoroughly aroused by dreadful greed and carried away by crime, no inclination towards what is right provides a foundation for honourable behaviour. For Rumour, the messenger of the truth at hand, reports whatever has been done bravely by Sforza, the leader, and whatever has been dealt with wisely by the high council; always twisting everything into a worse standpoint, they attribute it to the fates and attempt to distort it with evil stratagems. So great is the madness of this people. (fo. 86^r)

To be sure, Sforza rises above his men, for in the end it is impossible to confuse those driven by greed, seized by criminality, and lacking any understanding of what is right with a leader before whom even Neptune and Pluto, moved by admiration, withdraw in battle (fo. 94^r). Yet time and again, Filelfo's praise is qualified by the details of his presentation. At the end of book 6, for example, Sforza is betrayed by Giacomo and Francesco Picinnino, who withdraw from battle at a key moment and deprive Sforza of a decisive victory (fos. 95^v–7^r). The text makes it clear that they are motivated by fear, greed, and envy, and they appear ungrateful as well, for Sforza had shown them clemency after past indiscretions. Yet they could not put aside their old hatreds, for 'tunc omnia coram | Opprobia ante oculos quibus ipse paterque fuisset | Saepius affectus' ('all the insults by which he and his father had been afflicted again and again were present before their eyes', fo. 96^v). This point changes our entire perception of the situation, for what could have been portrayed as simple treason is instead nuanced as revenge, with the suggestion that Sforza is in part responsible for his own misfortunes.

In book 7, Sforza takes a break from battle and orders a series of athletic events modelled on book 5 of the *Aeneid*. His speech setting up the games (fos. 103^{r-v}) is based on *Aen.* 5. 45–71, which associates the athletic events with religious rites and expresses the hope that the gods will oversee a more prosperous future. Yet if war is to be a tool for divine justice, it is hard to see why Sforza should be optimistic, since the omniscient narrator has just said that most of the Milanese are motivated by 'utilitatis...species...inanis | Franciscive odium, contempto iure deoque' ('the illusion of empty utility and hatred for Sforza, in contempt for law and God', fo. 102^v). And as the first contest unfolds, we see what it is like to associate with people like this. Aeneas's games began with a ship race, but since Sforza's men are inland, this is not possible; instead, Filelfo moves the foot race from the second contest in the *Aeneid* to the first one in the *Sphortias.* Sforza begins the foot race by making a speech that offers a prize to everyone, as Aeneas had in *Aen.* 5. 304–14, but he also insists that there be no cheating. Of course the men do cheat, just as they did in the *Aeneid,* and Sforza settles the dispute that arises in the same way as Aeneas had, by distributing extra prizes. Sforza stands above all this, like Aeneas, restoring order and rendering justice, but at this point Filelfo has taken a scene that reflects badly on Aeneas's men and transferred it to the Milanese, whose shortcomings again tarnish Sforza at least a little by association.

Book 8 once more uses shifting perspective and indirect allusion to complicate the praise of Sforza. As usual, things start out clearly enough when Cosimo de' Medici, a nominal ally of the Venetians, delivers a stinging rebuke to the Venetians and leaves the field (fos. 115ʳ–16ᵛ). His former allies are tarred with the Virgilian negative value-words ('execranda cupido . . . bacchatur', 'detested desire raves'; 'trucis ira furoris', 'the anger of savage rage', fo. 115ᵛ), while Sforza, the putative enemy, is praised ('probitatisque viri, iurisque piique | . . . me causa monet', 'the cause of the man's uprightness and the law and what is pious warn me', fos. 116ʳ⁻ᵛ). But then Filelfo immediately juxtaposes another perspective, that of Juno, who dashes to earth to aid her Venetians, motivated by envy that the descendants of Aeneas fared better than the descendants of her Antenor, who settled near Venice (fo. 116ᵛ). Then she recounts the recent victories of Sforza and exclaims, 'non est, non est ut longius atram | Perpetiar pestem per nostros serpere luctus' ('it is not to be, it is not to be that I allow this black plague to creep any longer through our grief', fo. 117ʳ). A short time later Francesco Barbaro urges the Venetians to adopt a new course of action: placate the Florentines, rouse the Milanese against their leader, and win Sforza to their side (fos. 119ʳ⁻ᵛ). This will not be difficult, he argues, because Sforza knows he is hated by his own men and, as Barbaro puts it, because 'mitius omni | Illius ingenium caera solet esse sicana' ('his mind was generally softer than all the beeswax in Sicily'; fo. 119ᵛ; see Figure 4, with the lines in question beginning the page).

Filelfo continued to work sporadically on the poem—part of book 9, the first eighteen verses of book 10, and part of book 11 survive in one manuscript[93]—but our assessment of the *Sphortias*

---

[93] Only Rome, Biblioteca Casanatense, 415 (C.III.9) contains anything past book 8, but here book 9 (which was finished) lacks 417 verses, only the first eighteen verses of book 10 are present, and book 11 (which was also finished) lacks 532 verses (Giri, 'Il codice', 433, with plot summary and speculation on what might have been contained in the missing sections, 445–57). As Bottari has shown, Filelfo changed his plans several times on how long he intended the poem to be: in May 1455 he announced sixteen books to Piero de' Medici, then mentioned the same number in a letter to Panormita in June of 1456. However, in the same letter to Piero de' Medici, he also alludes with a certain trepidation to twenty-four or more books; by 1477, however, the number of books has gone down to fourteen ('La "Sphortias" ', 467 n. 38).

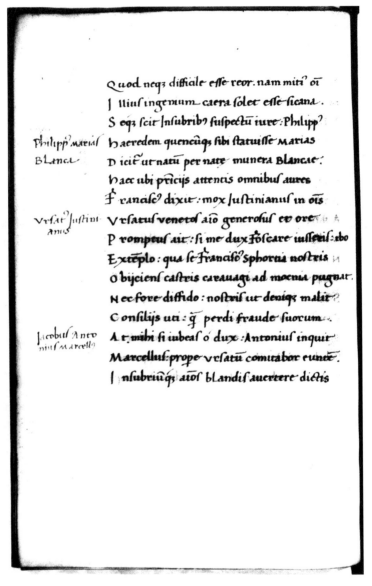

Figure 4. Filelfo's *Sphortias* with lines criticizing Francesco Sforza. Francesco Filelfo, *Sphortias*, Paris, Bibliothèque nationale de France, Ms. lat. 8126, fo. 186ᵛ (Bibliothèque nationale de France)

will have to rest on the eight books that were finished and systematically disseminated. This is more than enough, however, to show us why Filelfo's search for patronage failed. The first reason, as I have noted, is that Filelfo was more accomplished as a scholar than as a poet. But as my analysis of the *Sphortias* has shown, he also failed to provide what his potential patron would have expected. The dominant paradigm for laudatory epic was designed to flatter the vanity of anyone about whom such a poem was written, for he would expect to find his virtues praised and the vices of his enemies condemned. Filelfo, as we have seen, did some of this in the *Sphortias*, for one loses count of the flattering adjectives which accompany Sforza through the pages of the poem. Yet Sforza is also compared to a black plague and described as having a mind softer than Sicilian beeswax, and it is little wonder that the new ruler of Milan was not interested in subsidizing a work that continually called his abilities, actions, and motivations into question. Evidently the other self-made *condottiere*-princes to whom Filelfo sent the poem concluded that they, too, would be better off without a monument to their power that contained within it the seeds of its own resistance. These seeds came from another way of seeing the *Aeneid*, as a critique of power evolving from the acknowledgement of failure, and they took root and flourished in the mind of a perennial outsider, someone whose personal situation and character brought him near the rich and famous men of his day, yet left him always feeling like the marginalized Other.

Thus in my view, the *Sphortias* is a failure, but of a more complicated kind than the received opinion about the poem suggests. Anything but a straightforward encomium, the *Sphortias* became a model for how 'the product of discourse is at once controlled, selected, organised, and redistributed according to a certain number of procedures, whose role it is to avert its powers and its dangers'.[94] By calling into question the very power it helps to sustain, the *Sphortias* was a dangerous poem in the culture in which it was written. But this 'product of discourse' was 'controlled', as the princes of the day left Filelfo at the fringes of power and refused to extend to

---

[94] Michel Foucault, 'Discourse on Language', appendix in *The Archaeology of Knowledge*, tr. A. M. Sheridan Smith (New York: Harper & Row, 1972), 216; see also 'Truth and Power', in *Power/Knowledge*, 131.

him the support he needed to finish the project. And they did their job well, embracing the principles of laudatory epic that suited their interests and elevating them into a 'systematising theory', a 'globalising discourse' (the terms here are again Foucault's) that forces evaluation on its own terms and masks the signs of conflict and struggle that resistance engenders. The other *Aeneid*, the model for this resistance, thus became a kind of 'subjugated knowledge' that can only be revealed through 'a painstaking rediscovery of struggles together with the rude memory of their conflicts'[95]—conflicts like the one over the creation and suppression of the *Sphortias*.

The *Aeneid* therefore becomes a worthy model for the *Sphortias*, not because it presents the unqualified praise of Augustus that the prevalent epic theory of Filelfo's day said it should, but because both poems are implicated in a complicated series of power relationships that must be carefully unravelled. The approach to Augustan Rome that dominated much of the twentieth century, at least in the Anglophone world, was that of Ronald Syme, who depicted Augustus as the winner of a ruthless civil war whose goal, which he succeeded in obtaining, was power.[96] Ten years ago Karl Galinsky produced a subtler analysis that merits our attention here. As Galinsky notes, Augustus himself claimed that he held very little *potestas* (official power) after 27 BC.[97] To the extent that *potestas* derived from office,

---

[95] The passage from which these key terms were taken reads: 'only the historical contents allow us to rediscover the ruptural effects of conflict and struggle that the order imposed by functionalist or systematising thought is designed to mask. Subjugated knowledges are thus those blocks of historical knowledge which were present but disguised within the body of functionalist and systematising theory and which criticism—which obviously draws upon scholarship—has been able to reveal. . . . What emerges out of this is something one might call a genealogy, or rather a multiplicity of genealogical researches, a painstaking rediscovery of struggles together with the rude memory of their conflicts. And these genealogies . . . were not possible and could not even have been attempted except on one condition, namely that the tyranny of globalising discourses with their hierarchy and all their privileges of a theoretical *avant-garde* was eliminated' ('Lecture One: 7 January 1976', in *Power/Knowledge*, 82–3).

[96] Ronald Syme, *The Roman Revolution* (Oxford: OUP, 1939).

[97] 'Post id tempus auctoritate omnibus praestiti, potestatis autem nihilo amplius habui quam ceteri qui mihi quoque in magistratu conlegae fuerunt' ('After this time, I excelled all in *auctoritas*, although I possessed no more official power than others who were my colleagues in the several magistracies'). *Res Gestae* 34. 3, qtd. in Karl Galinsky, *Augustan Culture: An Interpretive Introduction* (Princeton: Princeton Univ. Press, 1996), 11, as part of a general discussion of *auctoritas*, 10–20.

this is true, for Augustus was a private citizen for most of the final years of his life. But at the same time he claimed that he surpassed everyone in *auctoritas*, which he presented as central to his rule. *Auctoritas* is difficult to define. It depends not on magistracies and governmental machinery, but on a sort of material, moral, and intellectual superiority that inheres in an individual. The kind of person who has it 'puts his stamp of approval, in a measurable and effective way, on an action which is to be undertaken by another person with the understanding, implicit in "measurable," that a certain degree of responsibility is taken on by the approver'.[98] In other words, *auctoritas* is reciprocal: it 'presupposes the approbation and voluntary allegiance of those on whom it is exerted'.[99] The model, in other words, is not a static, rigid one in which Augustus gives orders and everyone else obeys, but a dynamic, flexbile one, for *auctoritas* 'needs to be constantly reacquired and validated'.[100] In comparing *potestas* and *auctoritas*, Galinsky considers the latter to be 'actual power',[101] as manifested in a series of social interactions. Neither he nor the scholars he cites invoke Foucault by name, but Augustan *auctoritas* bears an uncanny resemblance to Foucaultian power.

There are many types of interactions in which this power can be manifested, one of which is literature. The exercise of power does not have to begin with the person in whom it is concentrated; in Augustan Rome, poets and artists regularly took the initiative and produced works of art and literature that were created under Augustus's *auctoritas*. Within the dynamic of this relationship, some things were obviously impossible, but the range of available options was wide, from patent sycophancy to respectful admonition. 'Optimists' and 'pessimists' place the *Aeneid* at different points on this sliding scale of options, but for our purposes it is sufficient to emphasize the artistic and creative options that open up once we envision the exercise of power in Augustan Rome not as rigid and unidirectional,

---

[98] Ibid. 13, quoting R. Heinze, 'Auctoritas', *Hermes*, 60 (1925), 46.
[99] Galinsky, *Augustan Culture*, 14, quoting J. Hellegouarc'h, *Le Vocabulaire latin des relations et des partis politiques sous la République*, 2nd edn. (Paris: Les Belles Lettres, 1972), 302.
[100] Galinsky, *Augustan Culture*, 15.
[101] Ibid. 14.

but as a kind of mutuality that cannot be legislated and depends on compromise. Virgil understood well what was possible within this system, positioned himself as the recipient of Augustus's patronage, and produced a poem whose subtlety and indirection allowed it to succeed in both practical and aesthetic terms. Working within a similar system, Filelfo failed, in part because he was not the poet that Virgil was, but also in part because he lacked Virgil's ability to find his place in the system and work within it. In both cases, art cannot be extricated from the exercise of power, so that in the end, the poets' ability to negotiate the exchanges of *auctoritas* has fundamental consequences for the success or failure of their work.

2

Colonization

We now know that these non-European peoples did not accept with indifference the authority projected over them, or the general silence on which their presence in variously attenuated forms is predicated. We must therefore read the great canonical texts, and perhaps also the entire archive of modern and pre-modern European and American culture, with an effort to draw out, extend, give emphasis and voice to what is silent or marginally present or ideologically represented . . . in such works.

(Edward Said, *Culture and Imperialism*[1])

In 1492, educated people knew that knowledge could be found in the Bible, the classics, and a few modern works of unusually great authority, as it had been for centuries. When the old world encountered the new,[2] however, all this changed, at least according to one version of the story. Now what people saw could no longer be reconciled with what they read, so that by the early seventeenth century knowledge had been freed from the confines of the library. Ancient history and geography had been replaced by new accounts derived from the experiences of the mariners, and ancient science had collapsed in the face of empirical research, so that antiquity was no longer the authoritative source of knowledge but the time of

---

[1] Edward Said, *Culture and Imperialism* (New York: Vintage Books/Random House, 1994), 66.

[2] In order to avoid overburdening this chapter with scare quotes, I shall not place them around terms like old world, new world, and the like. I am sympathetic to the effort to conduct discussion in non-Eurocentric terms, so I shall use 'encounter' rather than 'discovery' e.g. in the pages that follow. But it is impossible at this point to erase terms like Indian from the language, and I trust that my argument itself will do more to problematize the issues involved than anything else I might do.

New world encounters: experience over authority

collective childhood, in which inquiry groped towards the mature wisdom of the moderns. In other words, 'The encounter between Europe and the Americas juxtaposed a vast number of inconvenient facts with the elegant theories embodied in previously authoritative books....The encounter with naked inhabitants of a new world, in short, enabled intellectuals to make naked experience take the place of written authority.'[3]

There is, however, another version of the same story. This version recognizes that when a human being confronts something strange and new, the first temptation is to throw up one's hands in the face of novelty: everything is the opposite of what it is in Castile, as an old resident of sixteenth-century Cuzco advises a new arrival in colonial Peru. Yet the new cannot be processed on its own terms, but must be made intelligible on some level by reference to something familiar, for no other possibility exists. The familiar in turn obviously derives from previous experience, but it also depends on what one has read. And what was being read immediately after the encounter was not so very different from what was being read before it: a few more modern works, to be sure, but also the Bible and also the classics.[4] Thus

---

[3] Anthony Grafton, April Shelford, and Nancy Siraisi, *New Worlds, Ancient Texts: The Power of Tradition and the Shock of Discovery* (Cambridge, Mass., and London: Belknap Press of Harvard University Press, 1992), 1–7, with the quotation on 5. This position is not Grafton's, but the one to which he stands in opposition, as seen also in Hans Ulrich Gumbrecht, 'Wenig Neues in der neuen Welt: Über Typen der Erfahrungsbildung in spanischen Kolonialchroniken des XVI. Jahrhunderts', in Wolf-Dieter Stempel and Karlheinz Stierle (eds.), *Die Pluralität der Welten: Aspekte der Renaissance in der Romania* (Munich: Wilhelm Fink, 1987), 227–49. See also J. H. Elliott, *The Old World and the New, 1492–1650* (Cambridge: CUP, 1970).

[4] Ibid. 5–6; see also G. V. Scammel, 'The New Worlds and Europe in the Sixteenth Century', *The Historical Journal*, 12 (1969), 396, 409; Edward Said, *Orientalism* (New York: Vintage Books/Random House, 1979), 93; Michael T. Ryan, 'Assimilating New Worlds in the Sixteenth and Seventeenth Centuries', *Comparative Studies in Society and History*, 23 (1981), 519–38; Wilfried Nippel, *Griechen, Barbaren und Wilde: Alte Geschichte und Sozialanthropologie* (Frankfurt am Main: Fischer, 1990), 30–55; Anthony Pagden, '*Ius et Factum*: Text and Experience in the Writings of Bartolomé de Las Casas', *Representations*, 33 (Winter 1991), 147–62, repr. in Stephen Greenblatt (ed.), *New World Encounters* (Berkeley–Los Angeles and London: Univ. of California Press, 1993), 86–8; Peter Mason, 'Classical Ethnography and Its Influence on the European Perception of the Peoples of the New World', in Wolfgang Haase and Meyer Reinhold (eds.), *The Classical Tradition and the Americas*, i. *European Images of the Americas and the Classical Tradition* (Berlin and New York: Walter de Gruyter, 1994), pt. 1, pp. 135–72; Walter Cohen, 'The Discourse of Empire in the Renaissance', in Marina S. Brownlee and Hans Ulrich Gumbrecht (eds.), *Cultural Authority in Golden Age Spain* (Baltimore, Md., and

according to Columbus, there were pearls in the new world, but they were formed just like the ones in the old world, as described by Pliny; Vasco de Quiroga saw the Indians as characters in Lucian's *Saturnales*, simple and good in their primitive state;[5] and America in general was seen as an earthly paradise, a blend of the Elysian Fields from Homer, Horace, and Plutarch and the Saturnalian Golden Age as described by Hesiod, Ovid, and Virgil.[6] Artists, too, scanned new discoveries through classical lenses, as Figure 5 shows. This engraving, from Thomas Hariot's *A briefe and true report of the new found land of Virginia*... with illustrations by Theodore de Bry after the drawings of John White, shows that Amerindians entered European culture with the anatomy and pose of the gods and heroes of ancient culture, here with the three Indian maidens in the centre of the ring looking exactly like the 'Three Graces' from classical mythology.[7]

London: Johns Hopkins Univ. Press, 1995), 266; Anthony Pagden, *Lords of All the World: Ideologies of Empire in Spain, Britain and France c.1500–c.1800* (New Haven and London: Yale Univ. Press, 1995), esp. ch. 1, pp. 11–28; and John M. Headley, 'Geography and Empire in the Late Renaissance: Botero's Assignment, Western Universalism, and the Civilizing Process', *Renaissance Quarterly*, 53 (2000), 1119–55.

[5] Tzvetan Todorov, *The Conquest of America: The Question of the Other*, tr. Richard Howard (New York: Harper Collins, 1984), 17, 197; see also the important review of this book, Anthony Stephens, 'The Semiotics of Inhumanity: Tzvetan Todorov's "La Conquête de l'Amérique": La Question de l'autre', in Titus Heydenreich (ed.), *Columbus zwischen zwei Welten: Historische und literarische Wertungen aus fünf Jahrhunderten* (Frankfurt am Main: Vervuert Verlag, 1992), 83–96.

[6] Martin Snyder, 'The Hero in the Garden: Classical Contributions to the Early Image of America', in John W. Eadie (ed.), *Classical Traditions in Early America* (Ann Arbor: Center for the Coordination of Ancient and Modern Studies, University of Michigan, 1976), 144–55; and Stelio Cro, 'Classical Antiquity, America, and the Myth of the Noble Savage', in *Classical Tradition and the Americas*, i/1. 379–88, 395.

[7] The illustration is from Thomas Hariot, *A briefe and true report of the new found land of Virginia*... (Frankfurt am Main: Theodore de Bry, 1590), 58–9, accessible electronically through the University of North Carolina's Documenting the American South database at http://docsouth.unc.edu/nc/hariot/menu.html. In the introduction to the facsimile of the 1590 edn., Paul Hulton notes that 'De Bry often Europeanizes his Indian faces and postures' (New York: Dover Publications, 1972), p. xi. See also Michael Alexander (ed.), *Discovering the New World, Based on the Works of Theodore De Bry* (New York: Harper & Row, 1976); Hugh Honour, *The European Vision of America* (Cleveland, Ohio: Cleveland Museum of Art, 1975), 1–2, 5; *The New World in the Treasures of an Old European Library*, Exhibition of the Duke August Library, Wolfenbüttel, Exhibition Catalogue, 17 (Wolfenbüttel: Herzog August Bibliothek, 1976), 33, 70; and *The Age of Exploration: An Exhibition Commemorating the Quincentennial of Christopher Columbus's First Voyage to the Americas* (Provo, Utah: Friends of the Brigham Young University Library, 1992), esp. s. 13, 'Mistreatment of New World Peoples'.

Figure 5. Theodore de Bry, 'Their danses whych they use at their hyghe feastes'. Thomas Hariot, *A Briefe and True Report of the New Found Land of Virginia* (Cologne: Theodore de Bry, 1590), pl. 17 (University of North Carolina)

Thus as a growing number of scholars are concluding, America was not so much 'discovered' as the result of transoceanic travel but 'invented' in a process by which the new was accommodated to the old. And inevitably, as Edmundo O'Gorman trenchantly put it, 'it was invented in the image of its inventor'.[8]

---

[8] Edmundo O'Gorman, *The Invention of America: An Enquiry into the Historical Nature of the New World and the Meaning of Its History* (Bloomington: Indiana Univ. Press, 1961), 140. See also Marcel Bataillon's insightful review of this book in 'The Idea of the Discovery of America among the Spaniards of the Sixteenth Century', in Roger Highfield (ed.), *Spain in the Fifteenth Century, 1369–1516: Essays and Extracts by Historians of Spain*, tr. Frances M. López-Mirillas (New York: Harper & Row, 1972), 426–64; and the extension of O'Gorman's work in José Rabasa, *Inventing America: Spanish Historiography and the Foundation of Eurocentrism* (Norman, Okla., and London: Univ. of Oklahoma Press, 1993).

Grafton

While I prefer the second story to the first one, I also think it is important not to oversimplify the consequences of that narrative. For one thing, viewing the encounter through the lens of the classics does not provide much information by itself about the ideological stance of the viewer.[9] In the first place, the literature of Greece and Rome offers not one but many perspectives, ranging from the individualism of Homer to the utopia of Plato, from the republican vision of Lucan to the meditation on empire that we find in the *Aeneid*. Early modern writers selected what they needed from the classics, so that the earliest explorers saw themselves like Ulysses or Jason, as sailors pushing past the borders of the known world, while *conquistadores* like Hernán Cortés saw themselves as warriors like Hector and Achilles.[10] The temptation is to look at these sailors and *conquistadores* and, as Walter Mignolo put it, to see 'the rebirth of the classical tradition as a justification of colonial expansion',[11] but in fact this is not always the case. The Indians had their defenders in Madrid and London along with the apologists for the imperial project, and both groups had similar or identical classical educations. The most famous defender of the Indians is probably Bartolomé de las Casas, who was thoroughly steeped in the classics, but so was Juan Ginés de Sepulvéda, his adversary in the famous Indian rights debate; they simply cited different classical authorities to support their positions.[12]

[9] Grafton, *New Worlds*, 48.

[10] Jean-Pierre Sánchez, 'Myths and Legends in the Old World and European Expansionism on the American Continent', *Classical Tradition and the Americas*, i/1. 212–14, 232–3; and Kevin Sharpe, *Reading Revolutions: The Politics of Reading in Early Modern England* (New Haven and London: Yale Univ. Press, 2000), 317–18.

[11] Walter Mignolo, *The Darker Side of the Renaissance: Literacy, Territoriality, and Colonization* (Ann Arbor: Univ. of Michigan Press, 1995), p. vii, with the important review by Anthony Grafton, 'The Rest versus the West', *New York Review of Books* (10 Apr. 1997), 57–64, repr. in *Bring out your Dead: The Past as Revelation* (Cambridge, Mass., and London: Harvard Univ. Press, 2001), 77–93. See also Walter Mignolo, 'The Darker Side of the Renaissance: Colonization and the Discontinuity of the Classical Tradition', *Renaissance Quarterly*, 45 (1992), 808.

[12] Pagden, '*Ius et Factum*', 95; Bruno Rech, 'Bartolomé de las Casas und die Antike', in Wolfgang Reinhard (ed.), *Humanismus und Neue Welt* (Weinheim: VCH Verlagsgesellschaft, 1987), 167–97. Anthony Pagden, 'The Humanism of Vasco de Quiroga's "Información en derecho" ', in Reinhard (ed.), *Humanismus und Neue Welt*, 133–42, argues that Las Casas was not a humanist, but this does not mean that he did not know and use classical authors anyway.

In other words, as Lorna Hardwick has concluded, 'classical texts and allusions can ... [be] viewed as either liberating or repressive'.[13]

It is also important to note that the effort to see the new world in terms of the old was vexed in other ways as well. In a famous analysis of this problem, Tzvetan Todorov concluded that, if the Indian was seen as like the European, a human being with the same rights, the result was a movement towards assimilation and the projection of European values onto indigenous ones.[14] It was also possible, however, to start from difference, to concentrate on what remains after assimilation, the 'after-effect' or 'byproduct' that resists absorption. This fallout, as Michel de Certeau has repeatedly reminded us, will finally become the 'Other'.[15] In its most common constructions, the Other is either positioned as inferior to the European subject—a barbarian, a savage, a 'wild man'— or superior to it—a noble savage; both extremes function as the opposite of what the observers consider themselves to be.[16] The Others help the viewers in the process of self-fashioning, but they also

[13] Lorna Hardwick, 'Classical Texts in Post-Colonial Literatures: Consolation, Redress and New Beginnings in the Work of Derek Walcott and Seamus Heaney', *International Journal of the Classical Tradition*, 9 (2002), 239.

[14] Todorov, *Conquest*, 42.

[15] Michel de Certeau, 'Ethno-Graphy', in *Heterologies: Discourses on the Other*, tr. Brian Massumi, (Minneapolis: Univ. of Minnesota Press, 1986), 140. Notwithstanding Jeremy Ahearne's warnings that 'other' and 'same' are not stable categories in Certeau's work (*Michel de Certeau: Interpretation and Its Other* (Stanford, Calif.: Stanford Univ. Press, 1995), 18), the search for and study of the Other—what he calls 'heterology'—became a major concern in Certeau's later work. As Richard Terdiman explains, 'One way of understanding Michel de Certeau's work is as an incitation to understand and to cognize *nonrecuperable* resistance, to detect the voice of the other despite the pressures exercised by our own seemingly sovereign subjectivity and by homeostasis, by the inevitable return of the same. This is the project his heterology adumbrates' ('The Response of the Other', *Diacritics*, 22/2 (1992), 8).

[16] Giuliano Gliozzi (ed.), *La scoperta dei selvaggi: Antropologia e colonialismo da Columbo a Diderot* (Milan: Principate Editore, 1971), 14–15; Urs Bitterli, *Die 'Wilden' und die 'Zivilisierten': Grundzüge einer Geistes- und Kulturgeschichte der europäisch-überseeischen Begegnung* (Munich: C. H. Beck, 1976), 367–76; Hayden White, 'The Noble Savage Theme as Fetish', in *Tropics of Discourse: Essays in Cultural Criticism* (Baltimore, Md., and London: Johns Hopkins Univ. Press, 1978), 190–5; and Karl-Heinz Kohl, *Entzauberter Blick: Das Bild vom guten Wilden und die Erfahrung der Zivilisation* (Berlin: Medusa, 1981), 19. For an interesting discussion of how these issues were negotiated in the Dominican Republic, see Hilaire Kallendorf, 'A Myth Rejected: The Noble Savage in Dominican Dystopia', *Journal of Latin American Studies*, 27 (1995), 449–70.

tend to confirm them in their ethnocentrism and may in the end tell them very little about themselves.[17]

In this chapter, I shall be concerned with early modern attempts to construct a meaning for the American experience—to invent America—through the lens of the *Aeneid*, with a special focus on the tension between the efforts to assimilate the Indian to European values and the fallout from those efforts. In particular, we shall be trying to hear the voice of the Other in these texts, as a way to problematize and enrich the way they are often read.

This is a particularly auspicious time to undertake such an inquiry, in that several innovative approaches to the *Aeneid* developed by scholars of the classics now offer a model of how to proceed. The *Aeneid* itself is a poem about colonization—Latium, we recall, was already inhabited when Aeneas and his Trojan exiles landed—but, as Marilyn Desmond has noted, classical studies has just recently begun to develop a postcolonial reading of Virgil. Desmond cites the 'pessimistic', or 'Harvard', school and continues,

This strain of Virgil criticism, with its emphasis on the 'second voice' or the 'doubleness of vision' in the text, complements the focus of a critical attempt to dismantle imperial or colonial discourses of the sort exemplified by the 'imperial Virgil.' Although most versions of the 'imperial Virgil' encourage the reader to focus on the mythic program the *Aeneid* ostensibly represents and to ignore the play of differences in the text, the context of postcolonial cultural theory encourages us to consider the implications of difference that course through Virgil's text.[18]

[17] Stephen Greenblatt, *Renaissance Self-Fashioning from More to Shakespeare* (Chicago and London: Univ. of Chicago Press, 1980), 9. As Greenblatt put it elsewhere, 'We can be certain only that European representations of the New World tell us something about the European practice of representation' (*Marvelous Possessions: The Wonder of the New World* (Chicago: Univ. of Chicago Press, 1991), 7).

[18] Marilyn Desmond, *Reading Dido: Gender, Textuality, and the Medieval Mind* (Minneapolis: Univ. of Minnesota Press, 1994), 7. The discussion could also, of course, be extended from Virgil's text and its narrative focus on the founding of Rome to the territorial expansions of Augustus, the lens through which Virgil viewed the Roman past. Peter S. Wells, *The Barbarians Speak: How the Conquered Peoples Shaped Roman Europe* (Princeton: Princeton Univ. Press, 1999), makes an important contribution in this area, during which he notes, without elaboration, that 'many important similarities can be identified between Roman intentions and interactions in temperate Europe and Spanish activity both in Mexico and in South America' (264).

Accordingly, Ralph Hexter has looked carefully at Dido as a representative of Carthage, a foreign culture with which Rome had long,
extensive contact, and concludes that, in the *Aeneid*, Carthage is
thoroughly Romanized—that is, Carthage is assimilated to Rome,
whose values have been projected onto it.[19] Historically, the *Aeneid*
was being written at the same time as the *Colonia Iulia Concordia
Karthago* was being settled on the ancient site of Carthage and, as the
Roman city was literally built on top of its barbarian predecessor, so
the Romanized literary image covers up Carthage as it had been
known and experienced previously.[20] This does not mean, however,
that Virgil accepts this effacement without question. In a provocative
article that almost functions as an early postcolonial reading of the
Aeneid, Steven Farron argues that Virgil portrays Aeneas's mission as
brutal and destructive, leaving the reader's sympathies with Dido.
She becomes the symbol of Carthage, and by assigning Aeneas
responsibility for the destruction of the city, Virgil was condemning
the third Punic war as unjust, a 'disgrace'.[21]

The most subtle and influential analysis of the play of difference in
Virgil's text is that of Gian Biagio Conte. Conte begins by setting up a
dynamic tension between the epic code, an open system within which
epic can be recognized as epic, and the epic norm, an ideologically
oriented and historically contextualized bias within that code; an analogy would be to a piano keyboard and the selection of a key to compose
in. The norm generally presents itself as absolute but, according
to Conte, Virgil's signal achievement lay in showing that the Latin
epic norm was relative and contingent. This was accomplished by
opening the norm up to multiple points of view, making the text
polycentric: different points of view, represented by different characters,
coexist side by side, autonomous and able to conflict without any one

[19] Ralph Hexter, 'Sidonian Dido', in Ralph Hexter and Daniel Selden (eds.),
Innovations of Antiquity (New York and London: Routledge, 1992), 332–84. For a
more traditional survey of the ways in which Virgil's Dido reflects Roman views of the
Carthaginians, see N. M. Horsfall, 'Dido in the Light of History', in S. J. Harrison
(ed.), *Oxford Readings in Vergil's Aeneid* (Oxford and New York: OUP, 1990), 127–44.
[20] James Davidson, 'Domesticating Dido: History and Historicity', in Michael
Burden (ed.), *A Woman Scorn'd: Responses to the Dido Myth* (London: Faber &
Faber, 1998), 65–88.
[21] Steven Farron, 'The Aeneas–Dido Episode as an Attack on Aeneas' Mission and
Rome', *Greece and Rome*, 27 (1980), 34–47.

of them overcoming and annulling any of the others.[22] This recognizes the power over the reader that is exercised by Dido, Turnus, Mezentius, and Camilla as well as Aeneas; as Richard Thomas notes, 'Virgil remains unblinking in sustaining his focus on the exceptions, on those who lose and die.'[23]

It does not follow from this interpretation that the imperial programme is nullified. But it does mean, in the often-quoted phrase of R. O. A. M. Lyne, that there are 'further voices' in the text and that their presence 'probes, questions, and occasionally subverts the simple Augustanism that it may appear to project'. Lyne identifies several strategies by which these 'further voices' become audible. One strategy is allusion, by which, for example, Aeneas's character and actions are called into question in *Aen.* 12. 450 ff. by association with Ajax. Another is word choice: *exuviae* ('mementos/spoils') in *Aen.* 4. 651 insinuates pathos by suggesting that Dido is not the erotic victor, with whom the association usually rests, but the vanquished. A third category is imagery, as when Aeneas is linked to Cacus through the image of vomiting, which momentarily undercuts his heroic stature (do heroes actually vomit?). The inclusion or exclusion of information can also call into question the epic voice; one thinks here, for example, of *Aen.* 8. 370 ff., in which Venus and Vulcan's frivolity raises questions about the seriousness that characterizes Aeneas. Dramatic irony works similarly, as in *Aen.* 2. 355–9, where careful readers see that, contrary to their expectations, Aeneas at Troy is not like a wolf who feeds his young, but in fact works against the interest of those in his charge by fighting. And then there is what Lyne calls 'negative invention', by which Aeneas is characterized by what he fails to say, do, and feel at key moments.[24] Finally, there is a similar technique that Don Fowler has called 'deviant focalization', where the narrator and focalizer would be expected to

---

[22] Gian Biagio Conte, *The Rhetoric of Imitation: Genre and Poetic Memory in Virgil and Other Latin Poets*, ed. and tr. Charles Segal (Ithaca, NY, and London: Cornell Univ. Press, 1986), ch. 5, 'Virgil's *Aeneid*: Toward an Interpretation', 141–84. This analysis of Conte's has been extremely influential among classicists working on Virgil.

[23] Richard F. Thomas, 'The Isolation of Turnus: *Aeneid* Book 12', in Hans-Peter Stahl (ed.), *Virgil's Aeneid: Augustan Epic and Political Context* (London: Duckworth/Classical Press of Wales, 1998), 274.

[24] R. O. A. M. Lyne, *Further Voices in Vergil's Aeneid* (Oxford: Clarendon Press, 1987), 4–56, 145–206. At 217 n. 1, Lyne expresses explicit sympathy with the 'Harvard school'.

coincide but do not—where the text, in other words, shows the speaker seeing the world through the eyes of others as well as his or her own. Two examples may be found at *Aen.* 1. 21, where Juno's perspective intrudes into that of the narrator in the words 'belloque superbum' ('proud in battle'), and 1. 28, where 'genus invisum' ('the breed [she] hated') shows the same thing.[25]

The techniques identified here make audible the voice of the Other in Virgil's *Aeneid.* The result, as Conte puts it, is a poem that

proves to be not a glorification of the Augustan restoration but a meditation (modulated in various tones) on the reasons why one person or one people has emerged victorious [in] its painful struggle against another. That 'other' was not ignoble; it was, in fact, complete and necessary.... Victory necessarily involves destroying the rights of others; it may even require the victor to look through enemies' eyes. The epos becomes rich in contradictory registers, when right is divided—and so language along with it—as a whole age is torn apart.[26]

My argument in this chapter is that poems in the early modern period that pick up on the colonial theme in the *Aeneid* also pick up on the complexities with which Virgil treated this theme. The approach developed here involves listening for the voice of the Other not by trying to assess the correctness of the representation or its fidelity to 'reality', but by analyzing the representation itself, its style, narrative devices, references to other literary representations, and so forth. If, to paraphrase an old truism, America could represent itself

---

[25] Don Fowler, 'Deviant Focalization in Vergil's *Aeneid*', in *Roman Constructions: Readings in Postmodern Latin* (Oxford: OUP, 2000), 40–63, repr. from *Papers of the Cambridge Philological Society*, 216 (1990), 42–63. The approach developed in this paragraph emerged indirectly from Brooks Otis, *Virgil: A Study in Civilized Poetry* (Oxford: Clarendon Press, 1963), ch. 3, 'The Subjective Style', 41–96. Notwithstanding the criticisms of Antonio La Penna, 'Sul cosidetto stile soggettivo e sul cosidetto simbolismo di Virgilio', *Dialoghi di archeologia*, 1 (1967), 220–44, Italian scholars have produced a number of sensitively nuanced narratological studies in this tradition, one of which (Gianpiero Rosati, 'Punto di vista narrativo e antichi esegeti di Virgilio', *Annali della Scuola Normale di Pisa*, Classe de lettere e filologia (1979), 539–62) has traced points of interest back to Servius Danielis.

[26] Conte, *Rhetoric of Imitation*, 183–4. As Joseph Farrell points out, the voice of the Other may be unusually clear in the *Aeneid*, but it is potentially audible elsewhere in Roman literature as well, since a great many people who wrote in Latin during classical antiquity came to Rome from somewhere else; see *Latin Language and Latin Culture: From Antiquity to Modern Times* (Cambridge: CUP, 2001), 1–27.

it would, but since it cannot we must turn our attention to how that representation has been fashioned.[27]

The procedure adopted in this chapter is both similar to and different from the one used in the preceding chapter. There I began by looking at the author as Other, a poet whose position as marginalized outsider stimulated him to imitate the *Aeneid* with an authorial voice that critiqued the power structure of his day from an enforced distance. In this chapter I shall begin with the poems, to show how attention to textual strategies can recover the voice of the Other in various ways that are essentially internal to the text and its relation to other texts. Since parts of this procedure have traditionally been considered 'literary', I shall pay due attention to the literary theory of the period and consider how the interplay of genre and chronology allows the voice of the Other to emerge with more and more clarity in the poems under consideration.

1. ERCILLA'S *LA ARAUCANA*: EPIC AND THE VOICE OF THE OTHER

> Far from being writers—founders of their own place, heirs to the peasants of earlier ages now working on the soil of language, diggers of wells and builders of houses—readers are voyagers; they move across lands belonging to someone else, like nomads poaching their way across fields they did not write, despoiling the wealth of Egypt to enjoy it themselves. . . . Reading takes no measures against the erosion of time (one forgets oneself and also forgets), reading does not keep what it acquires, or it does so poorly, and each of the places through which it passes is a repetition of the lost paradise.
>
> (Michel de Certeau, *The Practice of Everyday Life* [28])

The reader of *Os Lusiadas* indeed becomes a voyager, by extension one of the heroes who spread Portuguese imperial power across the world

---

[27] Here I am paraphrasing Said, *Orientalism*, 21, although Greenblatt, *Marvelous Possessions*, 7–8, makes the same point.

[28] Michel de Certeau, *The Practice of Everyday Life*, tr. Steven Rendall (Berkeley–Los Angeles and London: Univ. of California Press, 1984), 174.

from Brazil to the Far East. The poem recounts the exploits of Vasco da Gama during his voyage to India, in the process of which, as Camões put it, the gods were determined 'to make of Lisbon a second Rome' ('de fazer de Lisboa nova Roma'; *Os Lusiadas*, 6. 7. 2, p. 142).[29] More specifically, as Camões makes clear from the beginning, Vasco da Gama is a second Aeneas ('ilustre Gama, | Que pera si de Eneias toma a fama', 'the illustrious Vasco da Gama [is more than a match] for Aeneas himself', *Os Lusiadas*, 1. 12. 7–8, p. 41), and the *Os Lusiadas* is to be the Portuguese *Aeneid*.

As we have seen so far, however, the question is, which *Aeneid*: an 'optimistic' one, focused on the celebration of empire and the values that made it great, or a 'pessimistic' one, in which the imperial project is probed, questioned, and occasionally subverted through the intermittent foregrounding of the voices of the colonized Other? In *Epic and Empire*, David Quint proposes a useful distinction 'between epics of the imperial victors and epics of the defeated',[30] then places the *Os Lusiadas* into the former category, which contains epics of conquest and empire that take the victor's side. I think this is right on target, although I would explain the point as well through reference to the early modern praise-and-blame theory that Camões himself explicitly invokes. The key statement is at the end of book 5, right in the middle of the ten-book poem. It begins like this:

> Quam doce é o louvor e a justa glória
> Dos próprios feitos, quando são soados!
> Qualquer nobre trabalha que em memória
> Vença ou iguale os grandes já passados;
> As envejas da ilustre a alheia história
> Fazem mil vezes feitos sublimados.
> Quem valerosas obras exercita,
> Louvor alheio muito o esperta e incita.   ·
>
> Não tinha em tanto os feitos gloriosos
> De Aquiles, Alexandro, na peleja,

---

[29] The text is taken from Luis de Camões, *Os Lusiadas*, ed. Frank Pierce (Oxford: Clarendon Press, 1972), with trs. from Luis Vaz de Camões, *The Lusiads*, tr. William C. Atkinson (Harmondsworth: Penguin Books, 1973). References will be placed in the text, with the Portuguese marked by book, stanza, and line, and the English by page number.
[30] David Quint, *Epic and Empire: Politics and Generic Form from Virgil to Milton* (Princeton: Princeton Univ. Press, 1993), 8; see the discussion of Camões on 113–25.

Quanto de quem o canta os numerosos
Versos; isso só louva, isso deseja.
Os troféus de Milcíades, famosos,
Temístocles despertam só de enveja;
E diz que nada tanto o deleitava
Como a voz que seus feitos celebrava.

How sweet are praise and glory to the doer of great and famous deeds! Your noble strives to leave behind him a name that will equal or surpass that of his distinguished forbears. Emulation of the illustrious achievements of others has called forth a thousand sublime exploits, and praise bestowed on his fellows is a powerful spur and stimulus to him who would be valorous himself. Alexander esteemed less the resounding deeds of prowess of Achilles on the field of battle than the harmonious verse in which Homer sang of them: this alone he extolled, and wished for himself. Miltiades's famous victory over the Persians filled Themistocles with envy, and nothing, he said, so delighted him as to hear his own exploits sung.   (*Os Lusiadas*, 5. 92–3, p. 138)

Just as in Petrarca's *Africa*, we see here the idea that the poet serves a necessary social function, that of praising virtuous deeds as a stimulus to even greater achievement. The immediate object of praise is Vasco da Gama (*Os Lusiadas*, 5. 99. 1–4, p. 138), but the larger goal is to praise the Portuguese people collectively:

Porque o amor fraterno e puro gosto
De dar a todo o lusitano feito
Seu louvor é sòmente o prossuposto
Das Tágides gentis, e seu respeito;

It is their sisterly love for the Portuguese people and a disinterested pleasure in bestowing due praise on their collective achievement that alone move the kindly nymphs in the matter.   (*Os Lusiadas*, 5. 100. 1–4, p. 140)

Camões takes up this point again at the beginning of book 7, where he systematically lists the faults of the Germans, the English, the French, and the Italians, who fight among themselves while the Portuguese risk everything for Christianity (*Os Lusiadas*, 7. 1–14, pp. 161–4). Given this level of patriotic fervor, it is no surprise that there is little effort to complicate the straightforward praise of Vasco da Gama and his countrymen. To be sure, as Quint points out, the giant Adamastor articulates the anti-Portuguese perspective in the middle of book 5 (*Os Lusiadas*, 5. 41–59, pp. 128–32), but Adamastor is only allowed to speak through Vasco da Gama, who is recounting his travels up to this point to the king of Malindi. Through Vasco da Gama, Adamastor reminds the reader that he is one of the giant sons of earth who declared war against Jupiter, who punished him for his wicked insolence. There is no 'deviant focalization' here, no effort to see the world sympathetically through the eyes of the Other nor to validate the goals and values of one's opponent. Camões took many things from the *Aeneid*, but not this; his Virgilianism is of the 'optimistic' variety.

This is not the case, however, with *La Araucana*. The author, a courtier to Philip II of Spain, participated himself in the colonial adventures in Peru and Chile, during which he composed an epic about his experiences. One approach to this poem has stressed what at one level seems obvious: *La Araucana* was dedicated to Philip II, with the presentation copy (see Figure 6) bearing the king's arms; the Indians depicted had rebelled against Spanish authority, and Ercilla's contemporaries understood clearly that the poem depicted the legitimate punishment of those who stood in the way of divinely sanctioned imperialism.[31] *La Araucana* contains three sections—accounts of the battles of St Quentin and Lepanto and the invasion of Portugal—that are not integral to the Spanish activity in Chile, but they do serve to emphasize the grandeur of Spain and its ruler and therefore seem to reinforce the pro-imperial theme.[32] Curiously, the poem does not have a dominant Spanish hero, but the pro-imperial line of criticism makes a virtue of necessity and posits that this space is filled by Philip II himself, thereby helping to construct and legitimate a national identity for Spain at a key point in its historical development.[33] Indeed, a study of the book trade in

---

[31] Francisco Javier Cevallos, 'Don Alonso de Ercilla and the American Indian: History and Myth', *Revista de estudios hispánicos*, 23 (1989), 5–17. Isaías Lerner, 'Felipe II y Alonso de Ercilla', *Edad de Oro*, 18 (1999), 87–101, observes that the fascination with power and its complexities threatens to obscure the obvious, that Ercilla was employed by Philip II in his new world imperial project.

[32] Luis Íñigo Madrigal, 'Alonso de Ercilla y Zuñigo', in Luis Íñigo Madrigal (ed.), *Historia de la literatura hispanoamericana*, 2nd edn. (Madrid: Cátedra, 1992), 196–8.

[33] Elizabeth B. Davis, *Myth and Identity in the Epic of Imperial Spain* (Columbia, Mo., and London: Univ. of Missouri Press, 2000), 10–11, 23–39.

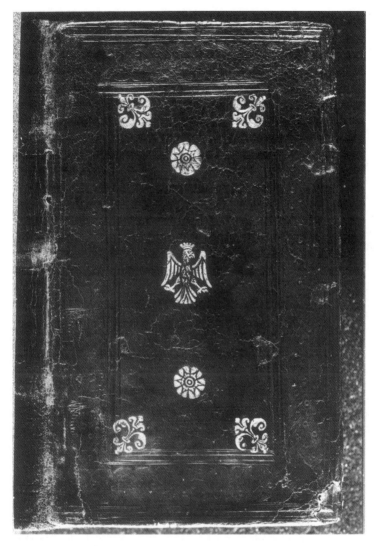

Figure 6. Arms of King Philip II of Spain. Alonso de Ercilla, *La Araucana* (Madrid: Pierreo Gosin, 1575), front cover (The Pierpont Morgan Library)

the new world reveals that *La Araucana* was the most widely disseminated representation of the conquest among the colonizers
themselves.[34]

Yet, as sometimes happens in literary criticism, the opposite interpretation has been developed with equal persuasiveness. Menéndez y
Pelayo, for example, notes that the natives had little direct influence
on much of Latin American literature, but a significant indirect
impact on poetry in Chile, for the determined resistance of the
Araucanians became the principal theme of early colonial literature
in that country.[35] This resistance was heroic and, in the process of
writing about it, Ercilla ended up 'presenting his clear preference for
his enemies'.[36] The female characters are treated with special sympathy, so that in the end one can argue that the poem is presented
from the perspective of the Indians.[37] From here, the next step is the
appropriation of the poem into the national culture of Chile:

The work of Ercilla, famous among Spanish men of letters from its first
appearance, holds a lofty national interest for us. Reading it, which is
agreeable for the majority, makes tenderness and energy, pride and enthusiasm
spring forth from the hearts of the Chileans, the most lively of sensations and
passions, because it is an historic and patriotic book apart from its literary

[34] Irving A. Leonard, *Books of the Brave*, 2nd edn. (New York: Gordian Press,
1964), 119–20, 164, 224.

[35] Marcelino Menéndez y Pelayo, *Historia de la poesía chilena (1569–1892)* (Santiago de Chile: Ediciones de los Anales de la Universidad de Chile, 1957), 9–10. This
study has been extracted from a larger work, *Historia de la poesía hispano-americana*
(Madrid: Librería Victoriano Suárez, 1913).

[36] Frank Pierce, *Alonso de Ercilla y Zúñiga* (Amsterdam: Rodopi, 1984), 101.

[37] On Ercilla's treatment of the Indian women, see José Toribio Medina, 'Las
mujeres de *La Araucana* de Ercilla', *Hispania*, 11 (1928), 1–12; and María Rosa
Lida, 'Dido y su defensa en la literatura española', *Revista de filología hispánica*, 4
(1942), 373–82; in a lightly retouched version this magisterial essay was reprinted as
María Rosa Lida de Malkiel, *Dido en la literatura española: su retrato y defensa*
(London: Tamesis, 1974). Cohen, 'Discourse of Empire', 275–6, claims that *La
Araucana* is presented from the perspective of the Indians and that this is done
primarily through its female characters (275); see also E. Michael Gerli, 'Elysium and
the Cannibals: History and Humanism in Ercilla's *La Araucana*', in Bruno M. Damiani
(ed.), *Renaissance and Golden Age Essays in Honor of D. W. McPheeters* (Potomac,
Md.: Scripta Humanistica, 1986), 83–93. As support for this position, one could note
that some Indians had reached higher levels of development than others, and that the
Peruvians and Mexicans were among those who therefore seemed more like the
Europeans; see Gliozzi, *La scoperta*, 1, 7–10; and Sergio Landucci, *I filosofi e i selvaggi,
1580–1780* (Bari: Editori Laterza, 1972), 9.

merit. The *Araucana* sings of our land, it exalts the valor of its sons and the faithfulness of its women.... For this reason, if the *Araucana* is a literary monument of the Spanish language, it ought to be for the Chileans a beloved national book as well: it is the baptismal certificate of our country.[38]

Thus Ercilla becomes, in the words of Pablo Neruda, the 'inventor and liberator' of Chile,[39] and *La Araucana* stands as an anti-imperialist poem.[40]

These two positions would seem to be impossible to reconcile, and as we might expect, the efforts to do so thus far have not been very satisfactory. Margarita Peña states simply that the poem supports both the Indians and the Spanish,[41] and Luis Leal suggests that it is both pro-Chilean and pro-Spanish,[42] but neither explains precisely how the same work can support two opposing positions at the same time. William Melczer at least attempts to do this, but his explanation strikes me as too subtle, arguing that Ercilla's ideological commitment differs from his moral commitment, so that he can identify both with the Spaniards' desire to conquer and the Indians' manifest virtues.[43] Elizabeth Davis describes both national readings

[38] *La Araucana de Don Alonso de Ercilla y Zúñiga, edición para uso de los chilenos, con noticias históricas, biográficas i etimolójicas*, ed. Abraham König (Santiago de Chile: Imprenta Cervantes, 1888), p. viii. This point is made forcefully by a number of other critics, e.g. Gaston von dem Bussche, in *Homenaje a Ercilla* (Concepción: Instituto de Lenguas, Universidad de Concepción, 1969), 3; and Alonso de Ercilla, *La Araucana*, ed. Isaías Lerner (Madrid: Cátedra, 1993), 50. Roberto González Echevarría, 'A Brief History of the History of Spanish American Literature', in González Echevarría and Enrique Pupo-Walker (eds.), *The Cambridge History of Latin American Literature*, i. *Discovery to Modernism* (Cambridge: CUP, 1996), 17–18, stresses the importance of José Toribio Medina, whose *Historia de la literatura colonial de Chile* makes *La Araucana* the foundation of Chilean literature and had great influence on those critics who followed him.
[39] Pablo Neruda, 'El Mensajero', in *Don Alonso de Ercilla, inventor de Chile* (Santiago de Chile: Editorial Pomaire, 1971), 12.
[40] Íñigo Madrigal, 'Alonso de Ercilla y Zuñigo', describes *La Araucana* as 'the first specimen of American "anti-imperialist" literature' (193), a point that is pursued by Barbara Simerka, *Discourses of Empire: Counter-Epic Literature in Early-Modern Spain* (University Park, Penn.: Pennsylvania State Univ. Press, 2003).
[41] Margarita Peña, 'Epic Poetry', in González Echevarría and Pupo-Walker (eds.), *Cambridge History*, 233–4.
[42] Luis Leal, '*La Araucana* y el problema de la literatura nacional', *Vórtice*, 1 (1974), 68–73.
[43] William Melczer, 'Ercilla's Divided Heroic Vision: A Re-Evaluation of the Epic Hero in "*La Araucana*"', *Hispania*, 56 (1973), 218–21.

Naïve judgment = bad!
split

of the poem and ends by assigning responsibility for what appear to be mutually contradictory lines of reasoning to 'Ercilla's own split subjectivity';[44] that, however, strikes me as simply another way of saying that the poet could not make up his mind where he was trying to go and left us with a bad poem. Fernando Alegría sees in *La Araucana* 'a marvellous union, the epic birth of a new people made with Spanish blood and Indian blood',[45] which sounds good but is difficult to support from the poem, where intermarriage between the Spanish and Indians does not take place.

Resolving such contradictory readings of *La Araucana* is an important critical desideratum, but at this point the matter seems intractable and there is clearly need for a different beginning place that will lead to a different resolution. In this section, I shall attempt to develop such a line of reasoning through a carefully controlled study of the allusive environment of the poem. At first glance it may seem almost perverse to try to stabilize the ideological stance of an early modern work through what used to be called 'source study', but I hope to show that reading the classics through the filter of postcolonial theory enables a new kind of allusion that can help solve problems like this.

For several generations, critics have agreed that Ariosto, Lucan, and Virgil are the most important models for *La Araucana*. The relationship between Ercilla's poem and the *Orlando furioso* has been thoughtfully studied by Maxime Chevalier, and there is little question that some parts of *La Araucana* owe a good deal to Ariosto.[46] A half-dozen scholars have worked on Ercilla's debt to Lucan, and again, there is little question that much can be learnt here. One of these scholars, Isaías Lerner, ends his analysis, however, with an unexpected conclusion: 'there is no doubt that the *Aeneid* was the text to which Ercilla had the greatest recourse to inscribe his

---

[44] Davis, *Myth and Identity*, 20–1.

[45] Fernando Alegría, *La poesía chilena, orígenes y desarrollo, del siglo XVI al XIX* (Berkeley–Los Angeles: Univ. of California Press, 1954), 39.

[46] Maxime Chevalier, *L'Arioste en Espagne: recherches sur l'influence du 'Roland furieux'* (Bordeaux: Institut d'Études Ibériques et Ibéro-Américaines de l'Université de Bordeaux, 1966), 144–64. Lía Schwartz Lerner, 'Tradición literaria y heroínas indias en *La Araucana*', *Revista Iberoamericana*, 38/81 (1972), 615–25, argues that the amorous portions of the poem in particular derive primarily from Ariosto and help us concentrate on the literary rather than the historical dimensions of the work.

own poem in the classical epic tradition. More than Lucan and more
than Ariosto, Virgil controlled the most important expressive, even
thematic instantiations of the *Araucana*.'[47] David Quint would not go
this far, but in what is undoubtedly one of the more thoughtful recent
studies of Ercilla's poem, he found himself returning to Virgil again
and again even when the thesis of his book required reading *La
Araucana* as a poem written in the tradition of Lucan.[48] Andrés
Bello in turn refers to Ercilla's poem as 'the *Aeneid* of Chile',[49] and
notwithstanding the hesitations of Frank Pierce,[50] it seems generally

[47] Isaías Lerner, 'Ercilla y Lucano', *Hommage à Robert Jammes* (Toulouse: Presses
universitaires du Mirail, *c.*1994), 691; James Edward McManamon, 'Echoes of Virgil
and Lucan in the *Araucana*', Ph.D. thesis (Illinois, 1955), 282–4, came to the same
conclusion. On Ercilla's debt to Lucan, see also Gilbert Highet, 'Classical Echoes in *La
Araucana*, *Modern Language Notes*, 62 (1947), 329–31; Dieter Janik, 'Ercilla, lector de
Lucano', in *Homenaje a Ercilla*, 83–109; and Gareth A. Davies, ' "El incontrastable y
duro hado": *La Araucana* en el espejo de Lucano', in A. Gallego Morell (ed.), *Estudios
sobre literatura y arte dedicados al profesor Emilio Orozco Díaz*, 3 vols. (Granada:
Secretariado de Publicaciones de la Universidad, 1979), i. 405–17.

[48] Quint, *Epic and Empire*, argues the general thesis that there are two rival epic
traditions, the Virgilian one, which is associated with the imperial victors, and that of
Lucan, the epic of the defeated (8–9). This is a rich, subtly nuanced book, however,
and I would not want to oversimplify Quint's position. The predominance of
Lucanian over Virgilian arguments in *La Araucana*, he argues, is tied to Ercilla's
sympathies for the Indians, but Quint recognizes that Ercilla also imitates Virgil and
that this imitation is important as well (157). In part this is due to the fact that the
Pharsalia never fully separates itself from the *Aeneid*: Lucan's own model was Virgil,
and Quint argues that Lucan in fact accepted Virgil's imperialist bias at the same time
as he lamented the loss of republican government within Rome (156–7). What is
more, Quint recognizes the 'further voices' within the *Aeneid* (11, 23, 52–3, 60, 78–9),
and this recognition offers at least the first steps toward linking Virgil to Ercilla's
widely recognized sympathies toward the Indians, although Quint does not develop
this point in detail.

[49] Andrés Bello, 'La Araucana', in *Obras completas*, ix. *Temas de crítica literaria*
(Caracas: Ministerio de Educación, 1956), 360; the same statement is made in the
introduction to Alonso de Ercilla, *The Araucaniad*, tr. C. M. Lancaster and
P. T. Manchester (Nashville, Tenn.: Vanderbilt Univ. Press, 1945), 11. A rudimentary
comparison of the two poems may be found in Menéndez y Pelayo, *Historia de la poesía
chilena*, 21 n. 3; and Frank Pierce, 'Some Themes and Their Sources in the Heroic Poem
of the Golden Age', *Hispanic Review*, 14 (1946), 95–103; while Vicente Cristóbal, 'De
la *Eneida* a la *Araucana*', *Cuadernos de filología, estudios latinos*, 9 (1995), 67–101,
compares how the two authors treat epic themes and motifs like the funeral games,
ecphrasis, similes linking the human and natural worlds, and so forth.

[50] Pierce, *Alonso de Ercilla*, recognizes some Virgilian elements in the poem
but concludes, surprisingly, that 'the *Araucana* does not follow the established
pattern of the Virgilian epic' and that Ercilla 'chose not to write his own "American
version" of the *Aeneid*' (70).

accepted that *La Araucana* owes a substantial debt to the *Aeneid*. Surprisingly, however, no one has attempted a thorough study of the subject, which, therefore, invites development.[51]

La Araucana was originally published in three parts. Part I (1569) tells of the campaign in Chile led by Valdivia, the revolt of the indigenous Araucanians, and the treacherous murder of the Spanish leader. The formation of an expedition from Peru, the storm that hit them off the coast of Chile, their arrival in Concepción, the building of a fort at Penco, and the battles that followed with the Indians are described in part II (1578). In part III (1589), the reader learns of the arrival of the Spanish commander in Concepción; raids, battles, and the further exploration of Chile; and the defeat of Caupolicán, the Indian leader. Ercilla based his account in history— he was personally involved in the events recounted in parts II and III—but *La Araucana* is a poem in the epic tradition and demands analysis in those terms.

For a Spaniard of the late sixteenth century, the epic poem *par excellence* was the *Aeneid*, and Ercilla loses no time in anchoring his poem intertextually in his Latin model. A good example of how this works may be found in canto 7, which depicts the sack of Concepción. Ercilla presents this account as a rewriting of the sack of Troy, which casts the defending Spaniards as new Trojans and the attacking Indians as reconstituted Greeks. All of this is made explicit in an epic simile:

> No con tanto rigor el pueblo griego
> entró por el troyano alojamiento,
> sembrando frigia sangre y vivo fuego,

---

[51] In preparing the analysis that follows, I have gone carefully through McManamon's dissertation and the notes to Lerner's edn. In order to avoid overburdening the notes, I shall not provide references to these two works but shall simply acknowledge my debt to both of them for signalling a good many of the structural and verbal parallels on which my analysis depends. McManamon, 6–10, follows José Toribio Medina, *La Araucana de D. Alonso de Ercilla y Zúñiga, edición del centenario, ilustrada con probados, documentos, notas históricas y bibliográficas y una biografía del autor*, 5 vols. (Santiago de Chile: Imprenta Elzeviriana, 1910–18), iii. 13 in assuming that Ercilla used a Spanish tr. of the *Aeneid*, probably the version of Hernández de Velasco, but he is forced to admit that there are few verbal similarities to this tr. I see no reason to deny Ercilla, who had received the standard education of his day, knowledge of the poem in the original, although he may well have used a Spanish tr. alongside the Latin.

talando hasta en el último cimiento
cuanto de ira, venganza y furor ciego,
el bárbaro, del robo no contento,
arruina, destruye, desperdicia
y aun no puede cumplir con su malicia.

    Grecian hosts with so much rigor
Entered no abode of Trojan,
Sowing fire and blood of Phrygian,
Ravaging Troy's last foundations,
As the savage discontented
With his vengeful theft and anger
Ruined, destroyed, and wreaked mad havoc,
Still his wicked ire unsated.

(La Araucana, 7. 48 [52])

Here we find not only an invitation to consider parallels between the events in Chile and Troy, but also to see in *La Araucana* a study of the same issues that emerge from a careful reading of the *Aeneid*. This makes Ercilla's poem a study of civilization and barbarism and of the forces that can transform one into the other. In this passage those forces are 'ira' ('anger') and 'furor' ('rage'), presented just as they had been in *Aeneid* 2, as a fire that threatens to burn out of control and consume everything of value in its path.

The associations between the two poems are found in larger structural units as well as smaller ones. A good example of such a larger unit is the storm that Ercilla uses to move from part I to part II. The situation in Chile has become desperate, and the Spanish ruler in Peru agrees to send reinforcements. Those coming by sea are drawing near their goal when they encounter a huge storm, which is immediately depicted in terms that every schoolboy would identify with *Aeneid* 1:

Allí con libertad soplan los vientos
de sus cavernas cóncavas saliendo,
y furiosos, indómitos, violentos,
todo aquel ancho mar van discurriendo,
rompiendo la prisión y mandamientos
de Eolo, su rey, el cual temiendo

---

[52] References to Ercilla's text are to Lerner's edn., and trs. are taken from *The Araucaniad*, tr. Lancaster and Manchester.

> que el mundo no arruinen, los encierra
> echándoles encima una gran sierra.
>
> There tempestuous blasts in freedom
> Whistle from their concave caverns,
> With indomitable violence
> Coursing o'er the expansive sea-waste,
> Breaking bonds, and flouting mandates
> Of King Aeolus, who fearful
> Lest they ruin the world, confines them
> In a mountain's crag-roofed dungeon.
>
> (*La Araucana*, 15. 58)

The Spanish find themselves in the same position as Aeneas and his men in *Aeneid* 1, where Aeolus, having been bribed by Juno, releases the winds to wreak havoc on the Trojan fleet. The Virgilian flavour of the passage even extends to word choice: 'indómito' ('untamed'), as Lerner observes in his note on the third line, is a Latinism which echoes *Aen.* 1. 52–3 and 1. 61–2.

Thus anyone who reads *La Araucana* in search of Virgilian parallels will have no trouble finding them, and once we have begun doing this, we quickly discover that the Indians are regularly associated with the enemies of Aeneas and his Trojans. The Indians, for example, tend to fight and die like Turnus. In canto 14, for example, Lautaro's death echoes that of Turnus at the end of the *Aeneid*:

> del rostro la color se le retrujo,
> los ojos tuerce y con rabiosa pena
> la alma, del mortal cuerpo desatada,
> bajó furiosa a la infernal morada.
>
> From his face the color vanished;
> Eyes he rolled; from mortal body
> Rushed his soul in rabid anguish
> Downward to the abode infernal.
>
> (*La Araucana*, 14. 18. 5–8)

> ... ast illi soluuntur frigore membra
> uitaque cum gemitu fugit indignata sub umbras.
>
> His limbs fell slack with chill; and with a moan
> his life, resentful, fled to Shades below.
>
> (*Aen.* 12. 951–2)

Both souls descend to the depths below, and both are 'furiosa' ('enraged'), bound to the wrath that always threatens to tear apart the fabric of civilization. Later Pinol dies the same way, and again his soul is 'furiosa' in death as in life.

If the Indian men resemble the Latins in how they fight, the Indian women resemble Dido in love. A good example is Tegualda, who resisted vigorously the allures of love until a foreigner, Mareguano, caught her eye. Then everything changed, just as in *Aeneid* 4:

> Sentí una novedad que me apremiaba
> la libre fuerza y el rebelde brío,
> a la cual sometida se entregaba
> la razón, libertad y el albedrío.
> Yo, que cuando acordé, ya me hallaba
> ardiendo en vivo fuego el pecho frío,
> alcé los ojos timidos cebados,
> que la vergüenza allí tenía abajados.
>
> Roto cun fuerza súbita y furiosa
> de la vergüenza y continencia el freno,
> le seguí con la vista deseosa,
> cebando más la llaga y el veneno.
>
> Strange oppression dimmed my senses,
> Snatched my liberty rebellious,
> And submitted to its dictates,
> Reason, free-born will, surrendered.
> When hypnotic spells were over,
> Flames allumed my icy bosom,
> Timid eyes I raised, impassioned,
> Which shamefastness had kept lowered.
> Having snapped with sudden fury
> Thongs of shame and moderation,
> Ardently my eyes pursued him,
> Nurturing the wound and venom.
>
> (*La Araucana*, 20. 61–62. 4)

The images used here certainly owe something to Petrarca as well, but Tegualda remains a Virgilian woman in love, an example of how casting off restraint gives free rein to the natural forces like passion that constantly threaten civilization.[53]

---

[53] On the role of the Indian women in *La Araucana*, see above, n. 37.

As James Nicolopulos has recently shown, the Virgilian underpinnings of part II of *La Araucana* are in many ways strongest in cantos
23 and 24.[54] Here Ercilla the soldier descends into a cave to receive a
prophecy about the future power of his country, just as Aeneas had in
Aeneid 6. Fitón, the seer, invokes Cerberus, Charon, Styx, Tartarus,
Cocytus, Phlegethon, the Furies—all the figures of the Virgilian
underworld. The vision climaxes in the battle of Lepanto, which
anchors *La Araucana* into Virgil's world in two ways. First, the battle
is explicitly compared to the Trojan War:

> No la ciudad de Príamo asolada
> por tantas partes sin cesar ardía
> ni el crudo efeto de la griega espada
> con tal rigor y estrépito se oía,
> como la turca y la cristiana armada
> que, envuelta en humo y fuego, parecía
> no sólo arder el mar, hundirse el suelo,
> por venirse abajo el alto cielo.

> 'Twas not so that Priam's city
> Was incessantly ignited,
> Nor were cruel Greek blades effectual
> Heard with such a clangorous clatter,
> As the fleets of Turk and Christian,
> Which in flame and smoke enveloped,
> Seared the sea, with cataclysms
> Rocked the earth and stormed the welkin.

> *(La Araucana*, 24. 42)

In addition, we should not forget that the battle of Lepanto took
place very near the spot where Octavian won his decisive naval
victory at Actium[55]—a victory celebrated in the *Aeneid*. At this
point, it appears that, as the *Aeneid* has often been interpreted as a
poem in praise of Augustus, so *La Araucana* can be interpreted as a
poem written in praise of Philip II, with the *Aeneid* as intertext
supporting Ercilla's imperial project.

---

[54] James Nicolopulos, *The Poetics of Empire in the Indies: Prophecy and Imitation in La Araucana and Os Lusíadas* (University Park, Penn.: Pennsylvania State Univ. Press, 2000).
[55] Quint, *Epic and Empire*, 158–9.

The problem with this interpretation, however, is that 'further voices' intrude, beginning almost immediately and growing more audible the further we proceed into the poem. On the one hand, these intrusions link the Indians not to the enemies of Troy, as the basic scheme linking *La Araucana* to the *Aeneid* dictates, but to the Trojans themselves and their allies. For example, in *La Araucana*, 2. 43. 1–2 the Indian Lincoya is described as 'De los hombros el manto derribando | las terribles espaldas descubría' ('laying the cloak aside from his shoulders, he uncovered his immense back'), which echoes *Aen.* 5. 421–3, 'Haec fatus duplicem ex umeris reiecit amictum, | et magnos membrorum artus, magna ossa lacertosque | exuit' ('he | threw down the double cloak that draped off his shoulders, | laid bare his giant joints and limbs, the | giant bones and sinews of his arms'). The passage in the *Aeneid* describes Entellus, the Trojan wrestler, however, not one of his adversaries, so that Ercilla's reference ennobles Lincoya by associating him with Virgil's hero and his people. Another example may be found during the description of the sack of Concepción. After the city is captured, the Indians loot it, carrying away its goods like ants who store things away for the winter (*La Araucana*, 7. 53). Virgil had described the Trojans making preparations to leave Carthage with the same simile (*Aen.* 4. 402–5), and while one might in the end wonder how much all this ennobles the Indians, it certainly links them again to the Trojans. Shortly afterwards, the soothsayer Puchecalco is slain by a putative ally for making a prophecy the Indians did not want to hear (*La Araucana*, 8. 39–44), reminding us of Laocoön (*Aen.* 2. 201–31) and, again, calling into question the basic linkage between the Indians and the antagonists of Troy. The next canto in turn offers a crescendo of 'further voices'. First a divinely instigated storm delays the Indians (stanza 9), then the Indian god Eponamon prophesies and disappears in a cloud of smoke (stanza 11), and finally the narrator compares Lautaro to a Hircanian tiger (stanza 72). The references—to the storm at the beginning of *Aeneid* 1, to Anchises's prophecy in *Aen.* 5. 740, and to Dido's rebuke to Aeneas in *Aen.* 4. 366–7—invite the careful reader to associate the Indians three times in rapid succession with Virgil's Trojans. In canto 10 the Indians, like the Trojans in *Aeneid* 5, celebrate with athletic games, and in *La Araucana*, 20. 75. 1–4 Tegualda pleas for the burial of her husband in exactly the same way as the mother of Euryalus pleaded for the burial of her son (*Aen.* 9. 485–6).

And finally, the Indian army is linked to Aeneas and his Trojans by a reference to nature: the earth trembles from the footsteps of marching soldiers (*La Araucana*, 21. 50. 1–4; *Aen.* 12. 444–5).

Other 'further voices' serve to undercut the exemplary position of the Spanish by associating them with those forces in the *Aeneid* that the Trojans struggle to control. At the end of canto 2, for example, the Spanish leader Valdivia turns aside from his mission to visit a gold mine, leading Ercilla the narrator to note at the beginning of the next canto that 'Codicia fue occasión de tanta guerra' ('Avarice was the war's occasion!' *La Araucana*, 3. 3. 7). This recalls Virgil's outburst at *Aen.* 3. 56–7, 'quid non mortalia pectora cogis | auri sacra fames!' ('To what, accursed lust for gold, do you | not drive the hearts of men!'), and links the Spaniards not to the Trojans, but to their perfidious 'allies' in Thrace who killed Polydorus to get the Trojan treasure that had been sent out of the city with him for safekeeping. In canto 7, in turn, the Spaniards in the city of Concepción found themselves un-nerved by Fama (rumour) and unable to brace themselves for the work they needed to do, just like the inhabitants of Carthage after Dido's affair with Aeneas. Here the Spaniards are associated with Carthage; in *La Araucana*, 9. 74. 7–8, by contrast, they are associated with the indigenous peoples of Italy as Ortiz dies with a faint but recognizable echo of Turnus ('y la alma del corpóreo alojamiento | hizo el duro y forzoso apartamiento', 'And the soul from corporal dwelling | Took its harsh, constrained departure'; see *Aen.* 12. 952, quoted above). Then a little later, the Spaniards building the fort at Penco are once again linked to the Carthaginians, the barbarian Other in Virgil's world:

> No con tanto hervor la tiria gente
> en la labor de la ciudad famosa,
> solícita, oficiosa y diligente
> andaba en todas partes presurosa.

> Not with so much zeal the Tyrians,
> Laboring for their lordly city,
> Anxious and alert to duty,
> Raced and dug in every area.

> (*La Araucana*, 17. 25. 1–4)

Up to the end of part II, Ercilla's conversation with Virgil is neither continuous nor, I would freely admit, absolutely essential to our understanding of his poetic project. At the end of the epic, however, *La Araucana* becomes a more explicitly Virgilian poem, in the sense that the issues that dominate the last several cantos are the same ones that dominate the end of the *Aeneid*.[56] And it is the *Aeneid*, I would argue, that ultimately guides us to an accurate understanding of Ercilla's attitude towards the colonial project in which he found himself implicated.

To see how this works, let us turn first to Ercilla's attitude towards the Indians. In the prologue to part I, Ercilla raises the possibility that he might appear biased towards the Indians, for they have defended their land with great constancy and firmness, redeemed and sustained their freedom with pure valour and obstinate determination, and in general are 'worthy of greater praise than I shall be able to give with my verses' ('digno de mayor loor del que yo le podré dar con mis versos'). As we have seen in the last chapter, the literary theory of the early modern period assigned praise to the protagonist of epic poetry, so this is certainly a 'further voice', a suggestion that praise-worthy virtue is not confined to the Spaniards. As Ercilla proceeds through the first two parts of the poem, the virtue of the Indians emerges again through an occasional acknowledgement of the Indians' valour or expression of sympathy for their cause:

> ¡Oh valientes soldados araucanos,
> las armas prevenid y corazones,
> y el usado valor de vuestras manos
> temido en las antárticas regiones.

> Oh, courageous Araucanians!
> Make your hearts and weapons ready!
> Steel your hands' accustomed valor
> Dreaded through the Antarctic regions![57]

> (*La Araucana*, 13. 17. 1–4)

---

[56] Nicolopulos finds the key Virgilian material in part II (*Poetics of Empire*, 11–12), but I think it is not until part III that the dialogue between Ercilla and Virgil becomes decisive.

[57] John Van Horne, 'The Attitude toward the Enemy in Sixteenth Century Spanish Narrative Poetry', *Romanic Review*, 16 (1925), 341–61, notes that other epics of this period also treat the Indians favourably, but even in representing Protestants and Muslims, Spanish poets recognized some ambiguity, assigning some virtues to their

This is not, however, the whole story. From the very beginning,
Ercilla has insisted that these virtues are accompanied by a character
flaw that any reader of Virgil cannot help but notice:

> En fin, el hado y clima desta tierra,
> si su estrella y pronósticos se miran,
> es contienda, furor, discordia, guerra
> y a solo esto los ánimos aspiran.
> Todo su bien y mal aquí se encierra,
> son hombres que de súbito se aíran,
> de condiciones feroces, impacientes,
> amigos de domar estrañas gentes.

> This land's watchword, as its climate,
> From the stars' prognostication
> Is, in fine, contentious fury;
> Discord, strife, its sole ambition.
> Thence stem all their good and evil.
> They are men of sudden anger,
> Fierce of temper, and impatient,
> Fond of quelling foreign varlets.
>
> (*La Araucana*, 1. 45)

In the cantos that follow, this point comes up again and again:
Lautaro addresses his countrymen 'ardiendo en furor' ('ablaze with
ire', *La Araucana*, 11. 73. 2), Tucapel is 'rabioso y vivo fuego' ('Singed
and blazing, wroth and rabid', *La Araucana*, 20. 11. 3) and 'ardiendo
en ira y de furor insano' ('Glowed insane with ire-stirred embers', *La
Araucana*, 22. 39. 2), and so forth; indeed, at the beginning of part II,

---

enemies and some shortcomings (especially cruelty) to their own countrymen.
Barbara Fuchs, *Mimesis and Empire: The New World, Islam, and European Identities*
(Cambridge: CUP, 2001), 44, makes the same points. Nevertheless Beatriz Pastor
Bodmer, *The Armature of Conquest: Spanish Accounts of the Discovery of America,
1492–1589*, tr. Lydia Longstreth Hunt (Stanford, Calif.: Stanford Univ. Press, 1992),
reminds us that in the decades preceding Ercilla's writing, the Indians were characterized as objects, 'pieces', or serfs, first as merchandise, then as primitive beings either
without reason (Alvar Núñez) or gentle savages (Las Casas), so that the way Ercilla
has depicted them is noteworthy. In developing this point, David A. Lupher places *La
Araucana* into the larger discussion about the virtues of the Indians among Spanish
writers, a discussion which ultimately turned classical references towards a critique of
Roman values (*Romans in a New World: Classical Models in Sixteenth-Century Spanish
America* (Ann Arbor: Univ. of Michigan Press, 2003), 297–309).

Caupolicán identifies this uncontrollable wrath as the great weakness of his people (*La Araucana*, 16. 67–8). The same problem thrusts its way to the fore again at the beginning of part III, where Ercilla as narrator states clearly that the combat between Tucapel and Rengo arises from this overpowering defect of character in the Araucanians:

> Y el Profeta nos da por documento
> que en ocasión y a tiempo nos airemos,
> pero con tal templanza y regimiento
> que de la raya y punto no pasemos,
> pues dejados llevar del movimiento,
> el ser y la razón de hombres perdemos
> y es visto que difiere en muy poco
> el hombre airado y el furioso loco.
>
> Tenemos hoy la prueba aquí en la mano
> de Rengo y Tucapel, que peleando
> por sólo presunción y orgullo vano
> como fieras se están despedazando;
> y con protervia y ánimo inhumano
> de llegarse a la muerte trabajando,
> estaban ya los dos tan cerca della
> cuanto lejos de justa su querella.
>
> We are cautioned by the prophet
> That whenever ire excites us,
> We should use control and patience,
> Nor o'erstep the line of licence.
> If we let emotion tow us,
> We are dispossessed of reason
> And the throne of man. The hothead
> And the lunatic are brothers.
> Proof of this today we proffer:
> Tucapel and Rengo fighting
> For vain pride and mere presumption,
> Snarling, rending flesh and members,
> Like wild beasts with wanton cruelty
> Edging close to death's abysm,
> Quite as near as is their quarrel
> Far removed from right's tribunal.
>
> (*La Araucana*, 30. 3, 7)

When 'ira' ('anger') and 'furor' ('rage') get so out of control that soldiers battle one another rather than the enemy, any collective enterprise is doomed to failure. It is true, as Michael Murrin has recently reminded us, that the Spanish army possessed an overwhelming technical superiority,[58] but within the terms of Ercilla's literary representation, the Araucanian army is defeated by its own character flaws, not by the guns and cannons of the invaders. And, I would argue, it is no accident that these character flaws are the same ones that characterize Dido, Turnus, and the other opponents of *pietas* in Virgil's epic world.

Let us turn now to the Spaniards with these same concerns in mind. It has become a critical commonplace to note that Ercilla freely censures his countrymen, and this is indeed true: they are characterized by 'intereses y malicia' ('self-interest, greed, and malice', *La Araucana*, 1. 68. 1), then as 'Gente vil, acobardada, | deshonra del honor y ser de España!' ('People vile and craven, | Shame of Spain, and Spain's dishonor', *La Araucana*, 7. 18. 6–7), and Valdivia in particular comes under steady reproach: 'Valdivia, perezoso y negligente, | incrédulo, remiso y descuidado' ('Plodding, indolent Valdivia, | Dull, suspicious, ever careless', *La Araucana*, 2. 90. 1–2). It would be misleading, however, to see only this, for in spite of their shortcomings Ercilla's countrymen remain 'nuestra gente española' ('we Spaniards', *La Araucana*, 5. 2. 2). The marquis of Cañete, who sent the decisive reinforcements from Peru to Chile, is praised for his even-handed justice (*La Araucana*, 12. 78. 5–8, 89), and part II begins with a reminder of the religious motives of the conquerors and the mercy they were prepared to offer to those who submit (*La Araucana*, 16. 29–30). Philip II is consistently presented as a model of virtue, especially at the battle of St Quentin (*La Araucana*, 18. 24–5). Indeed, as the Spanish commander García instructs his troops, Ercilla distinguishes the Spaniards from the Indians on precisely the point of greatest weakness in the Araucanians:

> Lo que yo os pido de mi parte y digo
> es que en estas batallas y revueltas,
> aunque os haya ofendido el enemigo,

---

[58] Michael Murrin, *History and Warfare in Renaissance Epic* (Chicago and London: Univ. of Chicago Press, 1994), 144–6.

jamás vos le ofendáis a espaldas vueltas;
antes le defended como al amigo
si, volviéndose a vos las armas sueltas,
rehuyere el morir en la batalla,
pues es más dar la vida que quitalla.
    Poned a todo en la razón la mira,
por quien las armas siempre habéis tornado,
que pasando los términos la ira
pierde fuerza el derecho ya violado.
Pues cuando la razón no frena y tira
el ímpetu y furor demasiado,
el rigor excesivo en el castigo
justifica la causa al enemigo.

    I request you, and command you,
In these skirmishes and conflicts,
Though the enemy betray you,
Never strike him with his back turned;
Rather, as a friend, defend him.
If he turns to you, arms loosened,
And refuses death in battle,
Rather spare his life than take it.
    Set your eagles' gaze on reason,
You who deal in war's profession,
For if wrath breaks through its limits,
Right is weakened, violated;
For when reason's curb restrains not
Maddened impulse, rage excessive,
O'ermuch rigor in chastisement
Justifies the foeman's cruelty.

(La Araucana, 21. 55–6)

The need for reason to control passion, of course, is precisely
Aeneas's struggle in the *Aeneid*, and I hardly think it coincidental
that García's instructions here would function as an excellent description of at least part of what is involved in Virgilian *pietas*.

    The great lesson of the *Aeneid*, of course, is that understanding this
point is one thing, but implementing it is quite another, and as we
move towards the conclusion of *La Araucana*, Ercilla's readers come to
the same realization. Everything begins unravelling in canto 26, where
the Spanish lose control in battle and abandon the very guidelines for
rational restraint that García had given a little while earlier:

como los nuestros hasta allí cristianos,
que los términos lícitos pasando,
con crueles armas y actos inhumanos,
iban la gran vitoria deslustrando,
que ni el rendirse, puestas ya las manos,
la obediencia y servicio protestando,
bastaba aquella gente desalmada
a reprimir la furia de la espada.

All till then humane and Christian,
Our men, passing licit limits,
With cruel steel and acts of monsters
Tarnished victory's escutcheon.
Hands outstretched in full surrender,
Oaths of loyalty and service
Failed to induce those hearts of granite
To repress their swords so ruthless.

(*La Araucana*, 26. 7)

Shortly afterwards the Spanish executed twelve captives as a lesson, a decision that Ercilla expresses his reservations about (*La Araucana*, 26. 23). A little later, near the end of the poem, Ercilla passes judgement on how the expedition in Araucania has resolved itself. This is the decisive passage, so I shall quote from it at some length:

Excelente virtud, loable cosa
de todos dignamente celebrada
es la clemencia ilustre y generosa,
jamás en bajo pecho aposentada;
por ella Roma fue tan poderosa,
y más gentes venció que por la espada,
domó y puso debajo de sus leyes
la indómita cerviz de grandes reyes.

No consiste en vencer sólo la gloria
ni está allí la grandeza y excelencia
sino en saber usar de vitoria,
ilustrándola más con la clemencia.
El vencedor es digno de memoria
que en la ira se hace resistencia
y es mayor la vitoria del clemente,
pues los ánimos vence juntamente.

of Bolivar!

La mucha sangre derramada ha sido
(si mi juicio y parecer no yerra)
la que de todo en todo ha destruido
el esperado fruto desta tierra;
pues con modo inhumano han excedido
de las leyes y términos de guerra,
haciendo en las entradas y conquistas
crueldades inormes nunca vistas.

Clemency, a noble virtue,
Generosity's transcendence,
Banished from all hearts ignoble,
Universally is lauded.
Rome attained her world dominions
More through kindness than through cruelty;
Necks of kings untamed were humbled
Chastened not by swords, but mercy.
Conquest has no claim to glory.
Grander and superior merit
Rests in wisdom's clement usage
Of the rights of victors' powers.
Conquerors meriting memorials
Match their ire with tempered mercy,
Carry off a double victory,
Banishing all vengeful passions.
If my own opinion errs not,
Too much blood has here been lavished
To destroy the total riches
Of this fructifying region.
Acts inhuman have exceeded
War's determined laws and limits.
Brute, unparalleled malevolence
Has polluted our invasion.

(*La Araucana*, 32. 1–2, 4)

In this environment, it is inevitable that everything will go wrong in the
final defeat of Caupolicán, and indeed it does: the captured Araucanian
hero offers to convert to Christianity and submit to Spanish rule, yet as
in the *Aeneid* there is no clemency and Caupolicán is tortured and
killed. Ercilla can only condemn the act and exculpate himself by
asserting that he was not present at the time (*La Araucana*, 34. 31). In

other words, *La Araucana* has ended in the same way as the *Aeneid*, with the forces of irrational passion overcoming reason in precisely those people who know what they should do but find that they simply cannot do it. Thus through the course of the poem, the narrator has become sadder but wiser along a Virgilian trajectory: initially ready to sing the deeds of Spanish heroism, in the last lines of the poem he can only confess his mistake and weep: 'conociendo mi error de aquí adelante | será razón que llore y que no cante' ('Knowing now my fault, I must | weep and sing no longer', *La Araucana*, 37. 76. 7–8).[59]

In the end, then, *La Araucana* is a profoundly Virgilian poem, one in which the echoes of the *Aeneid* go beyond mere epic decoration to the very ideological core of the poem. And just as Virgil's attitude towards the imperial enterprise resists easy simplification, so does Ercilla's. It is true that he has profound reservations about his countrymen and their abilities to encounter the indigenous peoples of Araucania according to the standards they have set for themselves, but that does not mean that the truth of the poem 'is the truth of a radical demythification of the process of conquest, which will lead the narrator to a complete rejection of it, and it is the truth of his realization of the superiority of pre-Columbian America'.[60] For one thing, it is hard to imagine any spaniard in the sixteenth century arriving at this position, and even harder to imagine why such a person would dedicate the poem to the Spanish king. But more importantly, the Indians are not superior to the Spaniards in this poem. Like Aeneas, the Spaniards failed to live up to their own standards, but within the value scheme of the poem, having these standards is better than not having them. That is, as Earl Fitz notes, Ercilla is more sympathetic to the Araucanians than to the Spaniards, but he considers the Spanish cause to be more just and proper.[61] There are 'further voices' as well, and we dare not suppress them, for they validate the Other in this poem and bring out the inevitable difficulties inherent in the imperial project. But as with the

[59] Pastor Bodmer, *Armature of Conquest*, 271, notes perceptively that through the course of the poem the narrator changes and grows into this final vision. Aeneas, too, grows into his understanding of *pietas*, and I suspect this resemblance is not accidental.

[60] Ibid. 272.

[61] Earl E. Fitz, *Rediscovering the New World: Inter-American Literature in a Comparative Context* (Iowa City: Univ. of Iowa Press, 1991), 58.

in coherent ?

Aeneid itself, we also dare not listen to these voices alone, for *La Araucana* is no more Caupolicán's poem than the *Aeneid* is Turnus's.[62]

Finally, it is worth focusing on the voice of the Other in *La Araucana* and reflecting briefly on how clearly it comes through in the poem. On the one hand, the Virgilian model makes it impossible to suppress this voice, for it is necessary for Ercilla and his countrymen to understand themselves. This by itself, however, tells us more about the Spaniards than the Indians. Beatriz Pastor Bodmer is quite pessimistic on this point, claiming that key female traits in the Indians are assimilated to the Renaissance model of Dido and key male traits to the European warrior code, with anything that could not be assimilated being either rejected or transformed.[63] Víctor Raviola Molina offers what to my mind is a more thorough analysis, noting the indigenous elements in Ercilla's treatment of theme and conflict, environment, customs, and characters. Yet he, too, acknowledges that the matter resists simplification: the love stories focus on the Indians, but they do so with features borrowed from the European Renaissance; many of the characters are drawn from history, but even the historical figures end up resembling epic characters; the vocabulary of the poem marks a pioneering effort to incorporate the voice of the colonized into the literature of the colonizer, but Ercilla made up some names in analogy with ones he actually heard; and, finally, the descriptions of Chile come from first hand observation, but epic conventions can be found here, too.[64] In the end, as Rolena Adorno suggests, reading *La Araucana* next to the *Aeneid* suggests that the formulaic prescriptions of the epic convention served to help contain and control the indigenous elements in the poem, providing

[62] In other words, as Walter Cohen puts it, 'an anti-imperialist subjectivity produces an imperialist objectivity of far greater plausibility and sophistication than any of the arguments previously presented by open apologists of empire' ('Discourse of Empire', 277). As Frederick A. de Armas has recently pointed out, in *La Numancia* Cervantes has also turned to the *Aeneid* to construct an imperial history of Spain that is simultaneously laudatory and subversive (*Cervantes, Raphael and the Classics* (Cambridge: CUP, 1998), 16–35).

[63] Pastor Bodmer, *Armature of Conquest*, 231–32; see also Menéndez y Pelayo, *Historia de la poesía chilena*, 22.

[64] Víctor Raviola Molina, 'Elementos indígenas en "La Araucana" de Ercilla', in *Don Alonso de Ercilla inventor de Chile*, 81–136. For lexica of indigenous words in the poem, see König's edn. of the poem, pp. xxxix–lv, 'Etimolojía de algunos nombres indíjenas'; and Medina's edn., iv. 425–99.

a predictable set of registers from which the Indians found it very difficult indeed to escape.[65]

2. *THE TEMPEST*: DRAMA AND THE VALORIZATION OF THE OTHER

> To achieve recognition is to rechart and then occupy the place in imperial cultural forms reserved for subordination, to occupy it self-consciously, fighting for it on the very same territory once ruled by a consciousness that assumed the subordination of a designated inferior Other. Hence, *reinscription*. ... That is the partial tragedy of resistance, that it must to a certain degree work to recover forms already established or at least influenced or infiltrated by the culture of empire.
>
>   Edward Said, *Culture and Imperialism* [66]

In contrast to *La Araucana*, where epic conventions helped shape the representation of history, Shakespeare has taken pains in *The Tempest* to create a space in which the flow of historical time can be temporarily suspended. The symbol of this suspension is the island on which the action of the play takes place for, as Roland Greene has noted, islands in the early modern period represent special places whose clearly defined borders make them autonomous from the world at large. And this autonomy in turn makes them good places from which to think about how things work elsewhere: their isolation makes it easy to focus attention on the principles of their own constructedness, but the insights gained there are applicable to other societies as well.[67]

Shakespeare's island is therefore both independent from and bound to the world around it. It is located, we are told, between Tunis and Naples, which puts it into the world that Aeneas and his men had traversed in *Aeneid* 3. But it is also situated between the old world of early modern Italy and the new world of the Virginia

[65] Rolena Adorno, 'Literary Production and Suppression: Reading and Writing about Amerindians in Colonial Spanish America', *Dispositio*, 11/28–9 (1985), 6.

[66] Said, *Culture and Imperialism*, 210.

[67] Roland Greene, 'Island Logic', in Peter Hulme and William H. Sherman (eds.), *'The Tempest' and Its Travels* (Philadelphia: Univ. of Pennsylvania Press, 2000), 138–45.

Company, some of whose members Shakespeare knew and whose experiences have clearly influenced what goes on in the play.[68] Other old world elements, ranging from overt references to Christian religion[69] to systematic engagement with the Moors who dominated the seas off North Africa in Shakespeare's day,[70] are rigorously suppressed, so that Virgil and colonialism, it seems, are the poles between which our response to the play should oscillate.

This seems clear now, but it was not always so. In fact, as recently as 1975, Geoffrey Bullough could omit the *Aeneid* from the sources and analogues to *The Tempest* in his *Narrative and Dramatic Sources of Shakespeare* and declare as well that '*The Tempest* is not a play about colonization.'[71] Since then, the growth of postcolonial studies has virtually guaranteed that the readings of *The Tempest* to which Bullough objects would proliferate, for as Howard Felperin has noted, 'It is perfectly consistent with the theory of a political unconscious that the ideological structures of a text should become visible as such only when they have begun to break down in the ambient culture.'[72] Not all responses to the colonial themes of the play, however, are recent: Trevor Griffiths has noted that, by the nineteenth

[68] Philip Brockbank, 'The Island of *The Tempest*', in *On Shakespeare: Jesus, Shakespeare and Karl Marx, and Other Essays* (Oxford: Basil Blackwell, 1989), 327.

[69] R. S. Conway, 'The Classical Elements in Shakespeare's *Tempest*', in *New Studies of a Great Inheritance: Being Lectures on the Modern Worth of Some Ancient Writers* (London: John Murray, 1921), 178.

[70] J. Brotton, ' "This Tunis, sir, was Carthage": Contesting Colonialism in *The Tempest*', in Ania Loomba and Martin Orkin (eds.), *Post-Colonial Shakespeares* (London and New York: Routledge, 1998), 36; and Richard Wilson, 'Voyage to Tunis: New History and the Old World of *The Tempest*', *ELH*, 64 (1997), 336–7.

[71] Geoffrey Bullough (ed.), *Narrative and Dramatic Sources of Shakespeare*, 8 vols. (London: Routledge & Kegan Paul, and New York: Columbia Univ. Press, 1957–75), viii. 241. Bullough was not alone in these opinions. Frank Kermode, in the introduction to his widely used Arden edn. of *The Tempest* (London: Methuen, 1954), asserted categorically that 'there is nothing in *The Tempest* fundamental to its structure of ideas which could not have existed had America remained undiscovered' (p. xxv), and in 1972 Howard Felperin would refer unproblematically to '[t]he absence of a literary source for *The Tempest*' (*Shakespearean Romance* (Princeton: Princeton Univ. Press, 1972), 247).

[72] Howard Felperin, 'Political Criticism at the Crossroads: The Utopian Historicism of *The Tempest*', in Nigel Wood (ed.), *The Tempest* (Buckingham and Philadelphia: Open University Press, 1995), 45–6. See also Ania Loomba, 'Shakespeare and Cultural Difference', in Terence Hawkes (ed.), *Alternative Shakespeares 2* (London: Routledge, 1996), 164–91.

century, the debates on evolution had begun focusing critical attention in this direction,[73] and interestingly enough, George Washington's one reference to Shakespeare is a description of the British army
as a Prospero whose plans were about to dissolve, leaving the rebel
colonists to take the position of a successful Caliban.[74] Thus there are
still a few naysayers, but even the ideologically reluctant generally
acknowledge that colonialism is an important discursive context of
the play, if not the dominant one.[75]

Whether or not Virgil forms one of these discursive contexts
remains more debatable. That Shakespeare knew the *Aeneid* cannot
be questioned,[76] and since James I both quoted from it in his
Basilikon Doron and was flattered in Virgilian terms in a triumphal

---

[73] Trevor R. Griffiths, ' "This Island's mine": Caliban and Colonialism', *Yearbook of English Studies*, 13 (1983), 159–80.

[74] Hulme and Sherman (eds.), *'The Tempest' and Its Travels*, 172.

[75] Leo Salingar, 'The New World in "The Tempest"', in Jean-Pierre Maquerlot and Michele Willems (eds.), *Travel and Drama in Shakespeare's Time* (Cambridge: CUP, 1996), 211–12, summarizes nicely the arguments against emphasizing colonialism in *The Tempest*; Alden T. Vaughan, 'Shakespeare's Indian: The Americanization of Caliban', *Shakespeare Quarterly*, 39 (1988), 137–54, concedes that colonial readings of the play bring it into contact with American culture in useful ways but argues that it was unlikely that these readings square well with Shakespeare's original intentions; and Edward Pechter, 'The New Historicism and Its Discontents: Politicizing Renaissance Drama', *PMLA* 102 (1987), 292–303, disagrees vigorously with efforts to place colonialism at the centre of interpretation, but even he has to admit that 'colonialism is obviously relevant' to *The Tempest* (296). More representative of contemporary critical opinion is the conclusion that 'The ensemble of fictional and lived practices, which for convenience we will simply refer to here as "English colonialism," provides *The Tempest*'s dominant discursive contexts' (Francis Barker and Peter Hulme, *Cannibalism and the Colonial World* (Cambridge: CUP, 1998), 198); see also Hulme and Sherman (eds.), *'The Tempest' and Its Travels*, 174–5; and Gerald Graff and James Phelan (eds.), *William Shakespeare, The Tempest: A Case Study in Critical Controversy* (Boston and New York: Bedford/St Martin's, 2000), whose extensive treatment of the colonial context of the play suggests how established this approach has now become.

[76] J. M. Nosworthy, 'The Narrative Sources of *The Tempest*', *Review of English Studies*, 24 (1948), 287–8 notes that trs. by Douglas, Phaer, and Stanyhurst made Virgil widely available in Shakespeare's time; that the *Aeneid* served as a frequent source in literature of the period like *Dido, Queen of Carthage* and *The Faerie Queene*; and that Hamlet even says clearly, 'One speech in it I chiefly loved: 'twas Aeneas's tale to Dido' (*Hamlet*, 2. 2. 447). For a survey of Virgilian allusions in Shakespeare's plays, see also T. W. Baldwin, *William Shakespere's Small Latine and Lesse Greeke* (Urbana, Ill.: Univ. of Illinois Press, 1944), ii. 456–96; for more recent work on Shakespeare and Virgil, see Craig Kallendorf, introduction to *Vergil: The Classical Heritage* (New York: Garland, 1993), 11–14.

again takes someone's view & cuts it down

procession a few years before the play was first produced,[77] there is no reason it could not provide a reference point for what goes on in the play. Yet critics are less than sure about what to do with all this. Barbara Mowat sees the *Aeneid* as one of several texts echoed in a play that lacks a 'controlling infracontext'; J. M. Nosworthy and Jan Kott feel that Shakespeare invokes, challenges, and then rejects the Virgilian material in his play; and Robert Wiltenburg concludes that 'the *Aeneid* is the main source of the play..., the work to which Shakespeare is primarily responding, the story he is retelling'.[78] My position is closest to Wiltenburg's, so I shall try in this section to provide the detailed justification that has been lacking for this position. In doing so, I shall also attempt to show that the Virgilian material merges with the colonial discursive context to guide us towards a reading of the play that respects the two interpretive poles between which Shakespeare's island world floats.[79] Finally, I shall consider

[77] At the end of *Basilikon Doron*, James took a line from Anchises's prophecy: 'And being content to let others excell in other things, let it be your chiefest earthly glory, to excell in your owne craft: according to the worthy counsell and charge of Anchises to his posteritie, in that sublime and heroicall Poet wherein also my diction is also included... *Parcere subiectis, & debellare superbos*' (Charles McIlwain (ed.), *The Political Works of James I* (Cambridge, Mass.: Harvard Univ. Press, 1918), 52, qtd. in Gary Schmidgall, *Shakespeare and the Courtly Aesthetic* (Berkeley–Los Angeles and London: Univ. of California Press, 1981), 83 n. 19). James was flattered in Virgilian terms in a triumphal procession of 1604, where one arch invented by Ben Jonson carries the motto 'Redeunt Saturnia Regna' (*Ecl.* 4. 6). Jonson explains the allusion thus: 'Out of *Virgil* to shew, that now those golden times were returned againe, wherein *Peace* was with us so advanced, *Rest* received, *Libertie* restored, *Safetie* assured, and all *Blessednesse* appearing in every of these vertues her particular triumph over her opposite evil' (Ben Jonson, *The Works*, ed. C. H. Herford, Percy and Evylyn Simpson, 11 vols. (Oxford: OUP, 1925–52), vii. 100, qtd. in Schmidgall, *Shakespeare*, 78).

[78] Barbara A. Mowatt, '"Knowing I Loved my Books": Reading *The Tempest* Intertextually', in Hulme and Sherman (eds.), '*The Tempest*' and Its Travels, 28; Nosworthy, 'Narrative Sources', 291; Jan Kott, 'The *Aeneid* and *The Tempest*', *Arion*, NS 3 (1976), 440; and Robert Wiltenburg, 'The "Aeneid" in "The Tempest"', *Shakespeare Survey*, 39 (1987), 159.

[79] Writing in 1998, Jerry Brotton could still argue that the Virgilian references in *The Tempest* had not been situated within discussions of the colonial contexts of the play ('"This Tunis, sir, was Carthage"', 23–42), and two years later Barbara A. Mowatt still felt that the image of Prospero that is supported by references to Virgil and Ovid could be perceived as ideologically at odds with texts that bring up the colonial implications of the play ('"Knowing I loved my books"', 28–9). In the 1990s, however, there were three serious attempts to bring the Virgilian and colonial interpretive discourses together. Donna B. Hamilton, *Virgil and The Tempest: The Politics of Imitation* (Columbus, Ohio: Ohio State Univ. Press, 1990) identifies a number of interesting new parallels

how our search for the voice of the colonial Other is affected by the generic switch from epic to drama.

Like the *Aeneid*, *The Tempest* opens in the midst of a storm, a point of contact that opens out into a broad dialogue between the two works.[80] In both cases the storm that brings the characters together is supernaturally inspired, and the role of Aeolus in *Aeneid* 1 is taken by Ariel at the beginning of the play. All the human characters escape drowning, and in both cases they come ashore in a deep cave with fresh springs and nymphs. The points of contact between play and epic, however, are not limited to geography and the weather. Ferdinand, for example, links the fury of the waves to his passion (*The Tempest*, 1. 2. 393), and in an obvious sense the raging waves reflect the raging emotions within Prospero as well, as he recalls his expulsion from Milan and begins his plan to redress his grievances. Indeed, although Prospero would prefer to assign rage to the lower creatures like Sycorax (*The Tempest*, 1. 2. 276), he finds himself provoked by Caliban, and each curses the other (*The Tempest*, 1. 2. 319–29).[81] As he struggles to control the *furor* ('rage') within himself, he begins to

between the *Aeneid* and *The Tempest*, but in trying to situate the *Aeneid* within both constitutional and colonial contexts at the same time, the book fails to develop a clear colonial reading of the play in Virgilian terms. The same problem arises in Heather James, *Shakespeare's Troy: Drama, Politics, and the Translation of Empire* (Cambridge: CUP, 1997), here in part because James finds the challenge to Virgilian imperialism not in the *Aeneid* itself, but in Ovid's rewriting of it. Finally, Margaret Tudeau-Clayton, *Jonson, Shakespeare and Early Modern Virgil* (Cambridge: CUP, 1998) from my perspective overstates Shakespeare's challenges both to Virgil and to the power structures of his own day, in part to emphasize a contrast she sees between the Virgilianism of Jonson and Shakespeare. The discussion below, I hope, will make clear my debt to all three of these books along with the differences in my own approach, which is intended to provide a more synthetic analysis of the play around the issues of Virgilian colonialism than these three scholars have done.

[80] I have relied primarily on the following sources, none of which is anywhere near complete, for parallels between the *Aeneid* and *The Tempest*: Nosworthy, 'Narrative Sources'; Wiltenburg, 'The "Aeneid" in "The Tempest" '; and Kott, 'The *Aeneid* and *The Tempest*'. In order to avoid overburdening the notes, I acknowledge my dependence on these three articles here. Citations are from The Arden Shakespeare edn. of Frank Kermode (London and New York: Methuen, 1954).

[81] P. Brown, ' "This Thing of Darkness I Acknowledge Mine": *The Tempest* and the Discourse of Colonialism', in Jonathan Dollimore and Alan Sinfield (eds.), *Political Shakespeare: New Essays in Cultural Materialism*, 2nd edn. (Manchester: Manchester Univ. Press, 1994; repr. of 1985 edn.), 315–46. See also Barbara J. Bono, *Literary Transvaluation: From Vergilian Epic to Shakespearean Tragicomedy* (Berkeley–Los Angeles and London: Univ. of California Press, 1984), 220–4.

take on the role of a new Aeneas in Shakespeare's play. The disorder in individuals, by extension, is transferred to a disorder in the state, for 'tempest' in Shakespeare's day also signified 'great trouble, business, or ruffling in a common weale'.[82] The 'common weale' aboard the storm-tossed ship is clearly troubled, for the boatswain rages at his noble passengers as violently as he does against the storm (*The Tempest*, 1. 1. 11–48). The ship of state in turn is equally storm-tossed for, as Prospero explains, he has lost his kingdom (and almost his life) to the rebellion of his brother Antonio. There is a possible allusion here to book 1 of the *Aeneid*. These themes are the same ones raised in Virgil's storm, which is compared in a famous simile to a political disorder that is calmed by an orator 'pietate gravem ac meritis' ('remarkable for righteousness and service', *Aen*. 1. 151).[83] This description fits Gonzalo, who is described in the list of characters at the beginning of the play as 'an honest old councillor' and who is challenged by the boatswain to restore order: 'You are a councillor; if you can command these elements to silence, and work the peace of the present, we will not hand a rope more—use your authority' (*The Tempest*, 1. 1. 20–3). He cannot do so, so that at this point the forces of fury clearly have the upper hand, for the storm rules the waves, the boatswain rules the ship, and Antonio rules Milan.

The corollary to this political theme is the play's colonial subplot. The matter comes up almost as soon as we meet Caliban, for he inhabited the island before Prospero came and still considers it his:

> This island's mine, by Sycorax by mother,
> Which thou tak'st from me. When thou cam'st first,
> Thou strok'st me, and made much of me; wouldst give me
> Water with berries in't, and teach me how
> To name the bigger light and how the less,
> That burns by day and night: and then I lov'd thee,
> And show'd thee all the qualities o'th'isle,
> The fresh springs, brine-pits, barren place and fertile:
> Curs'd be I that did so! All the charms

---

[82] Schmidgall, *Shakespeare*, 156–65, quoting Thomas Thomas's 1588 Latin/English dictionary.

[83] Viktor Pöschl, *The Art of Vergil: Image and Symbol in the Aeneid*, tr. Gerda Seligson (Ann Arbor: Univ. of Michigan Press, 1966), 23.

> Of Sycorax, toads, beetles, bats, light on you!
> For I am all the subjects that you have,
> Which was first mine own King, and here you sty me
> In this hard rock, whiles you do keep from me
> The rest o'th'island.
>
> (*The Tempest*, 1. 2. 333–44)

This is the story of colonization as it was played out again and again in the new world[84] and, as Stephen Orgel notes, Caliban's claim to the island is reasonable according to the international law of the day. Prospero, of course, sees things differently, but he never addresses Caliban's arguments; his claim, too, is legally defensible,[85] so that a space opens up between them, the space that invariably separates colonizer and colonized.[86] Caliban is helpless against Prospero's magic, leaving him only the option of cursing his oppressor, just as Dido could only curse Aeneas as he sailed off to conquer Italy.

The first act also begins rewriting the Dido-and-Aeneas subplot from the *Aeneid*. When Ferdinand first sees Miranda, he greets her with a literal translation ('Most sure the goddess', *The Tempest*, 1. 2. 424) of Aeneas's greeting to the disguised Venus ('O dea certe', *Aen.* 1. 328) after he came ashore near Carthage,[87] and their relationship quickly becomes one of the most important aspects of the play. Ferdinand plays Aeneas to Miranda's Dido, and by putting Ferdinand into Aeneas's place here, Shakespeare is splitting that role between Prospero and Ferdinand, for as we noted above, Prospero takes over from Aeneas the role of political leader and the burden of struggling to impose *ratio* ('reason') over *furor* ('rage'). There is, however, precedent for this division in previous Renaissance rewritings of the *Aeneid*: we recall that Sforza in Filelfo's epic functions as Aeneas except in the relationship with Lyda, where Carlo Gonzaga temporarily assumes this role. The same thing had happened in Petrarca's

[84] Patricia Seed, ' "This Island's Mine": Caliban and Native Sovereignty', in Hulme and Sherman, *'The Tempest' and Its Travels*, 202–11.

[85] Stephen Orgel, 'Prospero's Wife', in Margaret W. Ferguson, Maureen Quilligan, and Nancy J. Vickers (eds.), *Rewriting the Renaissance: The Discourses of Sexual Difference in Early Modern Europe* (Chicago and London: Univ. of Chicago Press, 1986), 58.

[86] Peter Hulme, *Colonial Encounters: Europe and the Native Caribbean, 1492–1797* (New York and London: Methuen, 1986), 124–5. See also John Gillies, *Shakespeare and the Geography of Difference* (Cambridge: CUP, 1994), 143–4.

[87] Hamilton, *Virgil and The Tempest*, 21.

Africa, presumably to keep the hero from being tainted with amatory failings.[88] How, we wonder, will Ferdinand handle this challenge?

It is worth pausing here to note that Shakespeare's Virgil is bound to his age, not ours, in several other ways as well. The idea that Virgil was a magician, which Comparetti put forth as typical of the Middle Ages,[89] remained alive in later centuries as well and accounts at least in part, I believe, for the role that magic plays in this drama. It may well be true that this association would have been stronger with the less well-educated members of the audience, but we should remember that the emerging principles of scientific empiricism had not generated explanations for everything and that the well-educated people who knew the *Aeneid* best often still retained some sympathy for the older way of seeing things.[90] Prospero's magic reflects aspects of this very ambivalence, for it works on the island but not off of it and can do almost anything except ensure the day-to-day survival of Prospero and Miranda.[91]

Several other important Virgilian details that are likely to escape a modern reader may well be linked to Cristoforo Landino, whose late fifteenth-century commentary remained influential in England through (*inter alia*) Gavin Douglas's partial appropriation of it.[92]

---

[88] See the preceding chapter, pp. 40–1, 55 for discussion of this point and references. I am not suggesting that Shakespeare had read Filelfo or Petrarca, only that this division of roles is reasonable within the mental framework of the time. On Ferdinand as an *alter Aeneas*, see Hamilton, *Virgil and The Tempest*, 40.

[89] Domenico Comparetti, *Virgilio nel Medioevo*, ed. Giorgio Pasquali, 2 vols. (Florence: La Nuova Italia, 1982; repr. of Florence, 1937 edn.), pt. 2: 'Virgilio nella legenda populare', tr. by E. F. M. Benecke as *Virgil in the Middle Ages* and repr. with a new intro. by Jan M. Ziolkowski (Princeton: Princeton Univ. Press, 1997); see, however, Pasquale's preface, i, pp. xv–xxxiv for a discussion of how modern scholarship has modified Comparetti's findings. I am grateful to Rita Wright for first stimulating me to pursue this point.

[90] Tudeau-Clayton, *Jonson, Shakespeare*, 7–8, 94–101, rightly emphasizes this point, referring to Gabriel Naudé's *Apologie pour tous les grands personnages qui ont esté faussement soupçonnez de magie* (Paris, 1625). See also Frances Yates, *Majesty and Magic in Shakespeare's Last Plays: A New Approach to Cymbeline, Henry VIII, and The Tempest* (Boulder, Colo.: Shambhala, 1978), 93–102.

[91] Hulme, *Colonial Encounters*, 128.

[92] Tudeau-Clayton, *Jonson, Shakespeare*, 25–6, 192, 209–11. It is difficult if not impossible to 'prove' that Shakespeare knew Landino's commentary, but a growing number of scholars suspect that he did, and the fact that extracts from Landino appeared in English in Douglas's version of the *Aeneid* makes it likely that at least the basic points of Landino's approach were circulating widely in Shakespeare's England.

In this commentary and the reworking of it in books 3 and 4 of Landino's *Disputationes Camaldulenses*, Aeneas's journey is seen as marking a movement from the active to the contemplative lives. This in fact is the very journey Prospero had made in Milan: 'thus neglecting worldly ends, all dedicated | To closeness and the bettering of my mind' (*The Tempest*, 1. 2. 89–90), he left a power vacuum into which his brother stepped. As part of this journey, *ratio* ('reason') must overcome *furor* ('rage'); the storm scene in *Aeneid* 1 was allegorized in this way in Landino's commentary,[93] and Shakespeare's rewriting in *The Tempest*, as we have seen, is compatible with this allegorization. Landino's allegory may also explain another puzzling aspect of Act 1 of *The Tempest*. As part of how he manipulates Ferdinand, Prospero attempts to cast him as a usurper on the island who wants to steal control of it (*The Tempest*, 1. 2. 454–7). He wants to see if he can arouse political ambition in him this way, and it is worth noting that, in Landino's allegory of *Aeneid* 4, Aeneas's attraction to Dido is also linked to the lust for political power.[94] Prospero, in other words, is simply casting Ferdinand into the role of Aeneas as he was understood in Shakespeare's age.

Thus by the end of Act 1, Shakespeare had initiated a rewriting of the *Aeneid* in which the storm reflects both the magic of Prospero and his fury at the characters from his past, along with a determination to work through once again the political and amatory values of Virgil's poem in a colonial setting. In what follows, I shall try to show that Shakespeare takes from Virgil not the precise substance of his colonial vision, but the process by which imperialism is questioned and qualified by 'further voices' that emerge in the drama.

In Act 2 the dialogue with the *Aeneid* proceeds in two principal directions. First Gonzalo addresses one of the other castaways in a speech that is designed to lift their spirits: 'Beseech you, sir, be merry;

On Landino's commentary, see Craig Kallendorf, *In Praise of Aeneas: Virgil and Epideictic Rhetoric in the Early Italian Renaissance* (Hanover, NH: Univ. Press of New England, 1989), 129–65, with bibliography.

[93] Cristoforo Landino, *Disputationes Camaldulenses*, ed. Peter Lohe (Florence: Sansoni, 1980), 159–66.

[94] Ibid. 166–98. This explanation, I believe, explains the problem articulated in James, *Shakespeare's Troy*, 207, about why Prospero seems to be trying to rouse in Ferdinand a passion he does not have. The association of Dido with political power was an unusual feature of Landino's commentary, so the glance in this direction in *The Tempest* increases the odds that Shakespeare knew something about it.

you have cause, | So have we all, of joy; for our escape | Is much beyond our loss' (*The Tempest*, 2. 1. 1–3). This speech resembles in tone and spirit the famous 'O socii . . .' ('O comrades . . .') address at *Aen.* 1. 198–207, in which Aeneas made similar arguments to his men when they found themselves in a similar position;[95] Gonzalo's speech, however, does not appear to do much good—a 'further voice' that calls into question both the Virgilian subtext and its efficacy in the world of this play.

Shortly afterwards comes the infamous 'widow Dido' exchange, a passage which is obviously referring to the *Aeneid* but which has resisted a fully satisfactory explanation.[96] Gonzalo refers to Dido as a widow, which starts a series of arguments, first about whether or not she remained a widow, then about whether Dido's Carthage was the same city as Tunis, to whose king Claribel had just been married. The passage is difficult to unravel, but two things at least are reasonably clear. First, as Donna Hamilton has pointed out, the argument over 'widow Dido' cannot be separated from the discussion that triggered it, Claribel's marriage.[97] Sebastian upbraids Alonso for marrying his daughter to the king of Tunis, for reasons that in themselves are important:

> Sir, you may thank yourself for this great loss,
> That would not bless our Europe with your daughter,
> But rather lose her to an African;
> Where she, at least, is banished from your eye,
> Who hath cause to wet the grief on't.
>
> (*The Tempest*, 2. 1. 119–23)

[95] D. D. Carnicelli, 'The Widow and the Phoenix: Dido, Carthage, and Tunis in *The Tempest*', *Harvard Library Bulletin*, 27 (1979), 389–433.

[96] Ibid. 389–433, offers the fullest analysis of the scene, which unfortunately still does not explain it very satisfactorily. See also J. M. Hooker, 'Widow Dido', *Notes and Queries*, NS 32 (1985), 56–8; Malcolm Pittock, 'Widow Dido', *Notes and Queries*, 231 (1986), 368–9; and John Pitcher, 'A Theatre of the Future: *The Aeneid* and *The Tempest*', *Essays in Criticism*, 34 (1984), 201. Adrianne Roberts-Baytop, *Dido, Queen of Infinite Literary Variety: The English Renaissance Borrowings and Influences* (Salzburg: Institut für Englische Sprache und Literatur, Universität Salzburg, 1974), 104–18, lists the other allusions to Dido in Shakespeare's plays and provides a brief discussion of them. James, *Shakespeare's Troy*, 198, suggests that the 'widow Dido' jokes unleash a bawdy and derisive revision of the *Aeneid* and any overly optimistic attempts to appropriate it into new contexts; this is the most insightful comment I have found on the scene.

[97] Hamilton, *Shakespeare and The Tempest*, 40–2. Hamilton approaches Claribel's marriage in relation to the discussions circulating at the time about how James might marry his children; this is certainly reasonable, but I think there is at least one other point of reference here as well.

In a play in which the relationship with the non-European Other becomes central, the fact that the king of Tunis is African cannot be overlooked. A sexual relationship with someone from this area proved a disaster for Aeneas, and Sebastian is arguing that the same will be true for Claribel; it is worth noting that, just days after the wedding, Alonso already agrees ('Would I had never | Married my daughter there!' *The Tempest*, 2. 1. 103–4).[98] The other point that seems clear here is that Virgil's version of the Dido story has become contested ground by this point. In the *Aeneid*, Dido began as a widow but sacrificed her chastity on the altar of libido; this version, however, had existed for centuries alongside another one in which she never met Aeneas, but chose death rather than remarry a neighbouring king.[99] Since the Ferdinand–Miranda subplot has been set forth as a retelling of the Dido story, which version becomes authoritative matters in this play, and the argument in this scene suggests that it may well not be Virgil's.

Some of the same difficulties that we encounter in the 'widow Dido' exchange also emerge in interpreting the famous 'Siena Sieve' portrait of Queen Elizabeth (see Figure 7). Dido was also called 'Elissa' or 'Eliza', a fact which Elizabeth panegyrists exploited regularly,

[98] Harry Berger, Jr., 'Miraculous Harp: A Reading of Shakespeare's *Tempest*', *Shakespeare Studies*, 5 (1969), 253–83. Patricia Parker, 'Fantasies of "Race" and "Gender": Africa, *Othello*, and Bringing to Light', in Margo Hendricks and Patricia Parker (eds.), *Women, 'Race', and Writing in the Early Modern Period* (London and New York: Routledge, 1994), 96–8, notes that the 'widow Dido' discussions recall a similar rewriting of the Dido and Aeneas story in *Othello*, which is also about a marriage between a European and an African Other. Leslie Fiedler, *The Stranger in Shakespeare* (New York: Stein & Day, 1972), suggests that Claribel's marriage reconciles the worlds that fell apart when Aeneas fled and Dido committed suicide (201), but I suspect that David Norbrook is more on target when he concludes that the efforts to discuss Claribel's marriage through the lens of *Aeneid* 4 actually highlight how difficult it is to bridge the historical and cultural differences involved in the exercise (' "What Cares These Roarers for the Name of King?": Language and Utopia in *The Tempest*, in Gordon McMullan and Jonathan Hope (eds.), *The Politics of Tragicomedy: Shakespeare and After* (London and New York: Routledge, 1992), 45). Finally, David Scott Wilson-Okamura focuses on Carthage rather than Rome as a template for colonization and notes that Shakespeare's rewriting of the *Aeneid* therefore serves as a warning against intemperance; see 'Virgilian Models of Colonization in Shakespeare's *Tempest*', *ELH* 70 (2003), 713–16.

[99] Basic information about the other, non-Virgilian Dido tradition may be found in Lida de Malkiel, *Dido en la literatura española*; and Kallendorf, *In Praise of Aeneas*, 58–76.

Figure 7. The 'Sieve Portrait' of Queen Elizabeth I. Attributed to Federico Zuccaro (Siena, Pinacoteca)

and this name in particular evoked the non-Virgilian Dido who died in order to preserve her chastity. The sieve, which was said to be Elizabeth's favourite device, reinforces this point, alluding to Tuccia, a vestal virgin who established her chastity by carrying water to the Tiber in a sieve. The Siena painting was one of several 'sieve' portraits

that appeared after 1579, when it was becoming increasingly clear
that the monarch was passing beyond her childbearing years. The
painting is also linked explictly to the *Aeneid,* in that the pillars
behind the queen contain scenes from book 4 of Virgil's poem.
Here, however, is where the interpretive difficulties emerge. On the
one hand, as we have seen, Landino had linked Dido to political
ambition, which makes her association with a powerful, politically
accomplished female monarch especially appropriate. Virgil's story,
however, is not about the Dido who kills herself to remain true to
Sychaeus, her dead husband, but the one who sacrifices her chastity,
then her life to a foreign visitor. Lowell Gallagher suggests that
the interpretive key is the sieve, which represents the act of separat-
ing good from evil in the iconographical literature of the period.
According to this interpretation, the painting invites the viewer
to focus on a queen whose role required her to discern the difference between a virtuous love, represented by the 'good' Dido, and
one intertwined with vice, represented by Virgil's 'bad' Dido. Given
that the painting dates to around the time when the Duke
d'Alençon was courting Elizabeth and raising the alarms of many
Englishmen,[100] this interpretation is certainly plausible enough. Nevertheless, in the painting as well as in the passage in the play, the
associative registers do not line up tidily, and there is probably something about all this that still escapes us over four hundred years later.

   In any case, later in this same scene, Gonzalo comes forth with his
utopian vision for the island, the ideal state he would set up there if
he could:

> Had I plantation of this isle, my lord,—
> And were the King on't, what would I do?
> I'th'commonwealth I would by contraries
> Execute all things; for no kind of traffic
> Would I admit; no name of magistrate;
> Letters should not be known; riches, poverty,
> And use of service, none; contract, succession,

[100] Lowell Gallagher, *Medusa's Gaze: Casuistry and Conscience in the Renaissance*
(Stanford, Calif.: Stanford Univ. Press, 1991), 127–40; see also Roy Strong, *Portraits of
Queen Elizabeth I* (Oxford: OUP, 1963), 66–8; Frances A. Yates, *Astrea* (London:
Routledge & Kegan Paul, 1975), 114–20; and Doris Adler, 'The Riddle of the Sieve:
The Siena Sieve Portrait of Queen Elizabeth', *Renaissance Papers*, (1978), 1–10.

Bourn, bound of land, tilth, vineyard, none;
No use of metal, corn, or wine, or oil;
No occupation, all men idle, all,
And women, too, but innocent and pure:
No sovereignty—
All things in common Nature should produce
Without sweat or endeavour: treason, felony,
Sword, pike, knife, gun, or need of any engine,
Would I not have; but Nature should bring forth,
Of its own kind, all foison, all abundance
To feed my innocent people.
I would with such perfection govern, sir,
T'excel the Golden Age.

(*The Tempest*, 2. 1. 139, 141, 143–52, 155–60, 163–4)

Many critics have suggested an intertextual relationship here with Montaigne's 'Cannibals';[101] this seems reasonable to me, and it has the merit of placing the passage firmly into the colonial discourse of the age. The new world, pointedly referred to here as a 'plantation', was often seen in precisely these terms, as a 'golden age' where all the shortcomings of European civilization could dissolve away into a new beginning. But we should not forget that the *locus classicus* for the Golden Age was Virgil's fourth eclogue:

Vltima Cumaei uenit iam carminis aetas;
magnus ab integro saeclorum nascitur ordo.
iam redit et uirgo, redeunt Saturnia regna;
iam noua progenies caelo demittitur alto.
Tu modo nascenti puero, quo ferrea primum
desinet ac toto surget gens aurea mundo,
casta faue Lucina: tuus iam regnat Apollo.

. . . .

ipsae lacte domum referent distenta capellae
ubera, nec magnos metuent armenta leones;
ipsa tibi blandos fundent cunabula flores.

---

[101] Paul N. Siegel, 'Historical Ironies in *The Tempest*', *Shakespeare Jahrbuch*, 119 (1983), 110; and William M. Hamlin, *The Image of America in Montaigne, Spenser, and Shakespeare: Renaissance Ethnography and Literary Reflection* (New York: St Martins Press). A good orientation to Montaigne's attitudes towards these issues may be found in Kohl, *Entzauberter Blick*, 21–32.

occidet et serpens, et fallax herba ueneni
occidet; Assyriam uulgo nascetur amomum.

(*Ecl.* 4. 4–10, 21–5)

Now is come the last age of the song of Cumae; the great line of the centuries begins anew. Now the Virgin returns, the reign of Saturn returns; now a new generation descends from heaven on high. Only do thou, pure Lucina, smile on the birth of the child, under whom the iron brood shall first cease, and a golden race spring up throughout the world. Thine own Apollo now is king! ...

Uncalled, the goats shall bring home their udders swollen with milk, and the herds shall fear not huge lions; unasked, thy cradle shall pour forth flowers for thy delight. The serpent, too, shall perish, and the false poison-plant shall perish; Assyrian spice shall spring up on every soil.[102]

In this speech, Shakespeare is therefore positing a Virgilian vision of how colonial power might be projected on this island. The audience, however, knows that the island is already inhabited and that the reality, at least for Caliban, is far removed from this. Once again, an imperial vision is at least partly overshadowed by a darker reality.

At this point in the play, power is the issue: in the first of two rebellious plots that drive the action here, Caliban joins with Stephano and Trinculo to overthrow Prospero. Their initial encounter is worth pausing over because of the ironic commentary it offers on the colonial encounter. The scene (2. 2) begins as Caliban, carrying wood and cursing his overlord, sees Trinculo and falls flat on his face before the seemingly divine European. Like many a colonizer in his first encounter with the Other, Trinculo is confused by the creature before him but quickly sees him as an Indian who could be commodified into a source of income back in England (*The Tempest*, 2. 2. 32, 57). In an ironic rewriting of Prospero's history on the island, Stephano resolves to give Caliban the gift of language as well—that is, he will loosen his tongue with a bottle of sack. Caliban's response is that of many other indigenous peoples: 'That's a brave god, and bears celestial liquor: I will kneel to him' (*The*

---

[102] The English tr. is that of H. Rushton Fairclough in the Loeb Classical Library edn. of Virgil (Cambridge, Mass.: Harvard Univ. Press, and London: William Heinemann, 1965), 29–31. On the appropriation of this poem by Judaeo-Christian culture, see Thomas Fletcher Royds, *Virgil and Isaiah: A Study of the Pollio* (Oxford: OUP, 1918), 74–85.

Tempest, 2. 2. 118–19).[103] It is easy to dismiss this plot as simple comic interlude, which in part it is, but it veers dangerously close to issues at the centre of discussion and in fact will resurface at a key moment in the Virgilian resolution of the play.

The other plot is very serious indeed, and is taken as such by Prospero. Here Antonio and Sebastian plan to rise up against Alonso and kill him in his sleep. Prospero deals with this plot in 3. 3, the harpy banquet scene whose connection with the *Aeneid* has long been recognized. In *Aeneid* 3, Aeneas and his men take refuge on the islands where the harpies live; the dreadful creatures swoop down on them as they are about to eat, foul their food, and give them a prophecy they do not want to hear. In *The Tempest*, Ariel assumes the form of a harpy—half human, half bird—and addresses the 'three men of sin' (*The Tempest*, 3. 3. 53), telling them both that the fates 'have Incens'd the seas and shores, yea, all the creatures, | Against your peace' (*The Tempest*, 3. 3. 72–4) and taken Alonso's son from him. The connection with the *Aeneid* is tight—Shakespeare even translates some Virgilian phrases in the text[104]—and the scenes perform some of the same functions in both works, but they are different as well. Alonso and his followers, for one thing, are not Aeneas, the man with the divine mission to found a new race, but usurpers whose illicit seizure of power has upset the moral, political, and natural order around them. In other words, Shakespeare is developing a meditation on imperialism that unfolds in Virgilian terms but is by no means a slavish imitation of the *Aeneid*.

[103] Gillies, *Shakespeare*, 146–47. In this scene Trinculo and Stephano have to try to figure out what kind of a creature Caliban is, a process that reproduces the reasoning of those first Europeans who encountered the indigenous inhabitants of the new world. Hamlin, *Image of America*, 116–18, and James Smith, *Shakespearian and Other Essays* (Cambridge: CUP, 1974), 188–203, make a persuasive case that by the end of this process, Caliban evolves as fully human.

[104] *The Tempest*, 3. 3. 55–6, the sea 'belched them up', translates *Aen*. 6. 297, 'eructat harenam', evoking judgement on the impenitent in Shakespeare's play through association with Virgil's description of the punishment of the wicked in the underworld. Shakespeare's Harpies clap their wings, just as Virgil's 'quatiunt... alas' (*Aen*. 3. 226) (Pitcher, 'A Theatre of the Future', 197–8; and Hamilton, *Virgil and The Tempest*, 74–8). Recent discussions of the scene in the *Aeneid* may be found in H. Akbar Khan, 'The Harpies Episode in *Aeneid* 3', *Prometheus*, 21/2 (1996), 131–44; and H. W. Stubbs, 'Vergil's Harpies: A Study in *Aeneid* III (with an Addendum on Lycophron, *Alexandra* 1250–2)', *Vergilius*, 44 (1998), 3–12.

The 'further voices' we have been hearing become much more
audible when we return to the unfolding relationship between Ferdinand and Miranda. Act 3, scene 1, begins with Ferdinand carrying
logs, a task to which Prospero has set him; since this has been
Caliban's job, we might view this as colonizer and colonized changing
places,[105] but in terms of the Dido–Aeneas associations at work here,
it also recalls Aeneas at work helping Dido build the city of Carthage
in *Aeneid* 4. Things quickly take a decisively un-Virgilian turn,
however, when Miranda declares, 'I am your wife if you will marry
me; | If not, I'll die your maid' (*The Tempest*, 3. 1. 83–4). At the
beginning of Act 4, Prospero announces his approval of the match,
but not without dire warnings of what will happen if sex precedes
marriage. Ferdinand immediately promises that the basest desire 'shall
never melt | Mine honour into lust' (*The Tempest*, 4. 1. 27–8), and
he does so with a specific allusion to 'the murkiest den' (*The Tempest*,
4. 1. 25) where Aeneas and Dido first made love (*Aen.* 4. 160–72).[106]
Prospero is satisfied with this promise and conjures up a masque in
honour of the upcoming marriage. This masque rewrites the harmonious vision promised by Jupiter to Venus at the beginning of the
Aeneid[107] by extending invitations to some Virgilian deities but not
others: Venus and Cupid are banished (*The Tempest*, 4. 1. 91–101), and
Juno, recognized 'by her gait' (*The Tempest*, 4. 1. 102; cf. 'et vera
incessu patuit dea', 'even | her walk was sign enough she was a goddess',
Aen. 1. 405), attends as the deity who presides over proper mar-
riages.[108] The Virgilian flavour of this masque is unmistakable, but
so is the challenge it offers to any effort to oversimplify the relationship
between the *Aeneid* and *The Tempest*. On the most obvious level, we
see immediately that in this rewriting of *Aeneid* 4, the tradition of the
other chaste Dido has won out over the version developed by Virgil.
Indeed, as Heather James has pointed out, the masque is designed to
exclude passion, indeed corporeality in any form.[109]

[105] Stephen Orgel, 'Shakespeare and the Cannibals', in Marjorie Garber (ed.),
Cannibals, Witches, and Divorce: Estranging the Renaissance (Baltimore, Md., and
London: Johns Hopkins Univ. Press, 1987), 55–6.
[106] Tudeau-Clayton, *Jonson, Shakespeare*, 215.
[107] Felperin, *Shakespearean Romance*, 47–8, 56.
[108] Hamilton, *Virgil and The Tempest*, 78–85; and Tudeau-Clayton, *Jonson,
Shakespeare*, 214.
[109] James, *Shakespeare's Troy*, 210.

The problem is that passion refuses to be excluded from Prospero's ideal world, for the masque vanishes suddenly when he remembers 'that foul conspiracy | Of the beast Caliban and his confederates' (*The Tempest*, 4. 1. 139–40). The issue must be important, for Shakespeare draws emphatic attention to it: Ferdinand notices how upset Prospero is (*The Tempest*, 4. 1. 143–4), Miranda notes that 'Never till this day | Saw I him touch'd with anger so distemper'd' (*The Tempest*, 4. 1. 144–5), and even Ariel admits that he was afraid to approach Prospero in this mood (*The Tempest*, 4. 1. 168–9). Indeed, in the famous revels speech, Prospero freely admits as much (*The Tempest*, 4. 1. 158–60).[110] And it is worth noting that in the speech making this admission, the Virgilian verbal texture is unusually strong, with two possible allusions linking Prospero directly to Aeneas. Prospero refers to his 'weakness' (*The Tempest*, 4. 1. 159) and his 'infirmity' (*The Tempest*, 4. 1. 160), in which he resembles Aeneas, who is 'curis ingentibus aeger' ('sick with heavy cares', *Aen.* 1. 208) at the point when he rallies his shipwrecked men on the shores of Carthage. And Prospero's comments about the evanescence of the visions he has crafted recall Aeneas's response ('pictura pascit inana', 'he feeds | his soul on what is nothing but a picture', *Aen.* 1. 464) to the scenes of Trojan history depicted in the Carthaginian temple.[111] Such links suggest that any effort to make sense of Prospero's role at this key point in the play would benefit from recognizing his position as an *alter Aeneas*.

Let us see how this might work. Act 5 begins with Prospero's announcement of how he wishes to end what he has arranged:

> Though with their high wrongs I am struck to th'quick,
> Yet with my nobler reason 'gainst my fury
> Do I take part: the rarer action is
> In virtue than in vengeance: they being penitent,
> The sole drift of my purpose doth extend
> Not a frown further. Go, release them, Ariel:
> My charms I'll break, their senses I'll restore,
> And they shall be themselves.
>
> (*The Tempest*, 5. 1. 25–32)

---

[110] Ibid. See also Berger, 'Miraculous Harp', 270–1.
[111] Schmidgall, *Shakespeare and the Courtly Aesthetic*, 169–70, 261.

Forsaking vengeance, having one's 'fury' ruled by one's 'nobler reason', is, of course, precisely what Aeneas proved unable to do at the end of the *Aeneid*. *The Tempest*, in other words, ends like the *Aeneid* should have, with the 'civilized' values of the colonizers triumphant over the forces of irrationality and darkness.[112]

In several other ways as well, *The Tempest* appears to end in a dream vision, a projection of European colonialist desires. Ferdinand, we understand, marries Miranda, rewriting the Dido story so that both reason rules over passion and the new Aeneas avoids intermarriage with a non-European Other.[113] The boatswain is properly obedient again (*The Tempest*, 5. 1. 221–39), and Prospero retakes his kingdom (*The Tempest*, 5. 1. 129–34). And Caliban, it appears, has grown as well. At the end of Act 4, in a scene modelled on the incident with the Golden Bough at the beginning of *Aeneid* 6, he and his co-conspirators come upon an array of glistening garments in a

---

[112] Wiltenburg, 'The "Aeneid" in the "Tempest" ', 167–8; Hamilton, *Virgil and The Tempest*, 133–4; and Robert S. Miola, 'Vergil in Shakespeare: From Allusion to Imitation', in John D. Bernard (ed.), *Vergil at 2000: Commemorative Essays on the Poet and His Influence* (New York: AMS, 1986), 241–58, repr. in Kallendorf, *Vergil*, 271–89. In adopting this reading of the end of the play, I am therefore disagreeing with Schmidgall, who sees both the *Aeneid* and *The Tempest* in black-and-white terms: 'Virgil's is a world of political absolutes in which good and evil are easily discerned. On the side of civic decency and harmony is Aeneas. On the other side are Juno and her factors Dido, Turnus, and Allecto. With their "high wrongs" the reader of the *Aeneid* is "struck to the quick." A similarly distinct division of the *dramatis personae* occurs in *The Tempest*' (*Shakespeare and the Courtly Aesthetic*, 167; see also 74–5). I also think that Jan Kott overstates his position in 'The Tempest, or Repetition', in Ralph Berry (ed.), *Shakespeare Today, Mosaic*, 10/3 (1977), 29, where he claims that *The Tempest* repeats the *Aeneid*, but in a bitter reading in which nothing is purified and the only lesson is that human plans and dreams fail.

[113] Jeffrey Knapp, *An Empire Nowhere: England, America, and Literature from Utopia to The Tempest* (Berkeley–Los Angeles and Oxford: Univ. of California Press, 1992), 240. As my discussion of the play shows, I believe that Barbara J. Bono, *Literary Transvaluation: From Vergilian Epic to Shakespearean Tragicomedy* (Berkeley–Los Angeles and London: Univ. of California Press, 1984), is wrong when she suggests that Dido's liaison with Aeneas is rewritten in *The Tempest* on the pattern of Claribell's marriage to the King of Tunis in order to unite the chastity of the 'good' Dido and the sexuality of the 'bad' one to form a chaste dynasty that unites former enemies (222). As Michael Mack, 'The Consolation of Art in the *Aeneid* and the *Tempest*', in Marc Berley (ed.), *Reading the Renaissance: Ideas and Idioms from Shakespeare to Milton* (Pittsburgh, Penn.: Duquesne University Press, 2003), notes, Claribel was married off into a loveless union for political expediency (75), and this marriage remains problematic throughout the play.

lime tree. Stephano and Trinculo are distracted by them and fall to fighting between themselves, but Caliban has learnt self-restraint and urges them to leave the garments alone (*The Tempest*, 4. 1. 221–55).[114] At this point he is still intent on murdering Prospero and retaking the island he considers his by right, so in a scene reminiscent of Spanish practice in the new world, Prospero unleashes his hunting dogs— whose names, Fury and Tyrant, are surely significant—on him. By the end of the play, however, Caliban announces, 'I'll be wise hereafter, | And seek for grace' (*The Tempest*, 5. 1. 294–5); Prospero has offered forgiveness rather than more vexed curses, and he receives submission in turn.[115] In other words, Prospero's plan has succeeded: order is restored, passion has yielded to reason, and the flow of historical events is contained within a plot of his making. Prospero renounces his magic, and he and the other Europeans return to their homes.

Yet once again, all is not as it first seems. In the earlier parts of *The Tempest*, the Virgilian material resisted easy schematization, and a closer look at the end of the play reveals that here, too, there are 'further voices', signs that even in Shakespeare's revised *Aeneid*, disaster lurks just below the surface. In renouncing his magic, Prospero recalls that 'to the dread rattling thunder | Have I given fire, and rifted Jove's stout oak | With his own bolt' (*The Tempest*, 5. 1. 44–6); this may recall a passage in the *Aeneid* ('uidi et crudelis dantem Salmonea poenas, | dum flammas Iovis et sonitus imitatur Olympi', 'I saw Salmoneus: | how brutal were the penalties he paid | for counterfeiting Jove's own fires and | the thunders of Olympus', *Aen*. 6. 585–6) which serves to link Prospero intertextually to one of Virgil's great sinners, suggesting how close his magic has come to evil.[116] In spite of what he has said, his brother Antonio has not repented, suggesting that, even here at the end, Prospero's vision is partial at best. When he pulls back the curtain in turn and shows Alonso that his son is still alive, Ferdinand and Miranda are arguing, which might make us wonder how much longer the rational forces that have restrained their sexual passion will dominate.[117] But most importantly, Prospero is finally forced at

[114] Hamilton, *Virgil and The Tempest*, 85–92.
[115] I am grateful to Disa Gambera for pointing this out to me in an unusually clear, forceful way.
[116] Pitcher, 'Theatre of the Future', 197.
[117] Fiedler, *Stranger in Shakespeare*, 245.

Moralizes residentials – doesn't take account of scholarly on

ha!

the end of the play to recognize how closely he is tied to Caliban. His words—'this thing of darkness I | Acknowledge mine' (*The Tempest*, 5. 1. 275–6)—say nothing clearly, but suggest a great deal: if we cannot separate ourselves cleanly from the forces of evil, then any victories are temporary at best. The evil without is bound to the evil within,[118] and all we can finally do is to forgive others and ask them to forgive us, as Prospero indeed does in the Epilogue.

In the end, then, Shakespeare's meditation on Virgilian values gives us a new *Aeneid*, but one that is not all that different from the old one and, I believe, akin spiritually to the powerful insights of its model. By making Prospero attempt to rouse political ambition in Ferdinand and then abandon the project, by having him reverse course and return from the contemplative life to take up again his duties in Milan, and by assigning to Prospero the role of Virgilian magician, then taking it away from him again, Shakespeare is, I believe, directing us away from the Renaissance commentary tradition represented by scholars like Landino to the text of the *Aeneid* itself.[119] If I am correct in this, then Shakespeare is (though perhaps by historical accident rather than conscious design) presenting an approach to the *Aeneid* that parallels that of Dante, who, according to Robert Hollander, also focused on Virgil's text rather than the commentaries to it.[120] Read carefully in conjunction with its source, Shakespeare's play, I believe, represents a powerful, and original, effort to come to terms with the text of the *Aeneid*. In some ways, *The Tempest* suggests that Virgil got it wrong, that self-control can succeed in deferring sexual activity to the right time and place and that reason can repress fury and offer compassion and forgiveness at key moments. But in showing what lurks just below the surface—in the argument of Ferdinand and Miranda, for example, and in the kinship to 'this thing of darkness' that Prospero must acknowledge—Shakespeare shows that he hears the 'further voices' in the *Aeneid* as well.

That leaves us with one final question: how clearly do we hear in particular the voice of Caliban, the colonized Other, in this play? Again, the answer is not simple. On the one hand, the dominant perspective throughout the play is Prospero's, which blocks Caliban's on both small

---

[118] Ibid. 250–3; Bono, *Literary Transvaluation*, 220–4.
[119] Cf. Tudeau-Clayton, *Jonson, Shakespeare*, 209–10.
[120] Robert Hollander, *Il Virgilio dantesco: Tragedia nella 'Commedia'* (Florence: Leo S. Olschki, 1983).

and large points. The title of the play offers a good example: the Indian word 'hurricane' had been available in English since 1555, but Shakespeare chose 'tempest' instead, thereby keeping the indigenous linguistic register from breaking in on the European one.[121] Indeed, as Caliban remarks to Prospero, 'You taught me language' (*The Tempest*, 1. 2. 365), and as Mary Sánchez rightly notes, imposing language also imposes a conceptual and value system, thereby trapping the native in the colonizer's system of thought and behaviour.[122] To carry this argument one step further, we might note that Shakespeare's dialogue with Virgil threatens to generate a Caliban who is little more than a projection of negative values created in reference not to the indigenous Other, but to European imperial ideology and literary tradition.[123] Indeed, Act 5, scene 1, presents a telling detail here. Miranda exclaims 'O wonder! | How many goodly creatures are there here! | How beauteous mankind is! O brave new world, | That has such people in 't!' (*The Tempest*, 5. 1. 181–4). Ironically, however, she is not referring in these lines to the island's native inhabitant but to Alonso and

---

[121] Peter Hulme, 'Hurricanes in the Caribbees: The Constitution of the Discourse of English Colonialism', in Francis Barker *et al.* (eds.), *1642: Literature and Power in the Seventeenth Century* (Colchester: Univ. of Essex, 1981), 55–83, with the basic argument repeated in *Colonial Encounters*, 94–101.

[122] Mary E. Sánchez, 'Caliban: The New Latin-American Protagonist of *The Tempest*', *Diacritics*, 6 (1976), 54–61. This point is made eloquently by the Cuban writer Roberto Fernández Retamar, who notes that 'we Latin Americans continue to use the language of our colonizers. . . . Right now we are discussing, as I am discussing with these colonizers, how else can I do it except in one of their languages, which is now also *our* language, and with so many of their conceptual tools, which are now also our conceptual tools. This is precisely the extraordinary outcry which we read in a work by perhaps the most extraordinary writer of fiction who ever existed. In *The Tempest*, William Shakespeare's last play, the deformed Caliban—enslaved, robbed of his island, and taught the language by Prospero—rebukes him thus: "You taught me language, and my profit on't | Is, I know how to curse. The red plague rid you | For learning me your language" ' ('Caliban: Notes Toward a Discussion of Culture in Our America', tr. Lynn Garafola, David Arthur McMurray, and Robert Márquez, *Massachusetts Review*, 15 (1974), 10–11; repr. in *Caliban and Other Essays*, tr. Edward Baker (Minneapolis: Univ. of Minnesota Press, 1989), 3–45, from *Casa de Las Américas* (Havana), 68 (Sept.–Oct. 1971)). The relationship between *translatio linguae* and *translatio imperii* (that is, between the transmission of language and the transmission of power) is explored at length in Eric Cheyfitz, *The Poetics of Imperialism: Translation and Colonization from The Tempest to Tarzan* (New York and Oxford: OUP, 1991).

[123] Schmidgall, *Shakespeare and the Courtly Aesthetic*, 173.

the other Europeans, so that Caliban and his like are symbolically erased through the very exclamation that should acknowledge their presence.[124]

Yet within these limits, Caliban occupies a space within the play that Prospero never succeeds in closing off. Occasionally his linguistic register intrudes: as Stephen Greenblatt notes, no one knows what 'scamel' means.[125] And as noted above, Caliban's claims to the island are never refuted; he is overpowered but on this point cannot be silenced. His curses have their own kind of power, which is tied to the island he considers his and leads in turn to an eloquence of his own:

> Be not afeard; the isle is full of noises,
> Sounds and sweet airs, that give delight, and hurt not.
> Sometimes a thousand twangling instruments
> Will hum about mine ears; and sometimes voices,
> That, if I then had wak'd after long sleep,
> Will make me sleep again: and then, in dreaming,
> The clouds methought would open, and show riches
> Ready to drop upon me, that, when I waked,
> I cried to dream again.
>
> (*The Tempest*, 3. 2. 133–41)

We should also not forget that in a way, Caliban wins: the Prospero who seeks the audience's leave to return to Milan will return the island to Caliban, which is the dream of all colonized people everywhere.[126] Thus while the main thrust of *The Tempest* is pro-imperial—it is difficult to imagine that Shakespeare is trying to get his friends in the Virginia Company to abandon their colonial project—the 'further voices', especially Caliban's, remind us of the cost of empire, just as in the *Aeneid*.[127]

[124] Gillies, *Shakespeare*, 146–7.

[125] Stephen Greenblatt, 'Learning to Curse: Aspects of Linguistic Colonialism in the Sixteenth Century', in *Learning to Curse: Essays in Early Modern Culture* (New York and London: Routledge, 1990), 31. See also Philip Brockbank, '*The Tempest*: Conventions of Art and Empire', in *Later Shakespeare* (London: Edward Arnold, 1966), 193; and Deborah Willis, 'Shakespeare's *Tempest* and the Discourse of Colonialism', *Studies in English Literature 1500–1900*, 29 (1989), 279, 283–7.

[126] Walter Cohen, *Drama of a Nation: Public Theater in Renaissance England and Spain* (Ithaca, NY, and London: Cornell Univ. Press, 1985), 401.

[127] Barker-Hulme, 203–4, and Erlich, 'Shakespeare's Colonial Metaphor', 63, both admit that G. Wilson Knight, for whom *The Tempest* celebrates England's 'will to raise savage peoples from superstition, taboos, and witchcraft...to a more enlightened existence' (qtd. from *Crown of Life*, 255), was at least partly right, and that there

It is worth noting as well that Caliban's voice has resonated clearly with a number of writers from the so-called Third World. In the 1960s and early 1970s, George Lamming, Aimé Cesaire, and Roberto Fernández Retamar in particular developed a reading that served in one sense as an allegory of colonialism,[128] but one that was also grounded 'in the words of the text, not in its own decision to find postcolonial themes present, to land a seventeenth-century play with a late twentieth-century agenda'.[129] This makes *The Tempest* today a Third-World play, as *La Araucana* is a Chilean epic.[130]

is a strong pro-imperialist thrust to the play. Recent critics, however, tend to see considerably more ambiguity in the play than this; see Siegel, 'Historical Ironies', 107; Stephen Greenblatt, 'Martial Law in the Land of Cockaigne', in *Shakespearean Negotiations: The Circulation of Social Energy in Renaissance England* (Berkeley–Los Angeles: Univ. of California Press, 1988), 155–7; Willis, 'Shakespeare's *Tempest*'; and Meredith Anne Skura, 'Discourse and the Individual: The Case of Colonialism in *The Tempest*', *Shakespeare Quarterly*, 40 (1989), who notes that while Shakespeare hardly succeeds in transcending the imperialism of his age, his acknowledgement of Prospero's relationship to Caliban at the end of the play comes closer to recognizing the Other than most colonial discourse of the time, including the earlier plays he himself had written (49). Indeed, Skura notes rightly that 'Shakespeare was the first to show one of *us* mistreating a native, the first to represent a native from the inside, the first to allow a native to complain on stage, and the first to make that New World encounter problematic enough to generate the current attention to the play' (58).

[128] George Lamming, *The Pleasures of Exile* (London: Michael Joseph, 1960); and Aimé Césaire, *Une tempête* (Paris: Éditions du Seuil, 1969), in English as *A Tempest*, tr. Richard Miller (New York: Ubu Repertory Theater Publications, 1985). Basic studies on the Third World appropriation of *The Tempest* include Charlotte H. Bruner, 'The Meaning of Caliban in Black Literature Today', *Comparative Literature Studies*, 13 (1976), 240–53; Robert Nixon, 'Caribbean and African Appropriations of *The Tempest*', *Critical Inquiry*, 13 (1987), 557–78; Thomas Cartelli, 'Prospero in Africa: The Tempest* as Colonialist Text and Pretext', in Jean E. Howard and Marion F. O'Connor (eds.), *Shakespeare Reproduced: The Text in History and Ideology* (New York and London: Methuen, 1987), 99–115; Roberto Fernández Retamar, *Caliban and Other Essays*, tr. Edward Baker (Minneapolis: Univ. of Minnesota Press, 1989) (thanks to Al Brilliant for this reference); Alden T. Vaughan and Virginia Mason Vaughan, *Shakespeare's Caliban: A Cultural History* (Cambridge: CUP, 1991); Mary Fuller, 'Forgetting the *Aeneid*', *American Literary History*, 4/3 (1992), 517–38; and Chantal Zabus, *Tempests after Shakespeare* (New York, and Houndmills: Palgrave, 2002), 1–101.

[129] Peter Hulme, 'Reading from Elsewhere: George Lamming and the Paradox of Exile', in Hulme and Sherman (eds.), '*The Tempest*' and *Its Travels*, 234.

[130] Sánchez, 'Caliban', 61.

In the end, the voice of the Other resounds more forcefully in *The Tempest* than in *La Araucana*, for notwithstanding the European filters that often block our vision, Caliban projects his own presence with clarity and vigour. Part of this impression probably derives from the fact that Prospero leaves the island to him while the Spaniards ultimately positioned themselves successfully in Chile. But in part I believe this impression also derives from the fact that these two Virgilian poems are written in different genres. Stephen Orgel is exactly right when he notes that 'Shakespeare, as he so often does, dramatizes both sides of the debate, and in the process renders a resolution to it impossible',[131] in the sense that once a series of characters have taken on life in a play, it is impossible for one perspective to suppress another completely. Caliban has begun to take on a life of his own, and once this happens, as the Prosperos learn, they never really possess the territory they have occupied nor the people who live there. As Caliban put it, 'This island's mine' (*The Tempest*, 1. 2. 331).

3. SOR JUANA INÉS DE LA CRUZ: LYRIC AND THE FEMALE OTHER BETWEEN TWO WORLDS

> ... if the effect of colonial power is seen to be the production of hybridization rather than the noisy command of colonialist authority or the silent repression of native traditions, then an important change of perspective occurs. The ambivalence at the source of traditional discourses on authority enables a form of subversion, founded on the undecidability that turns the discursive conditions of dominance into the grounds of intervention.
>
> (Homi K. Bhabha, 'Signs Taken for Wonders'[132])

---

[131] Orgel, *The Tempest*, 35–6. See also Richard Marienstras, *New Perspectives on the Shakespearean World*, tr. Janet Lloyd (Cambridge: CUP, and Paris: Éditions de la Maison des Sciences de l'Homme, 1985), 183–4.

[132] Homi K. Bhabha, 'Signs Taken for Wonders: Questions of Ambivalence and Authority under a Tree Outside Delhi, May 1817', in *The Location of Culture* (London: Routledge, 1994), 112, quoted in Roland Greene, *Unrequited Conquests: Love and Empire in the Colonial Americas* (Chicago: Univ. of Chicago Press, 1999), 4.

In 1536, less than twenty years after Cortés besieged Mexico City, a Franciscan seminary was established at Tlateloco. It was set up for the sons of the Mexican elite and quickly reached the highest levels of instruction, so that native-born students learnt Latin well enough to compose Virgilian dactylic hexameter verses.[133] An examination of the curricula of schools like this, along with libraries and books published in Mexico during the second half of the sixteenth and the first half of the seventeenth centuries, shows very little difference in the educational curricula of Spain and its colony in this period.[134] Not surprisingly, in an environment like this the indigenous Indian culture blended with the humanism of the European Renaissance so that the new world was seen as a revival of the old; as Octavio Paz put it, 'The resurrection of the Aztec world was its transfiguration in the imperial looking glass of humanism. Mexico-Tenochtitlan was an American Rome.'[135]

One of the most accomplished literary figures of this 'American Rome' was Sor Juana Inés de la Cruz. Born of a Spanish father and an Indian mother, she embodied the cultural hybridization of her country at this time. Before entering orders, she learnt to read and write in a school in Amecameca, then began reading in the library of her grandfather, Pedro Ramírez. One of the books in this library was an anthology of Latin poets, *Illustrium poetarum flores* (Lyon, 1590), edited by Octaviano de la Mirandola. This book, which is covered with marginalia, contained selections from the poetry of Virgil, confirming that Sor Juana knew this material from an early age.[136] She later amassed a library of some 4,000 books, which went well beyond the devotional books we would expect of a nun to include the

---

[133] Todorov, *Conquest of America*, 220.

[134] Ignacio Osorio Romero, *La enseñanza del Latín a los indios* (Mexico City: Universidad Nacional Autónoma de México, 1990), pp. v–vii, lxvii–lxviii. See also Mignolo, 'Darker Side of the Renaissance', 810–11.

[135] Octavio Paz, *Sor Juana Inés de la Cruz o las trampas de la fe* (Barcelona: Seix Barral, 1982), 58.

[136] Ibid. 115–16, 328. As Elsa Cecilia Frost, 'La formación clásica de los primeros evangelizadores novohispanos', *Silva*, 3 (2004), 162, notes, the early Spanish priests who initially evangelized Mexico also knew the classics well, and like Sor Juana, they, too, relied heavily on anthologies. Much has been written recently about Sor Juna, but a thorough analysis of her relation to the classical tradition remains a desideratum.

major works of Greek and Latin literature. Among them, clearly, was Virgil, whom she cited regularly in her poetry.[137]

This should not be taken as a given, for as Marilyn Desmond has pointed out, most of Virgil's readers through these centuries have been men, so that this reading experience has traditionally been tied to 'class-specific performances of masculinity'.[138] That is, reading the *Aeneid* has generally meant men responding to a poetic perspective fashioned by another man and constructing their own gender in the process. Yet as an increasing number of critics have been pointing out recently, women constitute a significant number of the 'further voices' within the *Aeneid*, and Virgil's treatment of them rewards analysis. On the one hand, as S. Georgia Nugent has observed, women in the *Aeneid* are constructed 'as the quintessential Other', separated, marginalized from, and subordinated hierarchically to the men, then sacrificed to their needs and goals. Dido comes to mind right away, but she in fact is joined by Amata, Camilla, and Juturna. The group of female exiles plays an important role in *Aeneid* 5, and Virgil even says they have a collective voice ('uox omnibus una', *Aen.* 5. 616), but 'in fact no woman ever speaks in this voice and no man ever hears it'.[139] And Lavinia, of course, survives the encounter with Aeneas and his men to marry him and unite the two peoples, but she is sacrificed as a person and treated as an object to be exchanged rather than a subject who wills her own actions. Virgil's female characters must be exorcized as a threat to Aeneas and his mission, yet he is clearly sympathetic to them and takes noticeable pains to

---

[137] Ignacio Osorio Romero, *Historia de las bibliotecas novohispanas* (Mexico City: Sep. Dirección General de Bibliotecas, 1986), 59–61; and E. Abreu Gómez, *Sor Juana Inés de la Cruz* (Mexico City: Monografías Bibliográficas Mexicanas, 1934), 332–3, 337–8, 344–5, 386.

[138] Desmond, *Reading Dido*, 8; see also 4. Some of the issues discussed in this section are also touched upon in Margaret W. Ferguson, *Dido's Daughters: Literacy, Gender, and Empire in Early Modern England and France* (Chicago and London: Univ. of Chicago Press, 2003). Charles Martindale makes the very interesting point that the 'male dominance of twentieth-century Virgilian scholarly discourse could be said to replicate the marginalisation of women within Virgil's own texts' ('Introduction: "The Classic of All Europe" ', in Charles Martindale (ed.), *The Cambridge Companion to Virgil* (Cambridge: CUP, 1997), 6 n. 10). As the next couple of paragraphs suggest, this situation is finally starting to change.

[139] S. Georgia Nugent, 'Virgil's "Voice of the Women" in *Aeneid* V', *Arethusa*, 25 (1992), 255; see also 256–92.

represent their point of view.[140] As part of what is repressed in Roman society, the feminine is written out of Virgil's text as slowly and painfully as possible.[141] In the process, women 'serve as signposts to the road not taken.... That is, Virgil's representational strategy enables him to show, often through women who question, refuse, or reject dominant ideological tenets of the *Aeneid*, that alternative modes exist.'[142]

A woman reader like Sor Juana would bring to the text a new sensitivity to these voices, but what is less obvious is that, in the Virgilian environment, the discourses of gender and colonialism intersect. Dido, for example, was a woman whose domination first by libido, then by rage, played the Other to Aeneas's rational self-control. But she was also a barbarian, the queen of Carthage whose city represented traits like cruelty and treacherousness that the Romans did not accept as part of their own self-construction. Thus listening to Dido offers a potential challenge both to gender constructions and to the imperial project of Virgil's *Aeneid* and of poetry written in imitation of it.[143] In the final section of this chapter, I shall look at how the discourses of gender and colonialism intersect in the Virgilian passages that Sor Juana wrote. In doing so, I shall follow a suggestion made by Roland Greene, who notes that lyric offers an

[140] Mihoko Suzuki, *Metamorphosis of Helen: Authority, Defiance, and the Epic* (Ithaca, NY, and London: Cornell Univ. Press, 1989), 93.

[141] Sarah Spence, *Rhetorics of Reason and Desire: Vergil, Augustine, and the Troubadours* (Ithaca, NY, and London: Cornell Univ. Press, 1988), 11–51.

[142] S. Georgia Nugent, 'The Women of the *Aeneid*: Vanishing Bodies, Lingering Voices', in Christine Perkell (ed.), *Reading Vergil's Aeneid: An Interpretive Guide* (Norman, Okla.: Univ. of Oklahoma Press, 1999), 263. The issues taken up in the paragraph receive further treatment in Grace Starry West, 'Women in Vergil's *Aeneid*', Ph.D. thesis (California–Los Angeles, 1975); Christine G. Perkell, 'On Creusa, Dido, and the Quality of Victory in Virgil's *Aeneid*', in Helene P. Foley (ed.), *Reflections of Women in Antiquity* (New York: Gordon & Breach Science Publishers, 1981), 355–77; Nadia Margolis, '*Flamma, furor*, and *fol'amors*: Fire and Feminine Madness from the *Aeneid* to the *Roman d'Eneas*', *Romanic Review*, 78 (1987), 131–47; Susan Ford Wiltshire, *Public and Private in Vergil's Aeneid* (Amherst, Mass.: Univ. of Massachusetts Press, 1989); Barbara Pavlock, *Eros, Imitation, and the Epic Tradition* (Ithaca, NY, and London: Cornell Univ. Press, 1990), 69–112; Ellen Oliensis, 'Sons and Lovers: Sexuality and Gender in Virgil's Poetry', in Martindale (ed.), *Cambridge Companion to Virgil*, 294–311; Sarah Spence, '*Varium et Mutabile*: Voices of Authority in *Aeneid* 4', in Perkell (ed.), *Reading Vergil's Aeneid*, 80–95; and A. M. Keith, *Engendering Rome: Women in Latin Epic* (Cambridge: CUP, 2000).

[143] Desmond, *Reading Dido*, 2, 32–3.

often-overlooked place to listen for signs of resistance to conquest. This genre has traditionally been seen as relatively divorced from politics, but Greene argues that

[w]hen victors do not see themselves as victors; when the vanquished imagine themselves as victors or are so imagined by the victors themselves; and most often, when a member of one of the classes conceives a position for himself—moral, political, or emotional—that varies from the standpoint of the class, the most available medium will often be lyric.[144]

As I shall attempt to show, I believe that the voices of the victors and the vanquished come together in the poetry of Sor Juana, who as a *mestiza* writes lyrics in which the cultural constraints of early modern Europe enclose, but finally cannot contain, the voice of the new world Other.

In 1680, to receive the newly appointed viceroy of New Spain, Don Tomás Antonio de la Cerda, Marqués de la Laguna and Conde de Paredes, erected two triumphal arches in Mexico City, one situated on the Plaza de Santo Domingo and planned by Don Carlos de Sigüenza y Góngora, the other beside the cathedral and planned by Sor Juana. Sigüenza y Góngora produced a pamphlet, *Teatro de virtudes politicas*, that described his arch, which proposed as models of political wisdom early Mexican rulers like Itzcóatl and Montezuma, but seen through the lenses of the Bible and Graeco-Roman antiquity. The plans for Sor Juana's arch rested on the same pattern of cultural syncretism. The booklet describing her arch, *Neptuno alegórico*, makes reference, for example, to the unfinished cathedral, comparing it to the wall around Troy, so that contemporary Mexico was seen in Virgilian terms. An account is also given of how Aeneas was saved from the winds by Neptune, who here represents the new viceroy. In this case, what we see in Sor Juana's work is pro-imperial. The commission for the arch came from the highest echelons of colonial society, and the ideological message it sets forth is one of seamless cultural continuity. No mention is made of the conquest, and Spanish power is projected here by someone whose absorption into that power was by no means a given.[145]

This absorption, however, is not complete, as we discover when we turn to Sor Juana's lyrics, although the distinctive voice of this

---

[144] Greene, *Unrequited Love*, 3–4.   [145] Paz, *Sor Juana*, 64–5, 206–15.

speaking subject only emerges gradually through its classicizing milieu. Sor Juana's poetry is learned and allusive; she generally does not provide much context for her mythological references but relies simply on allusion or reference, confident that her readers know the myths as well as she does.[146] Sometimes, as in Romance 46, l. 28 and Romance 50, ll. 76, 114, Virgil or one of the characters he created is simply added to a list of mythological figures.[147] In Romance 38, she flatters a fellow poet who has sent praises of her work through repeated references to Virgil: she is especially pleased with his praise for her because he is generally such a severe critic, such that if Virgil had written for him he would have had still more reason to burn his poem (ll. 57–60); in earlier days he could have been a Virgil himself for Augustus (l. 169); in his pen Spain enjoys even greater Sibylline oracles (l. 196), and so forth. In Romance 11, in turn, she seeks the rite of confirmation, speaking in a seriocomic tone of fever-induced delirium which serves as a pretext to cite classical sources, including Virgil; her inferno, as Paz put it, is a bookish one.[148]

These treatments strike most modern readers as fairly conventional, but things get more interesting when Sor Juana begins treating some of the famous heroines of antiquity. Romance 43, for example, begins like another poem of flattery, this time answering Elvira, her patron, with the claim that she could not find a classical model worthy of her. The unworthy models need to be listed, and Dido (ll. 41–5) and Lavinia (ll. 56–60) appear in the list. Romance 55 has attracted a good bit of attention from feminist critics, who have argued that in it the author subverts the male tradition of depicting heroic women by challenging misogynist myth from a woman's perspective.[149] Sor Juana's lyrics returned repeatedly to figures like Lucretia, Julia, Portia, and Thisbe, and it is easy to argue that these figures attracted her because in a way, their lives paralleled hers: they became famous but sacrificed a great deal, just as she did in achieving

[146] José Carlos González Boixo, 'Introducción', in Sor Juana Inés de la Cruz, Poesía lírica, ed. José Carlos González Boixo (Madrid: Cátedra, 1992), 44–5.

[147] Citations are from Juana Inés de la Cruz, Obras completas, 4 vols. (Mexico: Fondo de Cultura Economica, 1951–7); trs. are courtesy of Hilaire Kallendorf.

[148] Paz, Sor Juana, 185.

[149] Janice A. Jaffe, 'Sor Juana, Artemesia Gentileschi, and Lucretia: Worthy Women Portray Worthy Women', Romance Quarterly, 40 (1993), 141–55.

success as a poet, then renouncing her poetic vocation under pressure from her religious superiors.[150]

A look at two explicitly Virgilian love poems suggests at least in part why they were seen as so potentially subversive. Romance 3 turns on a specifically Virgilian problem: what is the nature and status of jealousy? In response to José Montoro, Sor Juana argues that jealousy is a disorder, a threat to rational control, but it is the only path to love and is therefore desirable. Dido, of course, is added to the list of jealous lovers in l. 65. Décima 100, entitled 'Alma que al fin se rinde al Amor resistido, en alegoría de la ruina de Troya' ('Soul that at the end gives in to the resisted Love, in allegory of the ruin of Troy'), is an extended conceit whose relevance to my argument demands that it be quoted in full:

> Cogióme sin prevención
> Amor, astuto y tirano:
> con capa de cortesano
> se me entró en el corazón.
> Descuidada la razón
> y sin armas los sentidos,
> dieron puerta inadvertidos;
> y él, por lograr sus enojos,
> mientras suspendió los ojos
> me salteó los oídos.
>
> Disfrazado entró y mañoso;
> mas ya que dentro se vió
> del Paladión, salió
> de aquel disfraz engañoso;
> y, con ánimo furioso,
> tomando las armas luego,
> se descubrió astuto Griego
> que iras brotando y furores,
> matando los defensores,
> puso a toda el Alma fuego.
>
> Y buscando sus violencias
> en ella al Príamo fuerte,
> dió al Entendimiento muerte,
> que era Rey de las potencias;

---

[150] Judy B. McInnis, 'Martyrs for Love: The Reflections of Sor Juana Inés de la Cruz in/on Lucretia, Julia, Portia, and Thisbe', *Hispania*, 80 (1997), 764–74.

y sin hacer diferencias
de real o plebeya grey,
haciendo general ley
murieron a sus puñales
los discursos racionales
porque eran hijos del Rey.
    A Casandra su fiereza
buscó, y con modos tiranos,
ató a la Razón las manos,
que era del Alma princesa.
En prisiones su belleza
de soldados atrevidos,
lamenta los no creídos
desastres que adivinó,
pues por más voces que dió
no la oyeron los sentidos.
    Todo el palacio abrasado
se ve, todo destruído;
Deifobo allí mal herido,
aquí Paris maltratado.
Prende también su cuidado
la modestia en Polixena;
y en medio de tanta pena,
tanta muerte y confusión,
a la ilícita afición
sólo reserva en Elena.
    Ya la Ciudad, que vecina
fué al Cielo, con tanto arder,
sólo guarda de su sér
vestigios, en su rüina.
Todo el Amor lo extermina;
y con ardiente furor,
sólo se oye, entre el rumor
con que su crueldad apoya:
'Aquí yace un Alma Troya.
¡Victoria por el Amor!'

    Love, astute and tyrannical,
caught me without warning:
with the cape of a courtier
he entered into my heart.
Unwary the reason

and without arms the senses,
they gave way unnoticed;
and he, to achieve his disturbances,
while he suspended the eyes
assaulted my ears.

    Disguised he entered, and sly;
but once he saw himself inside
the Palladium, he left
that deceitful disguise;
and, with furious spirit,
then taking arms,
he revealed himself an astute Greek
who, ires and furors erupting,
killing the defenders,
set fire to all the Soul.

    And seeking his violences
in the soul to strong Priam,
he gave death to Understanding,
who was King of the powers;
and without making distinctions
between royal and plebeian republic,
making a general law
rational discourses
died from his stab-wounds
because they were sons of the King.

    His fierceness sought Cassandra,
and with his tyrannical ways,
he tied the hands of Reason,
who was the princess of the Soul.
Her beauty in the prisons
of daring soldiers,
she laments the unbelieved
disasters she divined,
for despite the cries she gave
the senses did not hear her.

    All the palace burned
is seen, all destroyed;
Deiphobus there badly wounded,
here Paris mistreated.
Modesty takes also its care
in Polixena;

and in the midst of so much pain,
so much death and confusion,
reserves illicit affection
only in Helen.
 And the City, that was neighbour
to Heaven, with so much burning,
only retains of its being
vestiges, in its ruin.
Love exterminates everything;
and with ardent furor,
only is heard, amidst the noise
with which it supports its cruelty:
'Here languishes a Trojan Soul.
 A victory through Love!'

This poem rewrites *Aeneid* 2, but even on its most obvious levels it is a most un-Virgilian poem. Troy did not literally consume itself in the flames of love, but since Helen's departure with Paris started the Trojan War, the grounds for the comparison are certainly there. Indeed, the influential commentary of Landino allegorized *Aeneid* 2 in precisely this way, with Troy standing for *voluptas*, or unrestrained sensuality, against which Aeneas struggles.[151] There is a key difference, however, between Sor Juana's poem and Landino's allegory: reason prevails over sensuality in Aeneas and he leaves the city, while in Sor Juana's poem reason yields to love, after which 'Todo el Amor lo extermina' ('love exterminates everything', l. 55). Landino's allegory marks a victory for Aeneas; Décima 100 celebrates '¡Victoria por el Amor!' ('A victory through love!', l. 60).[152]

Within the parameters we have been exploring in this chapter, Sor Juana's poem is revolutionary. The *Aeneid* itself, as we have seen, records the triumph of imperialism, which it presents as necessary, even desirable, at the same time as it measures the cost in both human and political terms. The poems we have examined that were written in imitation of it preserved this tension, although we have seen that as we moved from epic through drama, the voice of colonial resistance is heard more audibly. Sor Juana's poem goes one step further. Here the

[151] This material is spread throughout Landino's commentary to *Aen.* 2 but summarized clearly in *Disputationes Camaldulenses*, 120–35.
[152] Paz, *Sor Juana*, 371–2.

voice of the narrator no longer suspends itself in temporary sympathy
with victims of imperialism before realigning itself with the imperial
project, but actually blends with the voice of the Other, the woman in
whom 'iras' ('ires') and 'furores' ('furors') overcome 'Razón' ('reason')
in a flaming burst of self-consuming glory. When love wins, empire
loses, and the vanquished become the victors.

As I noted earlier, gender and colonialism are connected here. In
Neptuno alegórico, Sor Juana assists in the projection of Spanish
power, a project gendered as masculine through the centuries. In
her love poetry, she moves away from public concerns to private ones
and cultivates a voice that, in the words of Roland Greene, 'is among
the sites of this resistance to conquest'.[153] Here, for the first time in
our inquiry, the Other becomes a speaking subject. No longer can we
say that Virgilian values are projected onto the objectified colonist,
whose resistance in turn has to be carefully sought out among the
'further voices' in a polyphonic poem. Here the voice of the Other
resounds clearly, and it should not surprise us that it challenges the
basic values of the European master narrative.

It is worth noting as well, however, that more than one voice can
still be heard in Sor Juana's writings, and that these voices alternately
project, then challenge, imperial power. It would be fashionable now,
I suppose, simply to explain this in terms of 'divided subjectivity',[154]
but I think the inquiry we have been conducting allows a more
satisfying explanation. Sor Juana was Spanish through her father
and Indian through her mother; like that of 'El Inca' Garcilaso de
la Vega, with whom she is often compared, her culture was hybrid.[155]
In a sense, as Edward Said has pointed out repeatedly, this is always
true: 'Partly because of empire, all cultures are involved in one
another, none is single and pure, all are hybrid, heterogeneous,

---

[153] Greene, *Unrequited Conquests*, 2. In general I agree with Walter Cohen, 'The
Literature of the Empire in the Renaissance', *Modern Philology*, 102 (2004), 1–34, who
notes that the Renaissance inherited from antiquity a propensity to see epic as the genre of
empire, lyric as its antithesis, and drama as occupying a more neutral, intermediate
position (33).

[154] This is the term used by Elizabeth Davis to account for the complexities of
Ercilla's ideology; see above, n. 33.

[155] Félix Duque, 'La conciencia del mestizaje: El inca Garcilaso y sor Juana Inés de
la Cruz', *Cuadernos Hispanoamericanos*, 504 (1992), 7–31; Greene, *Unrequited Conquests*, 204, 212; and Grafton, *New Worlds*, 154.

extraordinarily differentiated, and unmonolithic.'[156] But it is especially true in Latin America, whose interaction with the European narrative of conquest we have been studying. As writers like the Cuban Fernández Retamar have pointed out, history has in effect made it impossible to conceive of a non-hybrid culture in the Americas. 'El mestizaje', a mixture of the European, Indian, and African, is the essence of Latin America.[157] One of the elements in that cultural mix is Virgil's *Aeneid*, whose representation of colonial encounter and conquest provided in turn a model for how both the Europeans in the new world and the people they discovered saw themselves. It is often difficult to find the colonized within the narrative of the colonizer, but as Sor Juana's lyrics show, it can be done, so that the voice of the Indian emerges as well from the Virgilian heritage.

---

[156] Said, *Culture and Imperialism*, p. xxv; see also idem, *Orientalism*, 347, and for an extension of the argument, Lisa Jardine and Jerry Brotton, *Global Interests: Renaissance Art between East and West* (Ithaca, NY: Cornell Univ. Press, 2000). This position is the opposite of the one adopted by Frantz Fanon, who argues that while colonized, '[t]he native intellectual accepted the cogency of these ideas, and deep down in his brain you could always find a vigilant sentinal ready to defend the Greco-Roman pedestal. Now it so happens that during the struggle for liberation, at the moment that the native intellectual comes into touch again with his people, this artificial sentinal is turned into dust. All the Mediterranean values—the triumph of the human individual, of clarity, and of beauty—become lifeless, colorless knick-nacks' (*The Wretched of the Earth*, tr. Constance Farrington (New York: Grove Press, 1968), 46–7).

[157] Sánchez, 'Caliban', 59.

3

Revolution

1. MILTON'S *PARADISE LOST*: FROM COMMONWEALTH TO RESTORATION

These and other possible borrowings have been carefully cata-
loged [sic], but the question of their significance has been not
only unanswered but, until recently, unasked. For a long time
the prevailing model for the study of literary sources, a model
in effect parceled out between the old historicism and the new
criticism, blocked such a question.... [A] freestanding, self-
sufficient, disinterested art work produced by a solitary
genius...has only an accidental relation to its sources: they
provide a glimpse of the 'raw material' that the artist fashioned.
Insofar as this 'material' is taken seriously at all, it is as part of
the work's 'historical background,' a phrase that reduces history
to a decorative setting or a convenient, well-lighted pigeonhole.
But once the differentiations on which this model is based begin
to crumble, then source study is compelled to change its character: history cannot simply be set against literary texts as either
stable antithesis or stable background, and the protective isolation of those texts gives way to a sense of their interaction with
other texts and hence of the permeability of their boundaries.

(Stephen Greenblatt, *Shakespearean Negotiations*[1])

The year after Charles II returned to England and ended the republican experiment of Oliver Cromwell and his followers, John Boys

---

[1] Stephen Greenblatt, *Shakespearean Negotiations: The Circulation of Social
Energy in Renaissance England* (Berkeley-Los Angeles: Univ. of California Press,
1988), 95.

published his translations of the third and sixth books of the *Aeneid*. In the second of these translations (see Figure 8), Boys repeats the traditional argument that Virgil had two purposes in writing the *Aeneid*, to represent heroic virtue in the person of Aeneas and to praise the emperor Augustus, who claimed descent from the mythical founder of Rome.[2] Later on, Boys moves to bring the poem into the present by suggesting that as antiquity boasted of its Geryon, so the people of his day can proclaim their happiness in Charles II, whose 'inherent worth alone and noble personage seem to have design'd him for Empire' (pp. 86–7) The link is tightened in an epigram that Boys wrote to the king and placed at the end of the book:[3]

> Si dives, *Rex magne*, esset mihi vena *Maronis*,
>   Si foelix vatum principis ingenium,
> Ipse fores meus *Aeneas*, titulisque superbis
>   Te ornarem, *Heroi* quos dedit ille suo.

> Had I, *Great Monarch*, Maro's divine spirit,
>   Or did the Prince of Poets wit inherit,
> You should be my *Aeneas*, and what He
>   His *Heroe* gave, to you ascrib'd should be.

(fo. Gg2^r)

This seems clear enough, but one copy of the translation also carries a marginal note in a near-contemporary hand indicating that 'everybody

---

[2] John Boys, *Aeneas His Descent into Hell*…(London: Printed for the Author, 1661), fos. a4ᵛ–A1ʳ. The idea that Virgil wrote the *Aeneid* to praise Augustus, as we have seen in Ch. 1, goes back to Donatus, whose 4th-cent. commentary was printed regularly beginning in the 1470s. His approach was picked up by commentators like Jodocus Badius Ascensius, who wrote that Virgil's intention was 'ut et reipublicae et sibi quam plurimum per huius operis editionem prosit' ('that he profit both the state and himself as much as possible through the publication of this work'), by endowing Aeneas with every virtue, then setting him up to be imitated by Augustus (*Publii Virgilii Maronis poetae Mantuani universum poema*…(Venice: Joannes Maria Bonellus, 1558), fos. 123ᵛ–4ʳ). References to both of Boys's trs. will appear in the text.

[3] The royalist flavour of the book is intensified by the inclusion of a speech Boys intended to give when Charles II landed at Dover on 25 May 1660, but which was never given because Charles changed his route (fos. Ff4ᵛ–Gg1ᵛ). Boys's tr. of book 6 was well enough known to have been parodied, in a text entitled *Cataplus*, attributed variously to Charles Cotton, Andrew Marvell, and Sir Edward Sherburne, and published in London in 1672.

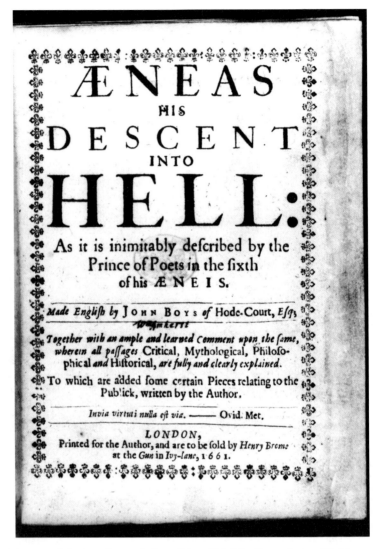

Figure 8. John Boys's translation of *Aeneid* 6. John Boys, *Aeneas His Descent into Hell*... (London: Henry Brome, 1661), title-page (The British Library)

knows that sweet Mr. John Boys might have said much more in praise
of Charles ye 2d. if he had pleased'.[4]

The implications of this position are worked out in Boys's translation to book 3.[5] Here, Boys begins, Virgil presents an allegory of a
well-ordered commonwealth, whose prince or supreme magistrate is
Aeneas. Initially it might seem that there is some ambiguity about
what kind of government, republic ('commonwealth...supreme
magistrate') or monarchy ('prince'), Boys has in mind, but the
ambiguity quickly disappears: Aeneas's goal in Italy is 'the foundation of a never-declining *Monarchy*' (p. 57). He then moves to link
Virgil's world clearly to his own by stepping back and addressing

<hr />

[4] The note is on p. 87 of a copy of the book in the Cushing Memorial Library at
Texas A&M University. There is an ownership note of Sir George Oxenden (1694–
1775), dated 1773, on the verso of the preliminary blank at the front of the volume,
but the marginal notes seem to me to be in an earlier hand. It is worth observing that
whoever he was, this annotator found himself irritated by Boys's politics. A good
many marginalia appear on pp. 156–61, where Boys turns to Livy and discusses how
Lucretia's husband avenges her violation by Tarquin and expels the king, ending the
monarchy in ancient Rome. Boys notes that everyone praises Brutus but queries
whether this conclusion is just. When he suggests that the rebels might have exaggerated their claims that Tarquin was an awful tyrant, the annotator notes that 'the
author who is a thorough King Ch[arles] I.[st] man, seems to have an eye to those times
in most of these queries' (159). Then when Boys observes that those who want to
change the government often offer a pretence of liberty which is retracted if they
succeed, the commentator explodes with 'It is a great pity an ingenious man can't
write a commentary on the 6th Book of Virgil without showing his own High Church
arbitrary Principles with regard to our government' (160–1). As Susanna Morton
Braund, *Latin Literature* (London and New York: Routledge, 2002), 25–36, notes,
Livy's account is itself embedded in the political events of his day; see also Lorna
Hardwick, *Reception Studies* (Oxford: OUP, 2003), 23–4. Steven Zwicker, 'Reading
the Margins: Politics and the Habits of Appropriation', in Kevin Sharpe and Steven
N. Zwicker (eds.), *Refiguring Revolutions: Aesthetics and Politics from the English Revolution to the Romantic Revolution* (Berkeley-Los Angeles: Univ. of California Press,
1998), 101–15 observes that mid-17th-cent. English books often contain marginalia
that show their readers engaging actively with the political implications of their texts.

[5] John Boys, *Aeneas His Errours, or his Voyage from Troy into Italy. An Essay Upon
the Third Book of Virgil's Aeneis* (London: Printed by T. M. for Henry Broome, 1661).
It is worth noting that Homer, too, was drawn into the mid-century political
controversies in a similar way. Ten of the verses in books 1–3 of the 1648 Cambridge
University Press edn. of the *Iliad* printed by Roger Daniel, e.g., have their first words
printed entirely in capital letters, with nine of these verses being *sententiae* that assert
the legitimacy, even supremacy, of monarchical government. Daniel was dismissed
from his position at the press in 1650, after printing the *Eikon Basilike*, presumably
for royalist sympathies. The likely editor of the volume was James Duport, who
published *Homeri poetarum omnium seculorum facile principis Gnomologia* (1669),

Charles II ('*most gracious Sovereign*...should I therefore compare
your Majesty with our Aeneas'), then working out the relationship in
three areas. First, Charles II demonstrates Virgilian *pietas* by rebuild-
ing churches and distributing justice, taking revenge in particular on
the 'horrid murderers' of Charles I (p. 58). Then he demonstrates a
wisdom and valour worthy of Aeneas, leading to an encomium of the
Stuart line: he and his countrymen, 'to our *ineffable* joy', see Charles
II, 'like another *Aeneas* in his promis'd *Italie*', seated on his paternal
throne (p. 60). Finally, as Anchises spoke prophetically of Aeneas, so
he will speak of his king, changing only one word in Virgil's lines:

> Hic *Carolina* domus Cunctis dominabitur [o]ris,
> Et nati nationum, & qui nascentur ab illis.
>
> Great *Charles* his house, with those who thence descend,
> Here far and near its Empire shall extend.

(p. 61; Aen. 3. 97–8)

Rather surprisingly, Boys did not begin the appropriation of Virgil's
Aeneid into royalist ideology at the Restoration, but rather continued a
trend that had extended through the interregnum. Richard Fanshawe,
for example, became secretary of war for Prince Charles in 1644, then
published his translation of book 4 in 1648, after Charles I had been
imprisoned by Parliament. Fanshawe's translation concludes with a
summary of Rome's civil wars that explicitly links these conflicts to
the civil wars in England. He then converts Anchises's warning to Aeneas
(to spare the humble and subdue the proud, *Aen*. 6. 853) into advice
for Charles, bringing his work into line with previous royalist translations like that of Sir John Harington, who had dedicated his version of
book 6 to Henry, prince of Wales, in 1604 and stressed how much a
future king could learn from Virgil's precepts. We see much the same
thing with John Ogilby's 1649 edition, revised in 1654. Ogilby equivo-
cates in places: Brutus, for example, is both praised for defending 'the
opprest Commonwealth' and ridiculed for defending 'specious
Liberty'. This, however, was enough to spare the book from Cromwell's
censors, while its royalist flavour was pronounced enough to win for
Ogilby both a royal warrant that protected the engravings in the 1654

---

which was dedicated to four students with royalist sympathies and treated prominently
the nine *sententiae* marked off in the 1648 edn. See Gregory Machacek, 'Royalist Homer',
Transactions of the Cambridge Bibliographical Society, 12 (2002), 331–2.

edition from piracy after the Restoration and the commission to write the poetry for Charles II's coronation.[6]

Perhaps the most interesting translation from this period is that of Sir John Denham. As Lawrence Venuti has shown, Denham's translation of book 2 was originally drafted in 1636 but not published until 1656, at a point when it could make a perceptible intervention into the unravelling political situation at the end of the commonwealth years. Denham had drafted a translation of several books of the *Aeneid* but chose to publish part of book 2 only. His selection focuses on the death of Priam—indeed, it ends there, even though Virgil's text continues on with Aeneas's departure from Troy. Denham's final lines accentuate the horror of regicide, with Priam's 'headless Carkass' lying on the shore for all to see. Denham has removed almost all the character and place names from these lines, inviting the reader to consider Charles I, whose mythological descent could be traced back to the Trojan royal line, in Priam's stead; the one place name left in the passage, Asia, alludes to the well-known orientalism of the Caroline court. Denham's architectural lexicon, in turn, absorbs the Trojan palace into the English castle, the seat of monarchy and aristocracy. It is also worth noting that Denham used the heroic couplet, which Dryden would later use as well—he virtually quotes eighty lines from Denham's translation in his own—representing the eventual triumph of what became the neoclassical translation form in post-Restoration aristocratic literary culture.[7]

Thus when a poet who had served in Cromwell's government and written well-publicized treatises in defence of republicanism sat down to write a long poem in the Virgilian mode, he found a somewhat complicated critical situation. The *Aeneid* should logically serve as the model for *Paradise Lost*, but it was generally interpreted in mid-seventeenth-century England as a royalist poem. The royalist translations of Fanshawe, Ogilby, and Denham, however, had managed to sail successfully through the stormy seas of the Commonwealth, which provided precedent for an approach to the *Aeneid* that was coloured in shades of grey rather than black and white. What would Milton do?

[6] Colin Burrow, 'Virgil in English Translation', in Charles Martindale (ed.), *The Cambridge Companion to Virgil* (Cambridge: CUP, 1997), 21, 24–7.

[7] Lawrence Venuti, 'The Destruction of Troy: Translation and Royalist Cultural Politics in the Interregnum', *Journal of Medieval and Renaissance Studies*, 23 (1993), 197–219.

Revolution

One position holds that, as the discussion so far might suggest, Milton found Virgil's poem uncongenial and looked elsewhere for his chief sources of inspiration. David Norbrook, for example, finds *Paradise Lost* to be anti-Augustan and associates the poem's ideology with that of Lucan and the general republican reassessment of literature from the middle of the century; Dryden, he claims, continued the tradition of royalist translations of Virgil, with his *Aeneid* being in some sense a response to *Paradise Lost*.[8] David Quint also stresses the affinities between Milton and Lucan, arguing that *Paradise Lost* takes its place within a division among epic poems between those that present the viewpoints of the victors (the *Aeneid*) and those that tell the story of the vanquished (the *Pharsalia*): 'the losers' story of Adam and Eve', he concludes, 'belongs to Lucan's rather than to Virgil's epic tradition'.[9]

The suggestion that the *Aeneid* is not in fact a major source for *Paradise Lost* receives some support from the difficulty that readers have had for centuries in tracing lines of affinity that support a meaningful interpretation of the poem. It is common knowledge that fragments of the *Aeneid* are embedded in *Paradise Lost*, but surprisingly, over three hundred years of critical activity has yet to clarify either the full extent of the relationship or what it might mean for our understanding of the two poems. Milton's first commentator, Patrick Hume, began the practice of identifying the Latin root of an unusual word in *Paradise Lost* and then citing passages from the *Aeneid* in which that word is used, generally without further comment. As Richard Thomas has reminded us, however, such references must then be interpreted.[10]

[8] David Norbrook, *Writing the English Republic: Poetry, Rhetoric and Politics 1627–1660* (Cambridge: CUP, 1999), 437–67.

[9] David Quint, *Epic and Empire: Politics and Generic Form from Virgil to Milton* (Princeton: Princeton Univ. Press, 1993), 269. Quint is a very sensitive reader, and further on in his chapter on *Paradise Lost* (268–324) he nuances his position, explaining that the poem divides, being Virgilian with the victory of God on the divine level and Lucanian on the human level, where the endless revolts of Adam and Eve and their successors against God turn the poem into a cyclical epic of the vanquished (303). Quint is also well aware that the *Pharsalia* alludes regularly to the *Aeneid,* which had suggested its own critique to Lucan, making any absolute divisions impossible (136, 156–7). Nevertheless Quint's study is based on 'two rival traditions of epic, which are here associated with Virgil and Lucan. These define an opposition between epics of the imperial victors and epics of the defeated, a defeated whose resistance contains the germ of a broader republican or antimonarchical politics' (8).

[10] Richard Thomas, 'Virgil's *Georgics* and the Art of Reference', *Harvard Studies in Classical Philology,* 90 (1986), 174.

Unfortunately those critics who have proposed interpretive patterns in Milton's allusions to Virgil remain divided on the most fundamental of issues. Davis Harding, for example, claimed that Satan rewrites Turnus, serving like his model as epic antagonist.[11] C. M. Bowra and Francis Blessington, however, linked Satan to Aeneas, but with different interpretations, with Bowra claiming that Satan indeed takes on Aeneas's grandeur but as part of Milton's larger critique of the value system of ancient epic,[12] while Blessington saw Satan as a parody of Aeneas, a posturer who fails to attain the nobility of his model.[13] In the face of such disagreement Charles Martindale has suggested that Milton's relationship to Virgil may well be exaggerated.[14]

In the end, however, this position seems counterintuitive. At the beginning of book 9, Milton describes his argument as 'Not less but more Heroic' (*PL* 9. 14) than the

rage

Of *Turnus* for *Lavinia* disespous'd,
Or *Neptune's* ire or *Juno's*, that so long
Perplex'd the *Greek* and *Cytherea's* Son

(*PL* 9. 16–19)

which seems to invite the reader to compare his poem to the one whose characters he mentions. Commentators have done just this for three hundred years and come up with dozens of parallels ranging from verbal echoes to entire Virgilian scenes that Milton has rewritten, and just because we have not succeeded so far in making sense of all this does not mean that there is not sense to be made. What is more, Milton has left us one further sign that should encourage us to continue thinking about the relationship between *Paradise Lost* and the *Aeneid*. When *Paradise Lost* was originally published in 1667, *much earlier* there were ten books, but when it was republished in 1674, there were twelve. The *Pharsalia* (or at least the part of it we have) has ten books, but the *Aeneid* has twelve. Over fifty years ago Arthur Barker

[11] Davis Harding, *The Club of Hercules: Studies in the Classical Background of Paradise Lost* (Urbana, Ill.: Univ. of Illinois Press, 1962), 44–51.

[12] C. M. Bowra, *From Virgil to Milton* (London: Macmillan, 1948), 229–30.

[13] Francis C. Blessington, *'Paradise Lost' and the Classical Epic* (Boston: Routledge & Kegan Paul, 1979), 1–8.

[14] Charles Martindale, *John Milton and the Transformation of Ancient Epic*, 2nd edn. (London: Duckworth, 2002), 107.

proposed that Milton restructured his poem to articulate its relationship to the *Aeneid* more clearly, and J. K. Hale has recently expanded on Barker's proposal, suggesting that the restructuring was part of a wider strategy to anchor Milton's literary career more firmly in Virgil's.[15]

Another approach has been to acknowledge that *Paradise Lost* owes a significant debt to the *Aeneid*, but to remove the two poems from their respective ideological settings and to argue that the move from prose to poetry marks Milton's withdrawal from, or at least indifference to, politics. This approach can be traced back to the 1695 edition of Patrick Hume, which marks the first time that a poem in English had been given the kind of commentary that had been reserved for the Greek and Roman classics. Hume's commentary, as I have noted, is rich in Virgilian parallels, but as Howard Erskine-Hill has shown, it also systematically sought to occlude Milton's political career and remove the poem from its historical circumstances, even going so far as occasionally to express political views that are decidedly un-Miltonic.[16] Hume's approach flows naturally into Samuel Johnson's claim that the subject of *Paradise Lost* 'is not the destruction of a city, the conduct of a colony or the foundation of an empire', but 'the fate of worlds, the revolutions of heaven and earth'.[17] This claim in turn plays into the romantic fixation on the solitary literary genius, removed from the press of daily life with his eye fixed on transcendental truths. As Coleridge put it, Milton 'was, as every true great poet has ever been, a good man, but finding it impossible to realize his own aspirations, either in religion, or politics, or society, he gave up his heart to the living spirit and light within him, and

---

[15] Arthur Barker, 'Structural Pattern in *Paradise Lost*', *Philological Quarterly*, 28 (1949), 17–30; and John K. Hale, '*Paradise Lost*: Twelve Books or Ten?', *Philological Quarterly*, 74 (1995), 131–49.

[16] e.g. in glossing the word 'Patriarchs' at *PL* 4. 762, Hume notes that all governments take their authority from Adam as the first patriarch and monarch, which is actually the counter-argument to the contractual theory of government invoked by Milton; the argument is repeated in Hume's gloss on *PL* 12. 26. See P. Hume (ed.), *The Poetical Works of John Milton* (London: Jacob Tonson, 1695); and Howard Erskine-Hill, 'On Historical Commentary: The Example of Milton and Dryden', in Erskine-Hill and Richard A. McCabe (eds.), *Presenting Poetry: Composition, Publication, Reception, Essays in Honour of Ian Jack* (Cambridge: CUP, 1995), 61–8, 74.

[17] Samuel Johnson, 'Life' of Milton, qtd. in David Armitage, 'John Milton: Poet against Empire', in David Armitage, Armand Himy, and Quentin Skinner (eds.), *Milton and Republicanism* (Cambridge: CUP, 1995), 215.

avenged himself on the world by enriching it, with the record of his own transcendent ideal'.[18] Coleridge's analysis rests on premises about the poet that seem dated now, but it does have the merit of explaining how an official in Cromwell's government survived the Restoration. Nigel Smith presents a modern version of this approach, arguing that *Paradise Lost* participates in an internalization of epic during the Civil War and Restoration.[19] Milton barely escaped proscription on Charles II's return: his *Defensio prima* and *Eikonoklastes* were called in and burnt, and he had to sue for pardon. Howard Erskine-Hill notes that some sort of deal in which Milton would agree not to write against the new government would have been the obvious way for him to win his release.[20]

Intuitively, however, this does not feel right either. Milton was a man of strong opinions, fervently held, and it is hard to imagine that someone who had proclaimed that 'poets truly so called', from Homer to Buchanan, were 'the sworn foes of tyrants'[21] would do a complete *volte face*. What is more, a seventeenth-century poet who really wanted to avoid commenting on current affairs would have been expected to turn to love sonnets, perhaps, but not to the epic, which was generally taken to be linked closely to the core values of a people and the collective definition and expression of those values.[22]

[18] Qtd. in Mary Ann Radzinowicz, 'The Politics of *Paradise Lost*', in Kevin Sharpe and Steven N. Zwicker (eds.), *Politics of Discourse: The Literature and History of Seventeenth-Century England* (Berkeley–Los Angeles and London: Univ. of California Press, 1987), 204.

[19] Nigel Smith, *Literature and Revolution in England, 1640–1680* (New Haven and London: Yale Univ. Press, 1994), 203–49.

[20] Howard Erskine-Hill, *Poetry and the Realm of Politics: Shakespeare to Dryden* (Oxford: Clarendon Press, 1996), 180.

[21] *Pro populo Anglicano defensio secunda*, ed. Eugene J. Strittmatter, in *The Works of John Milton*, gen. ed. Frank Allen Patterson, 18 vols. in 21 (New York: Columbia Univ. Press, 1931–40), viii. 76–9, qtd. in Blair Worden, 'Milton's Republicanism and the Tyranny of Heaven', in Gisela Bock, Quentin Skinner, and Maurizio Viroli (eds.), *Machiavelli and Republicanism* (Cambridge: CUP, 1990), 225–45.

[22] This is Radzinowicz's point, in 'The Politics of *Paradise Lost*', 'that *Paradise Lost* has a public role to play in the poet's own day' (206–7), a role she defines as 'paideutic', or educative: the epic poet gives a course in political education. And as Christopher Hill points out, at least one early reader agreed. Thomas Haak, a friend of Milton's, translated the first three books of *Paradise Lost* into German, then read the tr. to H. L. Benthem, a pastor in Hanover, in 1686–7. Benthem concluded that the poem was really about politics in Restoration England. See *Milton and the English Revolution* (London: Faber & Faber, 1977), 391.

Indeed, as Andrew Milner has pointed out, there is an obvious temptation to locate in the Restoration the basic stimulus for the writing of *Paradise Lost.* Once political success has gone to the worse cause, then the order governing the universe does not appear to be beneficent. This in turn can throw into doubt the very existence of God, which requires the effort to 'justify the ways of God to men' (*PL* 1. 26), to explain the temporary defeat of the godly as part of God's plan for the human race.[23]

Intuition, though, is not in the end enough on which to base a scholarly argument. Fortunately there is considerably more with which to work. Milton had written parts of *Paradise Lost* earlier in the 1650s, but his nephew Edward Phillips says that he began serious work on the poem two years before the Restoration and essentially had it finished five years later, although he delayed publication until 1667, when the government was sufficiently preoccupied with other concerns that censorship would be less likely.[24] In 1658 Milton also republished his *Defensio prima*, which he obviously saw as relevant once again to the political concerns of the moment. In this treatise Milton argued against tyranny in general and against non-elective, hereditary monarchy in particular. In chapter five of the *Defensio*, Milton had referred to the 'fraud and hypocrisy' ('dolo et simulatione') of Augustus, who had promised that he would lay down the principate and obey the laws, yet kept his legions armed under pretence of making war in the provinces. In doing so, he appeared to decline power but served as a *de facto* emperor ('nomen deinde principis aut imperatoris et αὐτοκράτορος sibi arrogare'), destroying the laws 'quod gladiator ille Spartacus potuit..., quasi Deus aut naturae lex omnes et homines et leges illi subjecessit' ('as Spartacus the gladiator might have done...as if God or the law of nature had put all men and all laws into subjection under him').[25] This chapter, moreover, happens to be the one that Milton reworked the most in

[23] Andrew Milner, *John Milton and the English Revolution: A Study in the Sociology of Literature* (Totowa, NJ: Barnes & Noble, 1981), 140.

[24] Norbrook, *Writing*, 433–6. Norbrook adds that the preponderance of evidence suggests that composition began in the mid to late 1650s, with the major biographies settling on 1658.

[25] John Milton, *Pro populo Anglicano defensio*, ed. Clinton W. Keyes, tr. by Samuel Lee Wolff, in Patterson (gen. ed.), *Works of John Milton*, vii. 320. On the republication of *Defensio prima*, see Martin Dzelzainis, 'Milton and the Protectorate in 1658', in Armitage *et al.* (eds.), *Milton and Republicanism*, 202–3.

preparation for republication, with additional material from Virgil being added for the 1658 edition (see Figure 9):

aut enim expulsi civitate Agyllina Mezentii tyranni antiquissimum exemplum Hetruria vicina praebuit, aut eâ fabulâ summus artifex decori Virgilius, quo jure apud cunctas gentes, idque ab omni vetustate, fuissent reges, regnanti etiam tunc Romae Octaviano Caesari voluit ostendere, Aeneid l. 8.

> At fessi tandem cives infanda furentem
> Armati circumsistunt, ipsúmque, domúmque:
> Obtruncant socios; ignem ad fastigia jactant.
> Ille inter caedes Rutulorum elapsus in agros
> Confugere, et Turni defendier hospitis armis.
> Ergo omnis furiis surrexit Etruria justis:
> Regem ad supplicium praesenti Marte reposcunt.

Vides hic justâ irâ inflammatos cives tyrannum non solùm ad necem repentino impetu quaesisse, non regno tantùm expulisse, sed profugum et exulem ad judicium, immò ad supplicium, bello suscepto, repetisse.

... for either their neighbour Etruria offered a very ancient precedent in the expulsion of the tyrant Mezentius from the city of Agylla, or Virgil, past master of the fitting and the beautiful, meant by that tale in the eighth Aeneid to show even Caesar Octavianus, who then ruled in Rome, what rights kings had among all nations—and this from the utmost antiquity.

> But while the madman yet meditates crimes unspeakable, the citizens, wearied out at last, in armed bands press round both him and his house, and slay his train, and hurl fire upon his rooftop. Slipping away from amid the slaughter, he betakes him to the territory of the Rutuli for refuge, and is defended by the arms of Turnus a stranger. 'Twas for this that all Etruria rose up in righteous rage: in open war they claim the king for execution.

Here you see that subjects, fired with righteous wrath, not only sought their tyrant upon a sudden violent impulse to murder him, not only drove him from his kingdom, but when he was a fugitive and an exile made war to get him back again for trial, yea for capital punishment.[26]

---

[26] Milton, *Defensio*, vii. 324–5. For the additions to the 1658 edn., see Robert W. Ayers, 'Appendix F: Variants in the London Editions of Milton's *Defensio*', in D. M. Wolfe (ed.), *Complete Prose Works of John Milton*, iv. *1650–1655* (New Haven and London: Yale Univ. Press, 1966), pt. 2, 1129–39. Andrew Barnaby notes that in his *Second Defence of the English People* (1654), Milton also links England to ancient Rome by echoing points of Anchises's prophecy of Rome's imperial destiny (*Works*, iv. 554–6; cf. *Aen*. 6. 679–892); see ' "Another Rome in the West?": Milton and the Imperial Republic, 1654–1670', *Milton Studies*, 30 (1993), 74–6.

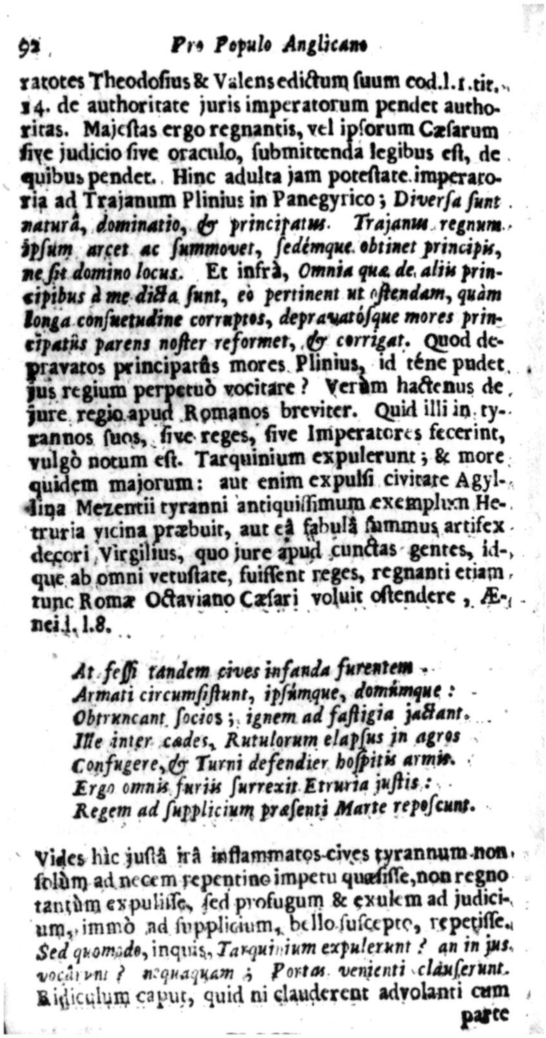

92   *Pro Populo Anglicano*

ratotes Theodofius & Valens edictum fuum cod.l.1.tit.
14. de authoritate juris imperatorum pendet autho-
ritas. Majeftas ergo regnantis, vel ipforum Cæfarum
five judicio five oraculo, fubmittenda legibus eft, de
quibus pendet. Hinc adulta jam poteftate imperato-
ria ad Trajanum Plinius in Panegyrico ; *Diverfa funt*
naturâ, dominatio, & principatus. Trajanum regnum
ipfum arcet ac fummovet, fedémque obtinet principis,
ne fit domino locus. Et infrâ, *Omnia quæ de aliis prin-*
cipibus à me dicta funt, eò pertinent ut oftendam, quàm
longa confuetudine corruptos, depravatófque mores prin-
cipatûs parens nofter reformet, & corrigat. Quod de-
pravatos principatûs mores Plinius, id téne pudet,
jus regium perpetuò vocitare ? Verùm hactenus de
jure regio apud Romanos breviter. Quid illi in ty-
rannos fuos, five reges, five Imperatores fecerint,
vulgò notum eft. Tarquinium expulerunt ; & more
quidem majorum : aut enim expulfi civitate Agyllina Mezentii tyranni antiquiffimum exemplum Hetruria vicina præbuit, aut eâ fabulâ fummus artifex
decori Virgilius, quo jure apud cunctas gentes, idque ab omni vetuftate, fuiffent reges, regnanti etiam
tunc Romæ Octaviano Cæfari voluit oftendere , Æ-
neid. l.8.

At feffi tandem cives infanda furentem
Armati circumfiftunt, ipfúmque, domúmque :
Obtruncant focios ; ignem ad faftigia jactant.
Ille inter cædes, Rutulorum elapfus in agros
Confugere, & Turni defendier hofpitis armis.
Ergo omnis furiis furrexit Etruria juftis :
Regem ad fupplicium præfenti Marte repofcunt.

Vides hìc juftâ irâ inflammatos cives tyrannum non
folùm ad necem repentino impetu quæfiffe, non regno
tantùm expuliffe, fed profugum & exulem ad judicium, immò ad fupplicium, bello fufcepto, repetiffe.
Sed quomodo, inquis, *Tarquinium expulerunt ?* an in jus
vocârunt ? nequaquam ; Portas venienti clauferunt.
Ridiculum caput, quid ni clauderent advolanti cum
                   parte

Figure 9. Milton's anti-monarchical reading of the *Aeneid.* John Milton, *Defensio pro populo Anglicano*... (London: Typis Neucombianis, 1658), 92 (The British Library)

key argument

Here we have proof that, right before he began to work systematically on *Paradise Lost*, Milton had his eye on Virgil as a source of insight into contemporary politics and that he was reading the *Aeneid* not as a straightforward royalist poem, but as a source for anti-monarchical sentiment as well, with a complexity of vision that reminds us of how Ogilby, for example, had used the *Aeneid* to help negotiate the transition from Commonwealth to Restoration.

It seems, then, that the *Aeneid* is a significant subtext for *Paradise Lost* and that the political valences of both poems might in fact work together in ways that can help us understand how Milton's political position evolved at the beginning of the Restoration. To test this hypothesis, I shall begin by searching for a pattern to Milton's Virgilian allusions that brings the two poems into a meaningful relationship with one another. I shall then step back from this pattern to suggest how Milton was able to find in the *Aeneid* and the circumstances of its composition a guide for himself at a difficult transitional moment in his life. This guide, as we shall see, allowed him to position himself in the changing political circumstances of his day in such a way that he could both comment on those circumstances and remain true to himself.

As Francis Blessington has noted, *Paradise Lost* begins *in medias res* just like the *Aeneid*, when a figure of manifest grandeur is driven by divine wrath across a body of water, then forced to explore a new land in search of a new home.[27] Indeed Satan's first words to Beëlzebub,

---

[27] Blessington, *Paradise Lost*, 6–7. There are two main modern sources for parallels between *Paradise Lost* and the *Aeneid*: the index to Patterson's Columbia edn. of the *Works of Milton*, under the lemma 'Vergil' in the second index volume, 2026–9, and the appendix to A. Verbart, *Fellowship in Paradise Lost: Vergil, Milton, Wordsworth* (Amsterdam and Atlanta, Ga.: Rodopi, 1995), 253–302. Both are extremely helpful, but neither is complete, so I have returned to the commentators of the long 18th cent., whose sensitivity to classical allusion is often greater than that of modern readers (A. Oras, *Milton's Editors and Commentators from Patrick Hume to Henry John Todd (1695–1801): A Study in Critical Views and Methods*, 3rd edn. (New York: OUP, 1967), 5–21). I have relied primarily on the edns. of Hume (1695); Richard Bentley, *Milton's Paradise Lost* (London: Jacob Tonson, 1732); J[onathan] Richardson [father and son], *Explanatory Notes and Remarks on Milton's Paradise Lost* (London: James, John, and Paul Knapton, 1734); Thomas Newton, *Paradise Lost. A poem in twelve books. The author John Milton. The second edition, with notes of various authors*, 2 vols. (London: For J. and R. Tonson and S. Draper . . . , 1750) (1st variorum); and Henry J. Todd, *The Poetical Works of John Milton. With notes of various authors . . .* , 2nd edn., 7 vols. (London: J. Johnson *et al.*, 1809) (2nd variorum), but will not normally reference each parallel to avoid overburdening the notes. Quotations from *Paradise Lost* are taken from John Milton, *Complete Poems and Major Prose*, ed. Merritt Y. Hughes (Indianapolis: Odyssey Press, 1957).

'If thou beest hee; But O how fall'n! how chang'd | From him' (*PL* 1. 84–5), echo Aeneas's words when he first saw Hector's ghost, 'ei mihi, qualis erat, quantum mutatus ab illo | Hectore qui redit' ('Oh this | was Hector, and how different he was | from Hector back from battle', *Aen.* 2. 274–5), making us wonder right away if Satan is a new Aeneas. Initially the answer seems to be 'yes', for Satan concludes this speech with another conspicuous gesture toward Aeneas:

> So spake th' Apostate Angel, though in pain,
> Vaunting aloud, but rackt with deep despair:
>
> (*PL* 1. 125–6)

> Talia uoce refert curisque ingentibus aeger
> Spem uultu simulat, premit altum corde dolorem.
>
> (*Aen.* 1. 208–9)

> These are his words; though sick with heavy cares,
> he counterfeits hope in his face; his pain
> is held within, hidden.

Then God withdraws the hail and thunderbolts from the fiery lake of Hell (*PL* 1. 169–77), just as Neptune calmed the seas and ceased to afflict Aeneas in the famous 'Quos ego…' scene at the beginning of the *Aeneid* (1. 124 ff.). Another series of allusions links Satan to Aeneas in Carthage. As Satan prepares to speak to the other fallen devils, 'attention held them mute' (*PL* 1. 618), just as when Aeneas began to tell his story to Dido, 'conticuere omnes attentique ora tenebant' ('A sudden silence fell on all of them; | their eyes were turned, intent on him', *Aen.* 2.1). Similarly the description of Pandaemonium, which Satan observes in *PL* 1. 728 ff., recalls the description of Dido's palace, which Aeneas observed in *Aen.* 1.710 ff., even down to the same number of lamps (*Aen.* 1. 726–7); what is more, the devils swarming to the newly constructed Pandaemonium (*PL* 1. 768–76) are depicted in terms of the famous bee simile that described the Carthaginian builders (*Aen.* 1. 430 ff.).

Book 2 of *Paradise Lost* rewrites Virgil's *descensus ad inferos*, suggesting that Satan in Hell parallels Aeneas in the underworld. In counselling war, Moloch claims that there will be no problem leaving Hell because 'Th' ascent is easy then' (*PL* 2. 81), echoing the Sibyl's advice to Aeneas, 'facilis descensus Auerno' ('easy— | the way that leads into Avernus', *Aen.* 6. 126). *PL* 2. 528 ff. is based on *pactce*

Aen. 6. 653 ff., suggesting that the devils in Hell parallel the blessed in Virgil's Elysian fields. When Satan announces his plan to leave Hell in search of Adam, he again describes the challenges of the journey in reference to Aeneas's descent to Hell, noting that 'long is the way | and hard, that out of Hell leads up to light' (*PL* 2. 432–3; cf. *Aen.* 6. 128–9, 'sed reuocare gradum superasque euadere ad auras, | hoc opus, hic labor est', 'But to recall your steps, to rise again | into the upper air: that is the labor; | that is the task'), with the ninefold restraint of Hell's fiery adamantine gates (*PL* 2. 436) recalling the details of Virgil's underworld (*Aen.* 6. 439, 552) and the 'four infernal Rivers' (*PL* 5. 575 ff.) giving a pronounced Virgilian flavour to Milton's Hell. Satan is also linked to Aeneas through references to other books of the *Aeneid*, brandishing his dart in *PL* 2. 786, for example, like Aeneas on his way to kill Turnus in *Aen.* 12. 919.

By this point, Satan appears to be a new Aeneas, described in terms and situations that link him systematically to Virgil's hero. The allusions diminish in book 3, where decorum perhaps makes it more difficult to link God's discussions with Jesus to classical literature; as the author of the first variorum commentary on *Paradise Lost*, Thomas Newton, explained, 'Milton's divine Persons are divine Persons indeed, and talk in the language of God, that is in the language of Scripture'.[28] In book 4, however, the allusive pattern resumes. Satan finds Adam and Eve in 'A Silvan Scene' (*PL* 4. 140) that closely resembles the 'siluis scaena coruscis' ('the backdrop…a black | grove thick with bristling shadows', *Aen.* 1. 164) of the Libyan shore on which Aeneas landed.

Signs that something may be wrong with this interpretation, however, begin to appear. When Satan enters Paradise, he is compared to a wolf entering a sheepfold (*PL* 4. 183–92), a comparison that echoes *Aen.* 9. 59–66, but which links Satan not to Aeneas, but to Turnus.[29] Milton's first description of Adam (*PL* 4. 288–94), in turn, recalls Virgil's description of Aeneas (*Aen.* 1. 588–93), although Adam's hyacinthine locks are perhaps closer to Odysseus's.[30] Our sense of confusion grows when Adam's first words to Eve, 'Whom fli'st thou?' (*PL* 4. 482), clearly echo Aeneas's last words to Dido in Virgil's underworld (*Aen.* 6. 466, 'quem fugis?' 'whom do you flee?'), suggesting again that perhaps Adam, not Satan, is the new Aeneas.[31] A reader who has

---

[28] Newton, *Paradise Lost*, i. 211.   [29] Blessington, *Paradise Lost*, 86–7.
[30] Harding, *Club*, 69–72.   [31] Verbart, *Fellowship*, 2.

noticed these clues will therefore not be totally unprepared when Milton settles the matter definitively in the final twenty-five lines of book 4. We see Satan, 'and on his Crest | Sat horror Plum'd' (*PL* 4. 988–9), which recalls the Chimaera on the helmet of Turnus in *Aen.* 7. 785–6. Then God hung 'his golden Scales' (*PL* 4. 997) in heaven, just as Jupiter had done before the final battle in the *Aeneid*, so that Satan, who must lose in his confrontation with the angels who have come to Adam's defence, is associated with Turnus, who had to lose to Aeneas so that Italy could be established. The confrontation ends by associating Satan with Turnus in a way that anyone who has ever read the *Aeneid* will recall instantly: Satan

fled,
Murmuring, and with him fled the shades of night.

(*PL* 4. 1014–15)

uitaque cum gemitu fugit indignata sub umbras.

and with a moan
his life, resentful, fled to shades below.

(*Aen.* 12. 952)

Until almost the very end of book 4, the clues suggest that Satan is the new Aeneas, the hero of Milton's rewritten *Aeneid*. But the clues are there to deceive: Satan is not the new Aeneas, but the new Turnus, just as he was in a group of minor (and now unread) epics written by Crashaw, Fletcher, and Beaumont, Milton's literary milieu from his Cambridge days.[32]

As long ago as Dryden, readers of *Paradise Lost* have been tempted to see Satan as the hero of the poem, even though they know that, theologically speaking, this cannot be. Part of Satan's appeal, I submit, is the strength of his association with Aeneas, the hero of the greatest epic of the ancient world and the one whose virtues are most compatible with Christian values. In Stanley Fish's now-famous

---

[32] As Colin Burrow notes, in both Richard Crashaw's tr. of Marino's *Sospetto d'Herode* and Phineas Fletcher's *Locustae*, Satan arouses Herod as Alecto aroused Turnus, and Joseph Beaumont's *Psyche* has Beëlzebub's inspiration of the serpent borrowing the cauldron simile from the inspiration of Turnus (*Aen.* 6. 226–7; cf. 7. 462–6). The writers of these poems, all of whom associated Satan with Turnus, were at Cambridge between 1600 and 1643. See *Epic Romance: Homer to Milton* (Oxford: Clarendon Press, 1993), 251–2.

phrase, however, such a reader has been 'surprised by sin',[33] having allowed himself or herself momentarily to be taken in by appearances and to forget what must be true, that the evils of Satan cannot really be associated with the virtues of Aeneas. Reading *Paradise Lost*, like living in the world, is a dynamic process in which perceptions must be corrected against the eternal verities. And for Milton the stakes were high: 'The rewards for reading that text were not earthly jouissance but eternal joy; the punishment for inept reading was eternal perdition.'[34] The Richardsons understood at least part of this when they tried to explain that Milton sent his Cherubim from the ivory gate, the portal of false dreams by which Aeneas left the underworld at the end of the first half of the *Aeneid*, because what he had just written 'was to be consider'd only as a Pure Fiction, and Poetical Invention,... [and] did not Answer the End'.[35] Indeed the entire scaffold of Virgilian underpinnings as they had been presented so far 'did not Answer the End'. We must therefore look elsewhere for the rewritten Aeneas in *Paradise Lost*.

Milton, like Virgil, tells parts of his story out of chronological order, so that the account of the battle in Heaven which led to Satan's expulsion does not come until book 6. Here there is no question about it: Satan is associated with Turnus, not Aeneas. At the decisive *aristeia* between Michael and Satan, the 'Uplifted imminent' (*PL* 6. 317) of both warriors' swords comes from *Aen.* 12. 728–9, 'corpore toto | alte sublatum consurgit Turnus in ensem' ('Turnus... | rises up to his full height; with sword | uplifted'). In the next lines Satan's sword is

---

[33] Stanley Fish, *Surprised by Sin: The Reader in Paradise Lost* (London: Macmillan, 1967), 1–56. Fish argues that an inevitable result of the Fall is a way of reading in which a temporary seduction to inattentiveness is corrected by the epic voice, by which we are challenged, instructed, and exhorted to observe more diligently. In a little-known passage of this discussion, Fish notes a Virgilian precedent for this technique, where Dido's appeals seduce the reader from his or her duty into sympathy with her, which is corrected by the voice of the epic narrator, who begins, 'At pius Aeneas' ('But...pious Aeneas', 47–8; cf. *Aen.* 4. 393–6). Fish's approach has been extremely influential but remains controversial: see John P. Rumrich, *Milton Unbound: Controversy and Reinterpretation* (Cambridge: CUP, 1996).

[34] S. N. C. Wood, 'Creative Indirection in Intertextual Space: Intertextuality in Milton's *Samson Agonistes*', in Heinrich Plett (ed.), *Intertextuality* (Berlin and New York: Walter De Gruyter, 1991), 204.

[35] Richardson, *Explanatory Notes*, 178–9.

broken by Michael's, which was taken from the armoury of God (*PL* 6. 320 ff.), just as Turnus's sword was broken by Aeneas's, which he had also received from a deity (*Aen.* 12. 731 ff.). A little later a collective reference to Satan's army, 'so thick a Cloud | He comes' (*PL* 6. 539–40), recalls the references to Turnus's troops as 'nimbus peditum' ('like a cloud … of the infantry', *Aen.* 7. 793) and 'nubem belli' ('the cloud of war', *Aen.* 10. 809).

Who, then, is the new Aeneas? In this context one might like to say 'the Son', whose army conquers Satan's and who, as Addison pointed out, could make sense as the hero of *Paradise Lost*.[36] In Milton's allusive system, however, this identification does not work. Satan's opponent in the *aristeia* in book 6 is Michael, not Jesus, and when Jesus on occasion is linked with a textual reference to the *Aeneid*, the association is generally not with Aeneas. In book 3, for example, Jesus offers himself in place of Adam to fulfil the terms of divine justice, using a repeated 'mee … mee' that recalls the 'me … me' of Euryalus's mother (*PL* 3. 236–8; *Aen.* 9. 427, 493–4).

There is another option, however. At the beginning of book 5, Raphael descends from God to warn Adam to keep his sexual passion from deflecting him from his proper duty to those who will come after him. When Milton writes 'Like *Maia's* son [Mercury] he stood' (*PL* 5. 285), he makes the link to the *Aeneid* explicit (cf. *Aen.* 4. 238 ff.), and Adam later addresses Raphael as 'Divine Interpreter' (*PL* 7. 72), which recalls the description of Mercury as 'interpres diuum' in *Aen.* 4. 378. If Raphael, not Satan, is the new Mercury, then Adam might be the new Aeneas for whom we are searching, with Eve being a new Dido.

And so they are. As Verbart notes,[37] Adam and Eve consummate their union in language that recalls the union of Dido and Aeneas, such that 'the Earth | Gave sign of gratulation' (*PL* 8. 513–14; cf. *Aen.* 4. 165–8). And for Adam, as for Aeneas, the relation between sex and duty is crucial. At *Aen.* 4. 265–76 Mercury reminded Aeneas that he had put the lesser before the greater in indulging his passion at the expense of his duty. He therefore had to break off his union with Dido and leave Carthage so that he could found Italy, as the gods had

---

[36] J. Addison, *Notes upon the Twelve Books of Paradise Lost* (London: For J. Tonson, 1720), 547.

[37] Verbart, *Fellowship*, 127–30.

commanded. Raphael likewise warns Adam that 'attribúting overmuch to things | Less excellent' (*PL* 8. 565–6) is a mistake and that Eve is 'worthy well | Thy cherishing, thy honoring, and thy love, | Not thy subjection' (*PL* 8. 568–70). Again, lest the point be missed, Raphael repeats it on his way out: 'take heed lest Passion sway | Thy Judgment to do aught, which else free Will | Would not admit' (*PL* 8. 635–7). In other words, Adam must be careful not to make Aeneas's mistake and elevate his passion for Eve above his willing obedience to God.[38]

Milton's story continues to unfold in Virgilian terms. At *PL* 5. 48 ff., Eve's distress at not finding Adam when she wakes up recalls Dido's dreams of being abandoned (*Aen.* 4. 465 ff.). And when the Fall takes place, it does so in decidedly Virgilian terms. When Eve eats, the earth responds much as it had at Dido's marriage:

> Earth felt the wound, and Nature from her seat
> Sighing through all her Works gave signs of woe,
> That all was lost.
>
> (*PL* 9. 782–4)

> prima et Tellus et pronuba Iuno
> dant signum; fulsere ignes et conscius aether
> conubiis summoque ulularunt uertice Nymphae.
>
> Primal Earth
> and Juno, queen of marriages, together
> now give the signal; lightning fires flash,
> the upper air is witness to their mating,
> and from the highest hilltops shout the nymphs.
>
> (*Aen.* 4. 166–8)

When Adam hears that Eve has eaten, his blood runs cold and his joints relax (*PL* 9. 888–91), linking him to Aeneas in several places: in the storm that opened the *Aeneid* (1. 92); in front of Polydorus, the bleeding bush (*Aen.* 3. 29–30); after a dream in which the gods told him his destiny lay not in Crete, but in Italy (*Aen.* 3. 175); and (most importantly) in response to Mercury's warning (*Aen.* 4. 279–80).[39]

---

[38] Blessington, *Paradise Lost*, 25–33. As Joy Connolly notes, James Harrington's 1659 tr. of *Aeneid* 3–6 consistently made Aeneas into a more passionate character than he was in Virgil's poem, which suggests that readers of Milton's time were sensitive to this issue; see 'Border Wars: Literature, Politics, and the Public', *Transactions of the American Philological Association*, 135 (2005), 122–6.

[39] Verbart, *Fellowship*, 291–2.

Eve is 'now to Death devote' (*PL* 9. 901), linking her yet again to Dido, who was 'pesti deuota futurae' ('doomed to face catastrophe', *Aen.* 1. 712).⁴⁰ Adam in turn resolves to die with her, 'not deceiv'd, | But fondly overcome with Female charm' (*PL* 9. 998–9), which is compatible with the sentiment of *Aen.* 4. 412, 'improbe Amor, quid non mortalia pectora cogis!' ('Voracious Love, to what do you not drive | the hearts of men?'). He eats, and 'Earth trembl'd from her entrails, as again | in pangs' (*PL* 9. 1000–1), re-echoing the passage in which the earth responded to the 'sin' of Dido and Aeneas (*Aen.* 4. 166–8). Now Death offers 'a passage broad, | Smooth, easy, inoffensive down to Hell' (*PL* 10. 304–5), another echo of 'facilis descensus Auerno' ('easy— | the way that leads into Avernus', *Aen.* 6. 126).

Once again Satan attempts to clothe himself in the image of Aeneas, returning to his legion of devils in Hell within a cloud (*PL* 10. 441 ff.), from which he bursts out as Aeneas had in his entry to Carthage (*Aen.* 1. 439 ff.); now, however, he can no longer deceive and is immediately turned into a snake (*PL* 10. 504 ff.).⁴¹ Adam remains the new Aeneas, 'arming to overcome | By suffering' (*PL* 11. 374–5) as Nautes had urged Aeneas to do in *Aen.* 5. 710. Michael appears in order to remove the mists from Adam's eyes (*PL.* 11. 411 ff.) as Venus did for Aeneas at the fall of Troy (*Aen.* 2. 603–5). This scene also rewrites Raphael's descent from Heaven, with the Virgilian resonances being strengthened when Adam's stupefaction echoes that of Aeneas at the appearance of Mercury in *Aeneid* 2 (*PL* 11. 263–5; cf. *Aen.* 2. 289–90).⁴² He gives Adam a vision of all that his descendants would accomplish, much as Anchises gave Aeneas a vision to encourage him: in fact, 'Things by thir names I call, though yet unnam'd' (*PL* 12. 140) echoes *Aen.* 6. 776, 'haec tua nomina erunt, nunc sunt sine nomine terrae' ('These will be names that now are nameless lands', *Aen.* 6. 776). The vision ends with Jesus, who will

⁴⁰ 'Devote' is a Latinism that invites the reader to compare Eve's situation to the Roman *devotio*, in which a leader sacrifices himself and his army to the infernal gods on behalf of his country.

⁴¹ S. M. Fallon, 'Satan's Return to Hell: Milton's Concealed Dialogue with Homer and Virgil', *Milton Quarterly*, 18 (1984), 78–81.

⁴² Andrew Laird, *Powers of Expression, Expressions of Power: Speech Presentation and Latin Literature* (Oxford: OUP, 1999), 299–300, notes that Raphael and Adam had spoken more or less as equals, but that Michael's exchange established a new hierarchy in which humans are clearly subordinated to immortals, in accordance with their newly fallen state.

'bound his Reign | With earth's wide bounds, his glory with the Heav'ns' *(PL* 12. 370–1), placing him in the same position as Augustus in Virgil's prophecy *(Aen.* 6. 791 ff.).

So encouraged, Adam and Eve trudge away from Paradise out into the world. And one last time, they do so in Virgilian terms, for over the receding gates stood the fiery arms and faces of the divine beings *(PL* 12. 641–4; cf. 12. 589–94), recalling the gods and goddesses that Aeneas saw above the walls of Carthage *(Aen.* 2. 604–20).[43] Unlike Aeneas, Adam has a companion, a point that Milton emphasizes in the final lines of the poem. But both have fallen, and a lifetime of toil awaits them both.

Milton has created a poem which must be read in the same way as sinners move through a fallen world: dynamically, and attentively, for appearances often deceive the unwary. The story of *Paradise Lost* is also the story of the *Aeneid,* and one of the attentive reader's jobs is to figure out how pagan poetry can support Christian truth. A good reading will escape the temptation to see Satan as the new Aeneas and settle on Adam, who, like Aeneas, allowed passion to invert his priorities temporarily but is sent on his way again to try to live in accordance with divine will.

The prevailing, although unexamined, tendency, however, has been to assume that Milton, like John Boys, saw Aeneas through the lens of Virgilian optimism, as a flawless hero who served as a sort of prototype for Augustus and as a suitable model for panegyrical praise. In writing about *Paradise Lost* for the *Spectator,* Addison was adamant that 'Aeneas is indeed a perfect Character' and that the *Aeneid* 'was designed to celebrate the Original of the Roman Empire'.[44] Writing over two centuries later, Davis Harding said

[43] Verbart, *Fellowship,* 72.

[44] Addison, *Notes,* 538, 536. In support of his point, Addison even goes so far as to cite Aristotle on the arousal of pity and fear when a good person with infirmities falls into misfortune *(Poetics,* ch. 13), only to deny the applicability of this point to the *Aeneid* or *Paradise Lost,* since in those poems the persons who fall into misfortune 'are of the most perfect and consummate Virtue' (ibid. 539). Further on Addison acknowledges difficulty in identifying the hero of *Paradise Lost;* he prefers not to address the question, but when pressed proposes the Messiah, since he has the requisite moral perfection (ibid. 547). A little later, however, he notes that when Eve ate, the earth trembled and lightning flashed in the heavens as when Dido 'yielded to that fatal Temptation which ruined her' (ibid. 578), seemingly unaware that this analogy associates Aeneas with Adam as the similarly flawed hero of Milton's poem.

essentially the same thing,[45] and twenty years ago James Sims con-
curred: 'As illustrated by the works of Camões and Milton, Renaissance writers saw Virgil as a greatly gifted propagandist for the Rome
of his emperor and patron Augustus.'[46]

I am by no means the first reader, however, to have noticed that
what Milton has actually written does not support this generalization
very well. Less than seventy-five years after the initial publication of
Paradise Lost, Bentley saw the problem quite clearly, as his comments
on *PL* 9. 13–19 show:

> Sad task, yet argument
> Not less but more Heroic than the wrath
> Of stern *Achilles* on his Foe pursu'd
> Thrice Fugitive about *Troy* Wall; or rage
> Of *Turnus* for *Lavinia* disespous'd,
> Or *Neptune's* ire or *Juno's*, that so long
> Perplex'd the *Greek* and *Cytherea's* Son …

The inclusion of Turnus in this list is remarkable, given that the same
Renaissance reading of the *Aeneid* that equated Aeneas with virtue
also equated his opponent with vice; as Bentley put it, 'Silly, as if the
Aeneid was wrote for *Turnus's* Sake and Fame, and not for *Aeneas's*
whose Name it bears.'[47] Bentley had a simple solution for the problem caused by lines that inject 'other voices' into the narrative and
complicate the straightforward 'optimistic' reading of the *Aeneid* that
he attributed to Milton: he excised them, using the circular argument
that lines suggesting sympathy for Turnus could not have been
written by Milton because they provide evidence for a reading of
the *Aeneid* that was not Milton's. Modern readers who do not wish to
go to this extreme are forced to argue that, since Adam gave into

[45] Harding, *Club*, 35.

[46] James Sims, 'A Greater than Rome: The Inversion of a Virgilian Symbol from
Camões to Milton', in P. A. Ramsey (ed.), *Rome in the Renaissance: The City and the
Myth* (Binghamton, NY: Medieval and Renaissance Texts and Studies, 1982), 335.

[47] Bentley, *Milton's Paradise Lost*, 266–7. *PL* 9. 13–19 is also bracketed off on p. 344
of the copy of the 1720 Tonson edn. of Milton's *Poetical Works* in the Cambridge
University Library, which contains annotations in Bentley's hand, along with the
note 'or the Arms & Man', suggesting that the remarks in the 1732 volume were the
result of mature reflection on Bentley's part. See John K. Hale, 'Paradise Purified:
Dr. Bentley's Marginalia for his 1732 Edition of *Paradise Lost*', *Transactions of the
Cambridge Bibliographical Society*, 19 (1991), 58–74.

temptation and Aeneas 'had resisted temptation or at least had extricated himself from it before his irresponsibility had consequences fatal to his mission',[48] then 'it is the contrast with the Virgilian epic that we are left with at the end' of *Paradise Lost*.[49] As Verbart puts it, Adam and Eve share a fate which is ultimately happy, resting in a satisfying matrimony that makes it difficult to condemn Adam's love for Eve; Aeneas, on the other hand, is left in miserable loneliness.[50]

This is not, however, what the allusions to the *Aeneid* seem to be stressing: Adam's love for Eve led to his fall, which parallels Aeneas's inappropriate affair with Dido. Both poems, in other words, stress the failure of their hero and the consequences of that failure. Critics from Addison to Sims were forced into their position by a key piece of external evidence: at the time they were writing, it was generally assumed that the 'pessimistic' reading of the *Aeneid* did not come into existence until after the Second World War and that the only reading of the *Aeneid* that was available to Milton was the 'optimistic' one, no matter how badly it seemed to fit the allusive system connecting the two poems. As we have seen in Chapter 1, however, this is simply not the case. The 'pessimistic' reading of the *Aeneid*, in other words, was available to Milton and is, I believe, the one that structures his allusive system. As a result, the dynamic allusive system in which a sinful Adam parallels a 'sinful' Aeneas enriches our reading of both poems, allowing us to see both an Aeneas whose repeated efforts to do what is right take on the resonances of the Christian effort to follow God and an Adam who provides the pattern for all

[48] William Porter, *Reading the Classics and Paradise Lost* (Lincoln, Neb., and London: Univ. of Nebraska Press, 1993), 115. Porter offers many thought-provoking observations but, like Bentley before him, strains mightily to fit Milton's reading of the *Aeneid* into the 'optimistic' paradigm into which he felt it ultimately belongs. He notes on the one hand that '[w]e need not assume, because of a lack of historical evidence to the contrary, that Milton was insensitive to the ambivalence of Vergil's vision', but then falls back on the assumption that Milton relied on a 'conventionally black-and-white reading of the *Aeneid*' (119).

[49] Blessington, *Paradise Lost*, 42. As Barbara Pavlock notes, in establishing a heaven-directed marriage as the goal for Adam and Eve, Milton differentiates himself from Virgil ('Milton's Critique of Classical Epic in *Paradise Lost* 9', in Craig Kallendorf (ed.), *Vergil: The Classical Heritage* (New York and London: Garland, 1993), 291–314).

[50] Verbart, *Fellowship*, 238–46.

people to follow as he loses sight of his proper priorities, makes a mistake, accepts the consequences of that mistake, and heads off to try again.[51]

If Milton's Virgil did something more than simply represent heroic virtue, as 'optimistic' critics from Donatus to Boys believed he had done, then it stands to reason that he probably did something more than simply praise Augustus as well. As we have seen above, Milton was mining the *Aeneid* for anti-monarchical sentiment at about the same time he was beginning serious work on *Paradise Lost*. The 'pessimistic' reading of the *Aeneid*, however, does not by any means make it into an openly anti-imperial poem, so that at this point we need to return to Milton's politics and ask more precisely how the *Aeneid* might have allowed him to position himself in English life as the late 1650s gave way to the early 1660s.

The traditional way to answer this question has used history to ground the meaning of a literary text, which in turn is understood to mirror, or (perhaps more precisely) to reflect indirectly, historical reality.[52] If that is the case, what historical events does *Paradise Lost* reflect? Here, unfortunately, we find little agreement among modern critics. During the Second World War, G. Wilson Knight and Malcolm MacKenzie Ross appropriated Milton for the embattled British crown and denied that he was anti-royalist at all.[53] Joan Bennett, however, draws on parallels with Milton's prose writings and identifies Charles I with Satan, arguing that both figures usurp power, abuse the traditionally regal sun imagery, corrupt the ideals of heroism, and enslave themselves and their followers in tyranny.[54]

---

[51] The analysis of which way meaning flows here is enriched by the fact that, as Fish points out, *Paradise Lost* was composed after the *Aeneid*, but since Adam was the first man, the events that Virgil portrayed had to have happened after the events in Milton's poem, so that in this sense *Paradise Lost* is the 'earlier' poem (*Surprised by Sin*, 37).

[52] Jean E. Howard, 'The New Historicism in Renaissance Studies', in Arthur F. Kinney and Dan S. Collins (eds.), *Renaissance Historicism: Selections from English Literary Renaissance* (Amherst, Mass.: Univ. of Massachusetts Press, 1987), 8. See also Wesley Morris, *Toward a New Historicism* (Princeton: Princeton Univ. Press, 1972), 3–13.

[53] G. Wilson Knight, *Chariot of Wrath: The Message of John Milton to Democracy at War* (London: Faber & Faber, 1942); and Malcolm MacKenzie Ross, *Milton's Royalism: A Study of the Conflict of Symbol and Idea in the Poems* (Ithaca, NY: Cornell Univ. Press, 1943); see Stevie Davies, *Images of Kingship in Paradise Lost: Milton's Politics and Christian Liberty* (Columbia, Mo.: Univ. of Missouri Press, 1983), 3–5.

[54] Joan S. Bennett, *Reviving Liberty: Radical Christian Humanism in Milton's Great Poems* (Cambridge, Mass., and London: Harvard Univ. Press, 1989), 33–58.

Christopher Hill extends this approach to topical allegory, noting that the angels' hurling mountains at their enemies may refer to the *levée en masse* that culminated in the Battle of Newbury, the Son intervenes in the battle in heaven with the same effect as Fairfax's New Model Army on earth, etc.[55] J. B. Broadbent in turn described Satan as 'the devils' Cromwell',[56] and by now a generation of critics have argued that Satan appropriates the language of English republicanism and becomes at some level a portrait of Cromwell, which makes *Paradise Lost* a retrospective reading of the failures of the 1650s and Milton an unregenerate republican, at least in theory, notwithstanding the disappointments he must have felt over how the experiment had worked out in practice.[57]

There are several problems here, it seems to me, but the worst one is tied to the basic assumption that literature is limited to a reflection of reality, for this forces us to look backwards only, to the past events that provided raw material for the poem. Recently, however, the so-called 'new historicists' have offered another paradigm that seems to offer more promise here.[58] As Hayden White has pointed out, history is not a collection of retrievable facts that are presented through descriptive science, but a construct that is shaped according

[55] Hill, *Milton*, 372. As Erskine-Hill, *Poetry*, notes, '[s]uch an approach is at present desperately unfashionable' (199), but in fairness it must be noted that Hill states clearly that '*Paradise Lost* is not a *roman à clef* in which Satan = Lambert (or Clarkson), Beelzebub = Fleetwood (or Coppe)' (398) and that 'the same narrative can refer to more than one series of historical events' (373).

[56] J. B. Broadbent, *Some Graver Subject: An Essay on 'Paradise Lost'* (London: Chatto & Windus, 1960), 115.

[57] See e.g. Worden, 'Milton's Republicanism', 235–45; and Armitage, 'John Milton', 215.

[58] For now-classic early treatments of the 'new historicism', see the essays in Kinney and Collins, *Renaissance Historicism*; H. Aram Veeser (ed.), *The New Historicism* (New York: Routledge, 1989); and Jeffrey N. Cox and Larry J. Reynolds (eds.), *New Historical Literary Study: Essays on Reproducing Texts, Representing History* (Princeton: Princeton Univ. Press, 1993). The lines of demarcation between 'old' and 'new' historicism are not always clear-cut (see e.g. Herbert Lindenberger, *The History in Literature: On Value, Genre, Institutions* (New York: Columbia Univ. Press, 1990), 2–19, 82–3; and Howard, 'New Historicism', 3–33), but a notable early effort to apply some of the principles that would be identified with the new movement as they are particularly relevant to this study is Annabel Patterson, *Pastoral and Ideology: Virgil to Valéry* (Berkeley–Los Angeles: Univ. of Calif. Press, 1987). The foremost practitioner of the 'new historicism' is Stephen Greenblatt, whose *Practicing New Historicism* (Chicago and London: Univ. of Chicago Press, 2000) (co-authored with Catherine Gallagher) offers a representative update, as do recent issues of the journal *Representations*.

to patterns of intelligibility available to the historian's own culture, using tropes and narrative structures that are also found in litera-ture.[59] I shall have more to say about this point shortly, but for now what is important is the idea that history is produced, not discovered, so that binaries like literature and history, text and context, are misleading. History is built from textual traces, and literature in turn becomes an agent through which reality is constructed. This throws the emphasis forward: what work can a given literary text do in history, as it is read and disseminated? As Jean Howard puts it, 'instead of a hierarchical relationship in which literature figures as the parasitic reflector of historical fact, one imagines a textualized universe in which literature participates in historical processes and in the political management of reality'.[60]

So, what happens when we shift paradigms and ask how *Paradise Lost* 'participates ... in the political management of reality'? And what happens when we ask how Milton's reading of the *Aeneid* might have helped him in this 'political management' as he moved through the 1650 and 1660s? These questions have not been asked in conjunction before, but enough information is available to suggest an answer.

Stevie Davies noted some years ago that *Paradise Lost* is saturated with imperial imagery, especially (although by no means exclusively) with the imagery of imperial Rome. Satan, for example, begins as a military commander but evolves into an emperor, with all the stand-ard accoutrements like an ensign and a standard bearer; indeed he seized power just as the Roman emperors did, using democratic rhetoric to mask his imperial aspirations. The bridge constructed to link earth and Hell in book 10 recalls the technical skill of the ancient Romans, bearing as well a resemblance to a triumphal arch. Satan attempts to celebrate a triumph in book 10, but he proceeds incorrectly (he sneaks back to Hell, for example, rather than entering with a public announcement), and the attempt fails dismally as the cheers he expects turn to hisses after the devils are turned into snakes.

---

[59] Hayden White, *Tropics of Discourse: Essays in Cultural Criticism* (Baltimore, Md.: Johns Hopkins Univ. Press, 1978), 58; and idem, ' "Figuring the nature of the times deceased": Literary Theory and Historical Writing', in Ralph Cohen (ed.), *The Future of Literary Theory* (New York: Routledge, 1989), 36.

[60] Howard, 'New Historicism', 15.

Here Milton is transferring his condemnation of the Roman emperors, in their associations with the Stuart kings, to *Paradise Lost*, but the poem also has a good emperor: Christ, who represents the ideal leader, one who is neither feared nor territorially ambitious and who receives the real triumph that eludes Satan.

Davies's analysis says virtually nothing about Virgil,[61] but it provides a foundation on which we can build. For one thing, the predominance of imperial imagery suggests that the author of *Paradise Lost* recognized that the political issue of the moment was absolute power and the decline of legitimate government into tyranny. Power was held by Cromwell when Milton was beginning the poem, but he had warned repeatedly in his prose writings that republican magistrates could become tyrants as well, which makes Milton's discussion of the issue potentially relevant first for Cromwell, then for Charles II in turn.[62] Davies also stresses the fact that 'Milton drew on the institutions of Rome, at that crucial period when Imperial Rome grew out of the ruins of the republic',[63] which turns out to parallel the movement in England from commonwealth to restored monarchy. In both cases, the moment is an unusually precarious one for which overly simplistic, reductive answers were unlikely to suffice.

It is worth noting as well that, although 'new historicism' does not enter explicitly into discussions of the *Aeneid* by most classicists, Virgil's epic is widely seen to 'participate . . . in the political management of reality' in a way that Howard would feel comfortable with. As Karl Galinsky has pointed out, Augustus's central claim was that he restored the *res publica*. This was more than a little disingenuous,

---

[61] Davies, *Images*, 89–126. Davies makes only one reference to the *Aeneid*, but it is a suggestive one: 'Imperial Rome inspired in Milton a dualistic approach: after all, the *Aeneid*, written under Augustus, was one of the fathers of the tradition without which *Paradise Lost* could never have existed' (96). Unfortunately her analysis, which is consistently suggestive, does not show how the *Aeneid* contributes to Milton's dualistic approach to imperialism. More illuminating is David Quint, 'The Virgilian Coordinates of *Paradise Lost*', *Materiali e discussione per l'analisi dei testi classici*, 52 (2004), 177–97, which discusses Satan's failed triumph in book 10 as well as some of the complex attitudes towards empire expressed in both poems.

[62] As David Armitage points out, Milton's *Defensio secunda* drew from Sallust and Macchiavelli to turn against Cromwell, who had become the English Sulla, a *dictator* who had extended his term and squandered republican liberty to become a tyrant ('John Milton', 206–24).

[63] Davies, *Images*, 93.

pessimistic
aeneid is
pretty adula-
tory

in that it was clear to his contemporaries that while he may well have been observing precedent, he was also stretching existing practices and institutions to the limits of what would be tolerated. Thus Dionysius, a contemporary of Augustus, indeed speaks of a revolution (*metabolē*), but it was one in which order was restored on the basis of traditional values. Syme felt comfortable calling this a 'revolution'; Galinsky hesitates, favouring the term 'evolution'. No matter what we end up calling such a process, however, it is clear that managing it must have required great political skill.

As classicists have long acknowledged, literature and the arts played an important role in effecting this change. The 'Altar of Augustan Peace' ('Ara Pacis Augustae'), for example, celebrates the return from Gaul and Spain of the man who guarantees peace for the Roman state. In both of these examples, as is the case in general in Augustan art, the emphasis is on Augustus as peacemaker, as the individual whose *auctoritas* (see the end of Chapter 1) ensures the prosperity of the state. Yet as such, the altar in particular represents a process of negotiation. It was built instead of giving Augustus a triumph, and outside the city limits rather than in the senate chamber, as the senate had suggested. Presumably Augustus was consulted about the pictorial programme but was not the designer, and the project originated with the senate, not with him. The artists were probably Greeks, but Augustus appears among the Roman people, not elevated above them like some eastern king. In this give and take, political reality is created: Augustan *auctoritas* is what it is depicted to be, in all its nuanced complexity.[64]

The *Aeneid* depicts this same process. Like many people of his generation, Virgil looked back with some nostalgia on the institutions of the republic that had endured for generations and made Rome great; at the same time, he recognized that things had changed and that the power of Augustus was a given in Roman political life. This does not mean, however, that straightforward adulation dissolving into sycophancy was the only option. The 'pessimistic' *Aeneid* gives us an Aeneas who is fundamentally patriotic, self-sacrificing, hard-working, and loyal—all values that could be transferred easily to the man who

---

[64] Karl Galinsky, *Augustan Culture: An Interpretive Introduction* (Princeton: Princeton Univ. Press, 1996), 3–9, 141–55. See also Ronald Syme, *The Roman Revolution* (Oxford: OUP, 1939).

saw himself as the successor to Rome's mythical founder. To be sure, Aeneas slipped now and again, and such failures constituted the veiled warnings to Virgil's patron that form the basis for the 'pessimistic' reading of the poem. But this is the strategy of indirection: on its surface the poem refers to

> hic uir, hic est, tibi quem promitti saepius audis,
> Augustus Caesar, diui genus: aurea condet
> secula qui rursus Latio, regnata per arua
> Saturno quondam: super et Garamantas et Indos
> proferet imperium.
>
> This,
> this is the man you heard so often promised—
> Augustus Caesar, son of a god, who will
> renew a golden age in Latium,
> in fields where Saturn once was king, and stretch
> his rule beyond the Garamantes and
> the Indians.
>
> (*Aen.* 6. 791–5)

The result is a richly textured approach to political power: openly respectful, even encomiastic at times, but containing a subtle warning that positions the poet in the realities of political life in a way that allows him to make a meaningful contribution during a period when the fundamental parameters were changing from republican to imperial. We have the benefit of hindsight at the beginning of the twenty-first century, but it is important to remember that when Virgil was writing his poem, Augustus was in the process of defining the role he would play on the stage of history. The *Aeneid*, like the 'Altar of Augustan Peace', contributes to that process, helping to create the history it also writes.

Milton's imperial motif also offers complexity of association. As Davies notes, *Paradise Lost* begins with a focus on one-man rule and, while imperial power may degenerate into the evil emperor who is tied to the corrupt community that begets him, it also can develop into the good emperor who safeguards the state.[65] Like Virgil, Milton had an obvious nostalgia for republicanism, and there are suggestions in the poem that a republic may well be the best form of government

---

[65] Davies, *Images*, 96–7.

on earth: man should rule over animals, not other men, in Adam's words, *PL* 12. 65–70, since a republic offered a better opportunity to remove a magistrate who was in danger of becoming a tyrant.[66] There is no question, however, that monarchy is the best form of government in absolute terms, for God is clearly an emperor, as Satan found out all too quickly. The result is a political vision that resists simplistic categorization. As Howard Erskine-Hill put it,

Milton was a political republican in opposing men who seemed to arrogate to themselves what was proper to God alone.... The republican poet had in common with royalist readers that he was a metaphysical royalist: the two sides of his thought are complementary, indeed symbiotic. This I think is a coherent view of Milton's consistent attitude before and after the revolution of 1660, whose restoration of legitimate monarchy reanimated the metaphor of kingship. The poet's mind was of wide resource, capable of discretion without betrayal of conviction. His belief in the kingship of the Messiah enabled him to reach out in his poem to a readership beyond that of falling or defeated republicans. Further, his desire to offer a political education through Christian epic is admirably fulfilled in its wide application of the image and terms of kingship, genuine and spurious, throughout the narrative.[67]

This is a message that could get past the censors.[68] And it is a message that is properly deferential to legitimate authority, while at the same

[66] Roger Lejosne, 'Milton, Satan, Salmasius and Abdiel', 106–17, and Dzelzainis, 'Milton's Classical Republicanism', 19–24, both in Armitage *et al.* (eds.), *Milton and Republicanism*.

[67] Erskine-Hill, *Poetry*, 195–6. J. Martin Evans, *Milton's Imperial Epic: Paradise Lost and the Discourse of Colonialism* (Ithaca, NY, and London: Cornell Univ. Press, 1996), argues that in his attitude towards colonialism, another aspect of imperialism, Milton was also deeply ambivalent, concluding that 'Milton's great "organ voice" is not a single euphonious instrument but a chorus of individual and sometimes discordant voices which echo the complex acoustics of Renaissance colonial discourse' (113). Milton may well have gotten this ability to see both sides of complicated questions from his experience with casuistry, the application of basic moral principles to daily life, under the assumption that while principles may be absolute, their application is often problematic. Indeed, the subject of *Paradise Lost* is moral choice, which brings the poem into the realm of casuistical discourse; see Camille Wells Slights, *The Casuistical Tradition in Shakespeare, Donne, Herbert, and Milton* (Princeton: Princeton Univ. Press, 1981), 3–34, 251–7; and Amy McCready, 'Milton's Casuistry: The Case of The Doctrine and Discipline of Divorce', *Journal of Medieval and Renaissance Studies*, 22/3 (1992), 393–428. I am grateful to Hilaire Kallendorf for these last two references.

[68] Hugh Wilson, 'The Publication of *Paradise Lost*, the Occasion of the First Edition: Censorship and Resistance', *Milton Studies*, 37 (1999), 18–41. Annabel Patterson, *Censorship and Interpretation: The Conditions of Writing and Reading in*

time warning that authority to proceed with care and adhere to its
ideals. This, in essence, was Virgil's message to Augustus, transferred
to England. As such, it makes *Paradise Lost* a poem for revolutionary
times, just as the *Aeneid* had been, and gives Milton a way not to look
back helplessly on the failures of Cromwell and the early commonwealth, but to look forward into the unfolding events of the moment,
remaining true to himself and continuing the interventions that had
marked his career up to that point.

carou

2. JOEL BARLOW, VIRGIL, AND THE AMERICAN REVOLUTION

> The older distinction between fiction and history, in which
> fiction is conceived as the representation of the imaginable
> and history as the representation of the actual, must give
> place to the recognition that we can only know the *actual* by
> contrasting it with or likening it to the *imaginable*.... In point
> of fact, history—the real world as it evolves in time—is made
> sense of in the same way that the poet or novelist tries to make
> sense of it, i.e., by endowing what originally appears to be
> problematical or mysterious with the aspect of a recognizable,
> because it is a familiar, form. It does not matter whether the
> world is conceived to be real or only imagined; the manner of
> making sense of it is the same.
>
>   (Hayden White, *Tropics of Discourse*[69])

Early Modern England, rev. edn. (Madison: Univ. of Wisconsin Press, 1984), notes
that the censorship system in place in Milton's day traced its origins to Quintilian,
Inst. 9. 2. 67, where one can speak out against the authorities so long as it is possible
to be understood differently, in which case everyone admires the ambiguity and no
one feels a need to make an example of the author (4, 12, 15). The result was a series
of 'strategies of indirection' (53) which allow us to move beyond a simplistic Whig
history that pits the government against its critics to the recognition that censorship
could actually encourage literary production by setting up a system of unwritten rules
through which writers could communicate by indirection without provoking a
confrontation (53–66). Patterson does not treat *Paradise Lost* but notes that it should
be examined from this perspective (259 n. 45), as is being done here.

[69] White, *Tropics of Discourse*, 98.

Milton, along with Shakespeare, was the modern author who had the greatest influence on colonial American writers, so it should not surprise us to learn that *Paradise Lost* was the only modern epic Joel Barlow knew first hand and drew from to a measurable degree in his *Vision of Columbus*. Ostensibly this poem focused on Christopher Columbus, whom the panoramic vision of life in the Americas from its discovery to the date of publication was designed to console, but the real focus of the *Vision* is the American Revolution, which brings it in line with *Paradise Lost*, which was read in America as a poem written by a Puritan rebelling against tyranny. By making the American Revolution central to the progress of Western civilization, Barlow endows it with Miltonic grandeur, and Columbus's relationship to the angel who stage-manages his vision is that of Adam to Raphael, who similarly explains to him events in which he cannot have participated. Some individual passages in the *Vision* (i.e. the Incan hymn to the sun) allude to *Paradise Lost*, and both poets handle certain themes and motifs (like battle scenes, which lack the classical epic's focus on the individual *aristeia*) in similar ways.[70]

Given its ambivalent critical reception, Barlow's *Vision of Columbus* and his *Columbiad*, as it was titled in its revised form, might seem a peculiar subject for a lengthy discussion in 2005. On the one hand, the poem was a best seller in its day, going through at least six editions and three reprints in the United States, Britain, and France in its initial version from 1787 to 1823, then six more editions, again in the United States, Britain, and France, in its revised form.[71] The revision was in fact 'the graphic arts event of the decade', being acknowledged from its own time until now as the first American example of fine printing that compared favourably with the products of the European presses.[72] In terms of its content, the *Critical Review*

[70] Leon Howard, *The Connecticut Wits* (Chicago: Univ. of Chicago Press, 1943), 147; and John P. McWilliams, Jr., *The American Epic: Transforming a Genre 1770–1860* (Cambridge: CUP, 1989), 23.

[71] Helen Loschky, 'The "Columbiad" Tradition: Joel Barlow and Others', *Books at Brown*, 21 (1967), 197–206. Publication information can also be found in James Woodress, *A Yankee's Odyssey: The Life of Joel Barlow* (Philadelphia and New York: J. B. Lippincott, 1958), 247–8. For full bibliographical descriptions of the various edns., see Jacob Blanck, *Bibliography of American Literature* (New Haven: Yale Univ. Press, 1955), i. 169–84.

[72] John Bidwell, 'The Publication of Joel Barlow's *The Columbiad*', *Proceedings of the American Antiquarian Society*, 93/2 (1984), 337–80. The importance of this book

declared that 'Mr. Barlow thinks with freedom and expresses himself with spirit', and the *London Monthly Magazine* pronounced the *Columbiad* 'magnificent, surpassed only by *Paradise Lost*'. The longest and most important notice was written by Francis Jeffrey in the *Edinburgh Review*, who concluded that as a philosophical and moral poet, Barlow 'has talents of no ordinary value'.

This same review, however, presents negative assessments as well. Jeffrey complains that the *Columbiad* has 'enormous—inexpiable,— and in some respects, intolerable faults', and that as an epic poet, Barlow's 'case is desperate'. The reviews in the *Monthly Anthology* and the *Boston Review* were sarcastic, and the *Philadelphia Portfolio* condemned the poem for 'ludicrous alliteration' and 'bathos'.[73] Some of this criticism strikes us as unfair today—Barlow's religious convictions were assailed even by his friends, and among the Americans, one can tell immediately whether a given reviewer was a Federalist or a Republican—but the poem has fared even worse among critics of the second half of the twentieth century. Roy Harvey Pearce complains of the 'dreary, insistent, intemperate, and homogenized descriptions of places, people, and events';[74] James Woodress, the author of the standard literary biography of Barlow, waxes eloquent about the *Columbiad* as 'a dinosaur in the clay pits of literary history', an example of 'attenuated verse suitable only for wall hangings in museum attics';[75] and Meyer Reinhold, an expert on the classical

can be judged from the fact that six copies of it went into Michael Papantonio's collection of early American bindings (Hannah Dustin French, 'A Mayo Binding of Barlow's "Columbiad" ', *Proceedings of the American Antiquarian Society*, 89/2 (1980), 369–70), three of which are now at the American Antiquarian Society (Marcus C. McCorison, 'Early American Bookbindings from the Collection of Michael Papantonio', *Proceedings of the American Antiquarian Society*, 93/2 (1883), 381–414).

[73] The early critical response to the *Columbiad* is surveyed in Charles Burr Todd, *Life and Letters of Joel Barlow, LL.D.* (New York: Da Capo Press, 1970; repr. of New York and London, 1886 edn.), 218–33; Howard, *Connecticut Wits*, 322–3; and Woodress, *A Yankee's Odyssey*, 85–9. A complete list of the early reviews can be found in McWilliams, *American Epic*, 253 n. 45; McWilliams notes that, seen as a group, the early reviews are actually contradictory, criticizing the poem for having no action and an excess of action, and so forth (63).

[74] Roy Harvey Pearce, *The Continuity of American Poetry* (Princeton: Princeton Univ. Press, 1961), 64.

[75] Woodress, *A Yankee's Odyssey*, 86.

tradition in America, states that it 'remains one of the most dismal failures in the history of American poetry'.[76]

Yet unlike most other 'dismal failures', this one will not go away. Like Reinhold, Michael André Bernstein refers casually and without explanation to the *Columbiad* as a 'failure', as if everyone knows this, but when he turns to William Carlos Williams a few pages later as part of a discussion on how to treat specifically American subject matter, Barlow's name slips back in again, since it turns out to be difficult to discuss this topic without him.[77] James E. Miller, Jr. in turn explains why this is so. Miller is writing about Walt Whitman, who, he feels, stands at the centre of the effort to write an epic that will sum up what it means to be an American, but when he sketches out a history of this effort, Miller begins with John Berryman and Allen Ginsberg, then works back through Ezra Pound, T. S. Eliot, Hart Crane, William Carlos Williams, Wallace Stevens, and Charles Olson, to arrive at two figures at the beginning: Timothy Dwight and Joel Barlow.[78]

I believe it is time for a fresh assessment of the poem, in part because in my reading at least, Barlow's epic has a good deal to say about larger issues of representation as they affect the writing of literary history, a topic which has been a matter of special concern to the 'new historicism'. Initially the poem appears to focus on Columbus, but as I mentioned above, the real subject is the American Revolution, and from its own day to the present, Barlow's poem has been valued primarily for its patriotic presentation of the origins of the republic and for its role in helping to launch a new national culture. It does not represent itself as a work of history *per se*, but as the quotation from Hayden White that begins this section suggests, many historians and scholars of literature are suggesting that the divisions between their two fields are by no means as rigid as they were once believed to be.

[76] Meyer Reinhold, 'Vergil in the American Experience', in *Classica Americana: The Greek and Roman Heritage in the United States* (Detroit: Wayne State Univ. Press, 1984), 237.

[77] Michael André Bernstein, *The Tale of the Tribe: Ezra Pound and the Modern Epic Voice* (Princeton: Princeton Univ. Press, 1980), 185.

[78] James E. Miller, Jr., *The American Quest for a Supreme Fiction: Whitman's Legacy in the Personal Epic* (Chicago and London: Univ. of Chicago Press, 1979), 13.

In the period immediately before White's *Tropics of Discourse* was published, which is when Pearce and Woodress were writing, the prevailing assumption was that the historian's task was to research the facts and tell the story he (or she, but usually he) discovered. White's contribution was to suggest that historical narratives are actually 'verbal fictions, the contents of which are as much *invented* as *found*'.[79] The example he gives, that of the French Revolution in two of its most famous accounts, is particularly relevant to the topic of this section. Michelet, White explains, wrote the French Revolution as a drama of romantic transcendence, but his contemporary Tocqueville wrote it as ironic tragedy. Neither was better informed than the other about the facts, but they had a different idea about the kind of story that fitted the facts they knew. The facts they sought out and presented are not always the same, but are the facts that fit the story they wanted to tell.[80]

Tropics of Discourse suggests that the story a historian tells, like that of a poet or novelist, must take 'some form with which we have already become familiar in our literary culture'.[81] By the eighteenth century Columbus had become many things to many people: an agent of Catholicism and Protestantism; a symbol of rationalism, Rousseauism, and scientific progress; of nationalism and worldwide unity; of freedom and slavery, of cultural self-affirmation and revolution; and so forth.[82] To tell Columbus's story, Barlow had to decide

---

[79] White, *Tropics of Discourse*, 85. Elizabeth A. Clark, *History, Theory, Text: Historians and the Linguistic Turn* (Cambridge, Mass.: Harvard Univ. Press, 2004), esp. ch. 5, 'Narrative History', 86–105, provides additional observations on the points raised in the next several paragraphs.

[80] White, *Tropics of Discourse*, 85.

[81] Ibid. 91. As Roger Chartier has pointed out, Paul Veyne had begun a similar analysis of the 'linguistic turn' in history two years before White published his analysis in *Metahistory* (1973); see 'Four Questions for Hayden White', in *On the Edge of the Cliff: History, Language, and Practices*, tr. Lydia G. Cochrane (Baltimore, Md., and London: Johns Hopkins University Press, 1997), 28–38, for an account of how these issues have been treated in recent historical writing.

[82] Herbert Knust, 'Columbiads in Eighteenth Century European and American Literature', in Mario Materassi and Maria Irene Ramalho de Sousa Santos (eds.), *The American Columbiad: 'Discovering' America, Inventing the United States* (Amsterdam: VU Univ. Press, 1996), 32–3. On earlier epics about Columbus based on classical models, esp. the *Aeneid*, see Heinz Hofmann, 'Enea in America', in Sesto Prete (ed.), *Memores tui: studi di letteratura classica ed umanistica in onore di Marcello Vitaletti* (Sassoferrato: Istituto Internazionale Studi Piceni, 1990), 71–98; and idem, '*Adveniat tandem Typhis qui detegat orbes*: Columbus in Neo-Latin Epic Poetry (16th–18th

in which Columbus he was interested, a decision that was inextricably bound to the form he chose.

Even those whose acquaintance with Barlow's poem is limited to brief selections in anthologies know that it is an epic, but the consequences of this generic choice for the meaning and appreciation of the poem have not, I believe, been adequately explored. It seems that Homer's *Iliad* was popular, perhaps to a surprising degree, in the colonial period, but the *Aeneid* was the epic poem that any American with even a grammar school education really knew. As Richard Waswo has shown, Virgil's epic served in many ways as the foundation myth for Western culture, telling the story of how Aeneas and his band of defeated Trojans sailed off to the west, uncertain of the precise location of their new home but certain that they had been predestined for great things.[83] Along the way they overcame obstacles that were both within themselves, like the emotions of anger and love that constantly threatened to deflect them from their goals, and in the outside world, like Turnus and the other indigenous peoples who already occupied the land in which they understood their future to lie. After finding their new home and fighting for it, Aeneas and his men won the climactic battle and settled down to create a new nation.

Centuries)', in Wolfgang Haase and Meyer Reinhold (eds.), *The Classical Tradition and the Americas*, i. *European Images of the Americas and the Classical Tradition* (Berlin and New York: Walter de Gruyter, 1994), part 1, 420–656, which goes a good way towards answering Jozef IJsewijn, *Companion to Neo-Latin Studies*, i. *History and Diffusion of Neo-Latin Literature*, 2nd edn. (Leuven: Leuven Univ. Press/Peeters Press, 1990), who noted that '[t]he full extent of the impact of Columbus' discovery on Neo-Latin literature is still to be assessed' (285). Shorter studies of poems in this tradition may be found in L. Bradner, 'Columbus in Sixteenth-Century Poetry', in Frederick R. Goff *et al.* (eds.), *Essays Honoring Lawrence L. Wroth* (Portland, Maine: Anthoensen Press, 1951); and Geneviève Demaron, 'La Tradition virgilienne dans les épopées du nouveau monde', *Annales Latini Montium Arvernorum*, 9 (1982), 37–45. As I have argued elsewhere ('Enea nel "Nuovo Mundo": Il *Columbeis* di Stella e il pessimismo virgiliano', *Studi umanistici piceni*, 23 (2003), 241–51), the 16th-cent. Neo-Latin *Columbeis* of Giulio Cesare Stella imitates the *Aeneid* from a 'pessimistic' perspective that is similar to Barlow's, but there is little, if any, chance that this poem was known to him. It is more likely that both Stella and Barlow were responding to the same features in the *Aeneid* as they composed poems on similar subjects.

[83] Richard Waswo, *The Founding Legend of Western Civilization: From Virgil to Vietnam* (Hanover, NH, and London: Univ. Press of New England, for Wesleyan Univ. Press, 1997).

The early Americans regularly identified themselves with Aeneas and the Trojans, for just as Aeneas had taken his men away from one dying civilization to establish a new one in the west, so the colonial settlers had fled the oppression and corruption of a dying Europe to go further west, where (they believed) great things had been ordained for them. For two hundred and fifty years, therefore, Virgil's works were read and studied in the United States from grammar school to college: the early colleges followed Harvard's lead in requiring an ability to read and understand Virgil as a prerequisite for admission, and the schools responded by preparing their students to pass the colleges' entrance examinations. Thomas Jefferson's affection for Virgil has often been quoted, and John Adams began a cult of veneration that lasted in his family for several generations.[84] It is therefore not surprising to find early American writers attempting their own epics and alluding to the *Aeneid* as they did so. Benjamin Tompson's *New Englands Crisis*, the first significant American epic, compares the treachery of the natives against the colonizers to the Trojan horse, then to Aeneas's being cloaked in mist at his arrival in Carthage, and contains a section entitled 'On a fortification at Boston begun by women. *Dux foemina facti*', which associates Boston with Dido's Carthage by quoting *Aen.* 1. 364 ('A woman leads').[85] Tompson's student was Cotton Mather, whose *Magnalia Christi Americana* draws from the beginning of the *Aeneid* at three key points in the narrative, first rewriting a Virgilian quotation on its title-page to make the American colonies into a new Rome, then associating the colonists with Virgilian *pietas* ('piety'), and finally rewriting the first phrase of the *Aeneid* at the point where the poem shifts from describing the travels of the Puritans to their battles with

---

[84] Reinhold, 'Vergil in the American Experience', 221–2, 232–3, 238–40; and McWilliams, Jr., *American Epic*, 34–5. Reinhold's essay has been severely criticized by John C. Shields, *The American Aeneas: Classical Origins of the American Self* (Knoxville, Tenn.: Univ. of Tennessee Press, 2001), 264 ff., who points out that it is difficult to reconcile Reinhold's claims that American students found the *Aeneid* distasteful (222) and that Virgil's poems failed to exercise any profound influence on American culture (250) with the easy familiarity educated people in early America had with the *Aeneid* and with the important role he found the poem to have played in the literature of the period.

[85] Ibid., pp. xl–xli. See also Bianca Tarozzi, 'Virgilio nella cultura americana', in *La fortuna di Virgilio* (Naples: Giannini Editore, 1986), 477–81.

rescue effort

the natives. This structural change in itself recalls the plan of Virgil's poem, which moves from Aeneas's travels to Italy to his battles with the people he encounters there.[86]

It is Barlow, however, who was referred to in the *New Haven Gazette* as the American Virgil,[87] an association that was taken up by Richard Alsop, who wrote, 'And in Virgilian Barlow's tuneful lines | With added splendour great Columbus shines.'[88] As a student first at Dartmouth College, then at Yale, Barlow had studied the *Aeneid* at length in the original Latin.[89] In the pages that follow, I shall argue that this intimate acquaintance with Latin epic is important and that Barlow's vision of the American Revolution was profoundly affected by his decision to view his subject through the lens of Virgilian epic, a decision whose consequences have never been explored at any length. More precisely, I shall suggest that it is the 'pessimistic' reading of Virgil that provides the decisive character of the *Vision*, and that the increasingly radical character of the *Columbiad* is tied directly to its increasingly Virgilian flavour. The result is a poem that is more profoundly revolutionary than *Paradise Lost*, and that is subtle and nuanced enough to merit more than a disparaging footnote in the annals of American literary history.

The *Vision* opens with Columbus declaring his sorrows in a way that recalls the beginning sections of the *Aeneid*. Virgil's poem begins in a storm at sea; in the *Vision*, Columbus recalls his sea voyages and the dangers he encountered there. In his first speech Aeneas wishes he were dead,

> . . . mene Iliacis occumbere campis
> non potuisse tuaque animam hanc effundere dextra

> why
> did your right hand not spill my lifeblood, why
> did not I fall upon the Ilian fields

> (*Aen.* 1. 97–8)

---

[86] Shields, *American Aeneas*, pp. xl–xli, 61–71.
[87] 'The Meddlar', *New Haven Gazette*, 1/4 (26 Jan. 1791).
[88] Qtd. in Woodress, *A Yankee's Odyssey*, 89.
[89] Howard, *Connecticut Wits*, 145.

as does Columbus, who wishes to see 'this drear mansion moulder to a tome' (p. 27).[90] In his second speech, Aeneas suggests to his comrades that

> . . . forsan et haec olim meminisse iuuabit.
>
> Perhaps one day you will remember even
> these our adversities with pleasure.

(Aen. 1. 203)

To Columbus, the new Aeneas, this time has not yet arrived, for he complains, 'But dangers past, fair climes explored in vain, | And foes triumphant shew but half my pain' (p. 27). For Aeneas some help arrives through an epic motif, the descent from heaven, as his mother, the goddess Venus, appears to him after he lands in Carthage and tells him where he has landed. Consolation, though, is bittersweet, as she disappears as soon as he recognizes her (*Aen.* 1. 314–417). Barlow uses a similar strategy. For Columbus an angel arrives with good news: 'Thy just complaints, in heavenly audience known, | Call mild compassion from the indulgent throne' (p. 28). What is more, Barlow captures a distinctly Virgilian sense of pathos by denying Columbus the consolation of direct colloquy with his heavenly Father: in the epic world, there is still a distance between the human and the divine that can never be fully bridged.

In the introduction to the *Vision of Columbus*, Barlow explains that his initial idea was that 'of attempting a regular Epic poem' on the discovery of America, but as he realized that what was important was not the discovery itself but its consequences, he also realized that those consequences 'must be represented in vision' (p. xxi). The vision he presents is one that is offered by the angel to Columbus at the end of his life, with the goal being to console him during his days in prison by showing him what will happen after he dies. This suggests that what is to follow will be modelled on the vision that Aeneas's father Anchises shows him in *Aeneid* 6, in which a parade of heroes from Aeneas's day to Virgil's encourages the hero of the poem to carry on with his duties.

Anchises begins by explaining reincarnation to Aeneas, helping him to understand the source and mystery of life as it unfolds through time:

---

[90] References are to *The Vision of Columbus: A Poem in Nine Books* (Hartford, Conn.: Hudson & Goodwin, 1787), accessed through Eighteenth Century Collections Online, and will be placed into the text.

> Principio caelum ac terras camposque liquentis
> lucentemque globum lunae Titaniaque astra
> spiritus intus alit, totamque infusa per artus
> mens agitate molem et magno se corpore miscet.

> First, know, a soul within sustains the heaven
> and earth, the plains of water, and the gleaming
> globe of the moon, the Titan sun, the stars;
> and mind, that pours through every member, mingles
> with that great body.

> *(Aen.* 6. 724–7)

Barlow's angel paints a similar picture:

> From that great Source, that life-inspiring Soul,
> Suns drew their light and Systems learned to roll,
> Time walked the silent round, and life began,
> And God's fair image stamped the mind of man.   (p. 28)

Then Virgil surveys the heroes of ancient Rome who will follow in
Aeneas's footsteps; Barlow presents Magellan, then Vasco da Gama,
then Drake, the other explorers who will continue what Columbus
has begun. These men and those who follow them will first conquer,
then bring culture to the new world:

> Here, here, my sons, the hand of culture bring,
> Here teach the lawns to smile, the groves to sing;
> Ye sacred floods, no longer vainly glide,
> Ye harvests, load them, and ye forests, ride;
> Bear the deep burden from the joyous swain,
> And tell the world where peace and plenty reign.   (p. 40)

Thus Columbus and his descendants are the fitting heirs of the
Romans, who, as Anchises had explained, were able to conquer and
bring peace, but not culture:

> excudent alii spirantia mollius aera
> (credo equidem), uiuos ducent de marmore uultus,
> orabunt causas melius, caelique meatus
> describent radio et surgentia sidera dicent:
> tu regere imperio populos, Romane, memento
> (hae tibi erunt artes), pacique imponere morem,
> Parcere subiectis et debellare superbos.

> For other peoples will, I do not doubt,
> still cast their bronze to breathe with softer features,

or draw out of the marble living lines,
plead causes better, trace the ways of heaven
with wands and tell the rising constellations;
but yours will be the rulership of nations,
remember, Roman, these will be your arts:
to teach the ways of peace to those you conquer,
to spare defeated peoples, tame the proud.

(*Aen.* 6. 847–53)

In book 2 of the *Vision*, Barlow begins to clarify how he understood the *Aeneid*. Here we meet Montezuma and Cortés, whom we
might logically expect to play certain roles: if the *Vision* tells the story
of how the government and culture of the civilization that succeeded
Rome continued its westward journey to the new world, just as it had
earlier travelled westward from Troy to Italy, then Cortés should play
the part of Aeneas, Montezuma should play the part of Aeneas's
adversary Turnus, and Barlow's sympathies should remain clearly
with the Spaniards. This is not, however, what we find. Montezuma is
described in consistently sympathetic terms: 'Mild in his eye a tem-
per'd grandeur sate, | Great seem'd his soul, with conscious power
elate' (p. 60). Columbus hopes that he and his people will be spared
conquest, but this is not to be, for motivated by avarice and acting
with 'harden'd guilt and cruelty', Cortés and his men, 'the blackest of
mankind', will steal Mexico's gold and bathe her fields in blood
(p. 60). Finally through their final encounter, Barlow rewrites the
end of the *Aeneid*, in which Turnus surrenders to Aeneas and pleads,
unsuccessfully, for mercy. Montezuma

Proffers the empire, yields the sceptred sway,
Bids vassal'd millions tremble and obey;
And plies the victor, with incessant prayer,
Thro' ravaged realms the harmless race to spare.
But prayers and tears and scepters plead in vain,
Nor threats can move him nor a world restrain;
While blest religion's prostituted name,
And monkish fury guides the sacred flame:
O'er fanes and altars, fires unhallow'd bend,
Climb o'er the walls and up the towers ascend,
Pour, round the lowering skies, the smoky flood,
And whelm the fields, and quench their rage in blood.   (p. 62)

Here the Spaniards give free reign to their 'rage', unrestrained by the mercy that Christianity teaches, for their 'blest religion' is 'prostituted' to the pursuit of gold. Barlow can only stress that 'virtues' inhere in the Mexicans, against whom Cortés has unleashed his 'impious arm'. These are key value words in Virgil's moral vocabulary, but everything seems confused: we would expect virtues to inhere in the Spaniards and Montezuma to be presented as a creature of rage.

When Columbus's vision reaches Peru, the confusion only grows worse. Here Manco Capac, the Peruvian ruler, takes on the role of Aeneas and Zamor, a chief from another tribe, that of the epic adversary. Manco's goal was to end human sacrifice by extending sun worship, but this goal is expressed in Virgilian terms, as he 'In savage souls could quell the barbarous rage |...| And teach the virtues in their laws to reign' (p. 67). His initial problem is that of Aeneas in Carthage: should he do his duty, to his country and the gods, or stay at home with Oella, who takes the role of Dido? The new Dido, unlike the old one, agrees to stay at home so that Manco, here a proper husband to her, can do what he should do. Manco is regularly described as 'pious' (e.g. p. 118), tightening his association with Aeneas; even when he thinks his native opponents have killed his son Rocha, he remains pious, praying and not giving way to his 'ire', and he is rewarded by learning that his son is still alive. Then Barlow rewrites the end of the *Aeneid* again, sending Manco to single combat against Zamor. As Turnus and Aeneas are described in similar ways at the end of the *Aeneid*, both giving way to the natural forces within them (cf. *Aen.* 12. 521–8), so 'meet the dreadful chiefs, with eyes on fire', at which point Manco 'rush'd furious on', after which 'he drives his furious way' (pp. 123–4). Here we fear he is about to lose control as Aeneas did, but as 'he drives his furious way', he is also praying, and moments later Manco does what Aeneas did not do:

> While Capac raised his placid voice again—
> Ye conquering hosts, collect the scatter'd train;
> The Sun commands to stay the rage of war,
> He knows to conquer, but he loves to spare.   (p. 124)

We recall Anchises's description of the glory of Rome—'parcere subiectis et debellare superbos' ('to spare defeated peoples, tame the proud', *Aen.* 6. 853), a line that echoes powerfully at the end of the *Aeneid*, when Aeneas fails to do precisely this (cf. *Aen.* 12. 950–2). Manco tries to stop Zamor's wound and offers him an honoured burial, but Zamor refuses and dies with a clear gesture towards Turnus:

> Thus pour'd the vengeful chief his fainting breath,
> And lost his utterance with the gasp of death.   (pp. 125–6)

> . . . ast illi soluuntur frigore membra
> uitaque cum gemitu fugit indignata sub umbras.

> His limbs fell slack with chill; and with a moan
> his life, resentful, fled to Shades below.
>
> (*Aen.* 12. 951–2)

In short, Barlow's rewriting of Virgil's cultural foundation myth does not proceed as we might have expected. If Spain is to the indigenous peoples of the Americas as the Trojans were to the indigenous peoples of Italy, then Aeneas's piety and virtue should have been transferred to Cortés, and Montezuma and Manco Capac should have played the roles of Turnus, the epic antagonist who is driven by rage and threatens all that the hero is working for. Instead Cortez is depicted as so thoroughly evil that our sympathies, like Barlow's, are clearly with Montezuma. The next scene does give us an evil Indian, Zamor, but his adversary is Incan, so that not only do the Spaniards not act with the piety and virtue they should, but now the character who does embody the Virgilian virtues is not even Spanish. In other words, when the 'savages' replay the plot of the *Aeneid*, they show the Europeans how it should have been done.[91] How can we explain this?

Part of the answer, I suspect, is tied to the historical record: in a preceding generation, we might have suggested simply that the ruthlessness of the Spanish invaders and the decimation of the indigenous populations speak for themselves. But if, as the 'new historicists' urge, we emphasize instead that history is text and facts require interpretation, then we should interrogate the nature of

[91] Danielle E. Conger, 'Toward a Native American Nationalism: Joel Barlow's *The Vision of Columbus*', *New England Quarterly*, 72/4 (1999), 558–9, brings up another relevant point, that as the British looked to Greece and Rome for their cultural roots, so Barlow looked to the Incas and Aztecs as representatives of new world antiquity. The same point is made by Richard Bauer, 'Colonial Discourse and Early American Literary History: Ercilla, the Inca Garcilaso, and Joel Barlow's Conception of a New World Epic', *Early American Literature*, 30/3 (1995), 203–32.

representation as we have it in Barlow's poem. For North Americans of English origins, the myth of the black legend, the evil, almost-Other Spaniard who symbolized repression and Inquisition, provided a filter through which the past could be interpreted, at least in part.[92] Since the *Vision*, however, is a Virgilian epic, the way in which the *Aeneid* was understood in Barlow's time provided another interpretive filter.

Let us begin with the fact that Barlow knew something about Ercilla's *La Araucana*. He states in one of the notes to the *Vision* that Ercilla's poem had unfortunately not been translated into English yet, but that he knew of it through a summary made by a Mr Hayley that reached him a few days before his poem went to press and through Voltaire, from whom he could have learnt at least that Ercilla was sympathetic to the native cause.[93] It would be dangerous to read too much into these observations, but we do not have to, since colonial American discourse contains enough other observations that square with a 'pessimistic' interpretation of the poem to let us feel confident that this interpretation was available to Barlow. Brockden Brown called the *Aeneid* 'a remarkable instance of servile adulation to tyrants',[94] which suggests at very least that, if Virgil had provided a straightforward encomium of Augustus as part of his praise for the Roman state, he should not have. Further criticism appeared in 1769, when John Wilson, a teacher in the Friends Latin School in Philadelphia, resigned his position over having to teach Ovid, Horace, and Juvenal, who, he believed, fostered lasciviousness, Epicureanism, and impudence, respectively. Virgil, he concedes, 'commonly is excepted from this guilty List yet with the impious Notion Of both the 2d and 8th Eclogues and his representing the Ungrateful Lustful Perfidious Aeneas as the particular Friend and Favorite of Heaven are shocking to every System of Morality.'[95] And

[92] This attitude comes through again and again in the accounts cited in Jeffrey Knapp, *An Empire Nowhere: England, America, and Literature from Utopia to The Tempest* (Berkeley–Los Angeles and London: Univ. of California Press, 1992).

[93] As Barlow notes, the conditions under which he worked were not always easy: 'It is usually presumed, that every Author must have read all that have gone before him . . . but these are not the only disadvantages that an Author, in a new country, and in modest circumstances, must have to encounter' (*Columbiad*, 68).

[94] *The Literary Magazine and American Register*, 4 (1805), 343, qtd. in McWilliams, *American Epic*, 22.

[95] Qtd. in Reinhold, *Classica Americana*, 235.

lest we think that Aeneas's failings were apparent only to obscure Quaker schoolmasters, John Quincy Adams also weighed his character and found it wanting, especially as regards the death of Turnus at the end of the poem. In his widely disseminated *Lectures on Rhetoric and Oratory*, Adams wrote that no reader should have 'to see the hero of Virgil, the pious Aeneas, steeling his bosom against mercy, and plunging his pitiless sword into the bosom of a fallen and imploring enemy, to avenge the slaughter of his friend'.[96] As we saw in Chapter 1, the 'pessimistic' reading of the *Aeneid* begins here, in the capacity to see shortcomings in Aeneas and to take the first steps away from a straightforwardly encomiastic vision of the poem.

In America, as in Europe, the 'optimistic' reading of the *Aeneid* dominated, in the eighteenth century as well as the twenty-first.[97] But the other reading was there as well, latent in the text and audible to those who proved able to go beyond criticism of Aeneas to hear Virgil's hesitations and doubts. When Barlow made Aeneas speak through the mouth of Manco Capac and sympathized with Montezuma at the expense of the evil Cortés, he showed that he was sensitive enough to read his source 'against the grain', so to speak, and to move his poem beyond the black-and-white moral configurations that have made so many epics built on Virgil's foundations so hopelessly dull.

However great his sympathies for Turnus, Dido, and what they represent, Virgil did not suggest that it would have been better had the Roman Empire never been founded. Similarly Barlow clarifies what is lost in colonizing the new world and how the colonizers fall short of their expressed values, but his theme is progress, and he

[96] John Quincy Adams, *Lectures on Rhetoric and Oratory* (Cambridge, Mass.: Hilliard & Metcalf, 1810), i. 245.

[97] In 18th-cent. culture, the reception of Virgil was tied to the assessment of Augustus in a curious way, as Howard D. Weinbrot has shown. The ancient sources record a range of responses to Augustus, almost all of which were available to 18th-cent. scholars. Whether Augustus was viewed favourably or unfavourably tended to depend on the viewer's politics, with royalists being more positively disposed in general than republicans. The consensus, however, was that Virgil was an apologist for the emperor, with debate centring on whether this was a good or a bad thing; see *Augustus Caesar in 'Augustan' England: The Decline of a Classical Norm* (Princeton: Princeton Univ. Press, 1978), esp. 120–49. Weinbrot has captured very well the dominant approach to the *Aeneid* in the long 18th cent.; this is the approach to which the group of readers in this chapter were responding.

spends the remainder of his epic describing how the new world becomes a better place once its history becomes entangled with that of Europe. Book 4 recounts the events from Cortés to William Penn, with an eye on European kings, writers, and religious reformers. Books 5 and 6 cover the French and Indian War, then the American Revolution, with Cornwallis's surrender at the end of book 6 being the climax. The success of the revolution leads to a paean to peace, then a litany of the new world's cultural accomplishments, ranging from Benjamin Franklin in science to West and Copley in art. Book 8 describes the progress of knowledge, which is presented as a balance of passion and reason in what becomes a versification of the prevailing faculty psychology of the day. The final book 9 ends in an Enlightenment dream, with a general council convened to establish political harmony throughout the world.

Initially the vision opened up to Columbus seems to be a straightforward transferral into Barlow's poem of the dream that Anchises opened up to Aeneas, in which Augustus would establish a new golden age that extends beyond the Garamantes and the Indies (cf. *Aen.* 6. 791 ff.). Barlow, however, emphasizes a couple of themes that are only suggested in the *Aeneid* (or more precisely, in a 'pessimistic' reading of the *Aeneid*). Let us look, for example, at how Barlow describes the encounter of peoples from the two worlds:

> From eastern tyrants driven, and nobly brave,
> To build new states, or seek a distant grave,
> Thy generous sons, with proferred leagues of peace,
> Approach these climes, and hail the savage race;
> Pay the just purchase for the uncultured shore,
> Diffuse their arts and share the unfriendly power;
> While the dark tribes in social aid combine,
> Exchange their treasures and their joys refine.   (p. 144)

This version of the encounter would find few takers today, but it makes more sense when we examine it through Barlow's Virgilian filter. The *Aeneid* does not dwell on the fact that Rome grew from the union of Aeneas's Trojan exiles with the indigenous peoples they met when they arrived there, but this is clearly implied at the end of the poem: indeed Maffeo Vegio's thirteenth book of the *Aeneid*, which was still being printed in Barlow's day and was still well enough known to have been parodied thirty years before the publication of the *Vision*,[98] collects the hints Virgil left about how this must have been done and makes them explicit for the literal-minded reader. In stressing that American culture results from the old world coming together with the new, Barlow is making explicit what Virgil had only suggested.

It is immediately clear, however, that in doing so, he is also making the 'other voices' in Virgil more audible than they were in his source. The native inhabitants in the new world are clearly described as a 'savage race' dwelling on an 'uncultured shore', but when he explains that the European settlers were 'from eastern tyrants driven', Barlow suggests that on the moral level, the governments of Europe may not have been much more advanced than those in America. This suggestion is amplified in Barlow's description of the culture whose literary masterpiece he is imitating in the *Vision*:

> They see, in all the boasted paths of praise,
> What partial views heroic ardor raise;
> What mighty states on others' ruins stood,
> And built, secure, their haughty seats in blood;
> How public virtue's ever-borrowed name,
> With proud applause hath graced the deeds of shame;
> Bade Rome's imperial standard wave sublime
> And patriot slaughter spread to every clime;
> From chief to chief, the kindling spirit ran,
> The heirs of fame and enemies of man.   (p. 248)

For Barlow, the hesitations Virgil felt about Rome's ability to reach and maintain her own ideals go one step further, to the conclusion that Rome and her successors are not able alone to progress in accordance with Enlightenment values. Only when the 'nobly brave' leave Europe and join with the inhabitants of the new world do we get 'a new creation' where 'reason triumphs o'er the pride of power' (p. 145).

[98] A modern edn. of Vegio's *Book XIII of the Aeneid* may be found in Maffeo Vegio, *Short Epics*, ed. and tr. Michael C. J. Putnam, with James Hankins (Cambridge, Mass., and London: Harvard Univ. Press, 2004), 2–40, with discussion and bibliography in Craig Kallendorf, *In Praise of Aeneas: Virgil and Epideictic Rhetoric in the Early Italian Renaissance* (Hanover, NH, and London: Univ. Press of New England, 1989), 100–28. The parody is [John Ellis], *The Canto Added by Maphaeus to Virgil's Twelve Books of Aeneas, from the Original Bombastic, Done into English Hudibrastic...* (London: R. and J. Dodsley, 1758).

Twenty years later Barlow republished the *Vision*, as a new poem with
a new title. Several copies of the *Vision* with Barlow's manuscript
revisions survive, and they confirm that the changes are significant
indeed, ranging from countless alterations in wording to additions of
material that generate a tenth book for the *Columbiad*.[99] What is
more, the later poem reflects two key changes in emphasis.

First, the *Columbiad* transforms the *Vision* from a fairly conventional poem in the Christian humanist tradition to a document of
radical republicanism, in which the elements of traditional Christianity recede far into the background and the ideological emphasis
on liberty presses insistently forward. In the original poem, Columbus's vision is presented by an angel, and the religious roots of the
new world are clearly set in the Protestantism of Barlow's New
England. In the *Columbiad*, the vision is introduced by Hesper, the
personification of lands to the west whose roots are in the classical
world, not in Christianity. The de-emphasis on religion was sufficiently pronounced that Noah Webster, a long-standing friend, refused to review the *Columbiad* because his reading of it convinced
him that Barlow had become an atheist, and another old friend, the
Abbé Gregoire, circulated an open letter in which he protested the
ugliness with which Catholicism was treated in the poem. Barlow
insisted that there was nothing in the poem that was incompatible
with the traditional teachings of Christianity, but this is not the
defence that he would have given for the *Vision*.[100]

Epic poems traditionally begin with an invocation to a deity, who
is asked to inspire the poet. Virgil invoked Calliope, the muse of epic
poetry; in the *Columbiad* Barlow invokes Freedom:

> Almighty Freedom! give my venturous song
> The force, the charm that to thy voice belong;
> Tis thine to shape my course, to light my way,
> To nerve my country with the patriot lay,

[99] Dorothy W. Bridgwater, 'The Barlow Manuscripts in the Yale Library', *Yale
University Library Gazette*, 34 (1959), 57–63. References to the *Columbiad* are to my
copy of the 1st edn., *The Columbiad a Poem* (Philadelphia: Fry & Kammerer, for C.
and A. Conrad & Co., Philadelphia, and Conrad, Lucas, & Co., Baltimore, Md.,
1807), and will be placed into the text.

[100] Todd, *Life and Letters*, 218–33, which reproduces extensive quotations from
Barlow's correspondence with Webster and Gregoire.

To teach all men where all their interest lies,
How rulers may be just and nations wise:
Strong in thy strength I bend no suppliant knee,
Invoke no miracle, no Muse but thee.

(1. 22–30)

This emphasis extends throughout the poem. The *Vision*, for example, had been dedicated to Louis XVI, which made sense given France's assistance during the Revolutionary War. Since then, however, the French monarchy had been overthrown and Barlow, in Paris, had allied himself with the revolutionaries. The *Columbiad*, therefore, was dedicated to Robert Fulton, the American inventor of steamboat fame and a close family friend, and the poem takes on a pronounced anti-French flavour, with the French settlers in the new world described as enslaved by a 'feudal genius', having a 'crampt soul that fears to think alone' (5. 136–8). This makes it harder to explain how the French ended up intervening in the Revolutionary War, but Barlow comes up with an ingenious explanation: Louis XVI's counsellors were actually crypto-Republicans who believed

That no proud privilege from birth can spring,
No right divine, nor compact form a king;
That in the people dwells the sovereign sway,
Who rule by proxy, by themselves obey;
That virtues, talents are the test of awe,
And Equal Rights the only source of law.

(7. 39–44)

It was unlikely that arguments based on these principles would persuade Louis XVI to send troops to America, so 'By honest guile the royal ear they bend' (7. 49), encouraging the king to outmanœuvre his archenemy, the English, while actually luring 'him on, blest Freedom to defend' (7. 50). In a similar way the English king is made the cause of the Revolutionary War, not the English people, who 'lend a listening ear' (5. 381) to the just complaints of the colonists, nor the colonists themselves, who are pushed reluctantly into a war they do not want to fight.

The second major change in emphasis results from the fact that the *Columbiad* is a markedly more classical poem than the *Vision*. A number of epic devices, like the opening invocation mentioned above, appear for the first time in the revision or are noticeably better developed there than they were in the original version. When Washington crosses the Delaware, for example, he contends with two personified forces of nature, Flood and Frost, who recall similar forces like *Fama* ('rumour') in the *Aeneid* (*Aen.* 4. 173–97). Later we meet Atlas, a figure from the *Aeneid* as well (*Aen.* 4. 246–58), who joins with Earth in an eloquent condemnation of slavery in the Americas that is logically consistent with Barlow's feelings about freedom but is hardly a given in literature of this period (8. 201–430). Appropriate epic references like this one abound:

> In vain sage Washington, from hill to hill,
> Plays round his foes with more than Fabian skill,
> Retreats, advances, lures them to his snare,
> To balance numbers by the shifts of war.

(5. 825–8)

Here Washington is compared to Quintus Fabius Maximus 'Cunctator', the Roman general who wore down Hannibal by refusing to meet him in pitched battle, thereby earning the nickname 'the delayer'. Similarly the Americans rally against Burgoyne's invasion as the Greeks had rallied against Xerxes (6. 309–35), Arnold turning the tide against Burgoyne is compared to Achilles re-entering battle in the *Iliad* (6. 591–8), and the danger of losing Freedom through inattention is illustrated by reference to the theft of the golden fleece (8. 95–130). Another extended paean to Freedom appears in an account of the exploits of Sir Walter Raleigh, where Prometheus is invoked as a type of heroic striving for liberty (4. 397–512). Indeed details from the classical world sometimes intervene in quite unexpected ways: for example when Lucinda, the beloved of the British officer Heartly, pleads for her life against the Mohawks, she 'runs to grasp their knees' (6. 664) as she would have done in the *Iliad*. (It doesn't work—she is scalped forthwith.)

The increased classical 'feel' of the *Columbiad* is enhanced considerably by the eleven plates that Barlow commissioned for the revised version of the poem. Several of these plates are in a neoclassicizing style that was already beginning to look a bit dated by the time the *Columbiad* was published: the last one, for example, entitled 'The Final Resignation of Prejudice' (opposite p. 327; see Figure 10), has a nude figure clearly derived from ancient sculpture in the foreground

THE FINAL RESIGNATION OF PREJUDICES.

COLUMBIAD

Painted by Smirke. *Engraved by Goulding*

Figure 10. The Final Resignation of Prejudice. Joel Barlow, *The Columbiad a Poem* (Philadelphia, Penn., Fry and Kammerer, 1807), after p. 380 (University of Cincinnati Library)

and a series of buildings designed to copy Greek and Roman archi-
tecture in the background. What is more, several plates depict subjects from antiquity: 'Cesar [sic] Passing the Rubicon' (opposite
p. 185), 'The Rape of the Golden Fleece' (opposite p. 289), and
'Initiation to the Mysteries of Isis' (opposite p. 380). The subject of
each of these plates is mentioned in the text, but the reference in the
Columbiad is in each case a passing one. The plates, in other words,
give these scenes an importance that is out of proportion to the role
they play in Barlow's story, but they contribute toward the cumula-
tive impression that the *Columbiad* is a more classical poem than *The
Vision of Columbus.*

The *Columbiad* is thus anchored more firmly into the ancient epic
world in general than the *Vision* had been, but more specifically it is a
decidedly more Virgilian poem than its predecessor. This is clear
from the beginning, which now clearly recalls Virgil:

> Long had the Sage, the first who dared to brave
> The unknown dangers of the western wave...
>
> (*Vis.* 22)

> I sing the Mariner who first unfurl'd
> An eastern banner o'er the western world,
> And taught mankind where future empires lay
> In these fair confines of descending day.
>
> (*Col.* 1. 1–4)

> Arma uirumque cano, Troiae qui primus ab oris
> Italiam fato profugus Lauiniaque uenit
> litora...
> ...dum conderet urbem
> inferretque deos Latio; genus unde Latinum
> Albanique patres atque altae moenia Romae.

> I sing of arms and of a man: his fate
> had made him fugitive; he was the first
> to journey from the coasts of Troy as far
> as Italy and the Lavinian shores....
> until he brought a city into being
> and carried his gods to Latium;
> from this have come the Latin race, the lords
> of Alba, and the ramparts of high Rome.
>
> (*Aen.* 1. 1–3, 5–7)

In the next few lines Barlow mentions Columbus's 'virtuous steps'
(1. 7), which recalls the *pietas* that characterizes Aeneas from the
beginning of Virgil's poem. As Barlow points out in a note, the evening
star Hesper gave its name to the western regions, so that Italy was
called 'Hesperia' by the Greeks (p. 28); John C. Shields in turn notes
that Italy is also called 'Hesperia' in the *Aeneid*,[101] so that changing the
name of Columbus's heavenly visitor also serves to strengthen the
Virgilian contours of the *Columbiad*. *Aeneid* 6 is invoked specifically
once more in book 9 of the *Columbiad*, where Barlow expands the role
of the arts in his vision of cultural progress. Culture heroes like these
are present in the *Aeneid* as well, where they join kings and generals
in Elysium right before Anchises's vision proper begins. In *Col.* 9.
233 ff. Elysium is mentioned by name, and Barlow's reference to
'Illusions all, that pass the Ivory Gate' (*Col.* 9. 240) cannot refer to
anything other than the ivory gates of false dreams through which
Aeneas passes as he leaves the underworld (cf. *Aen.* 6. 893–9).

This being so, we cannot help but be puzzled at what Barlow has to
say about Virgilian epic in the introduction to the *Columbiad*. In the
Vision he had noted that his subject matter did not fit well into what he
called a 'regular epic form' (p. xxi), by which he meant that it had to be
presented in a vision, not as straight narrative. The *Columbiad* repeats
this point (p. v), but with the insistence that the poem is an epic
nonetheless, and one that is accommodated well to the classical unities
(p. vi). Barlow then discusses Homer, Lucan, and Virgil, and it is here
that the argument takes a surprising turn. First he criticizes Homer,
for defending military glory, advocating plunder and conquest by
arms, and upholding the divine right of kings (a 'pernicious doctrine',
pp. vii–viii). Lucan's republican ideology is good, but his skills as a poet
are limited (pp. ix–x). Given that Barlow had strengthened the ties
between his poem and Virgilian epic in his revisions, we would expect
that Virgil would escape criticism. On one level he does, when Barlow
praises his 'interesting variety of incidents, such weight of pathos, such
majesty of sentiment and harmony of verse' (p. ix). But then he writes,

The moral tendency of the Eneid of Virgil is nearly as pernicious as that of
the works of Homer.... Virgil wrote and felt like a subject, not like a citizen.

[101] Shields, *American Aeneas*, pp. xxix–xxx; see Shields's more general treatment of
the *Columbiad*, 255–8.

Barlow contradicts our author!

The real design of his poem was to increase the veneration of the people for a master, whoever he might be, and to encourage like Homer the great system of military depredation.   (pp. viii–ix)

Initially this judgement does not seem to make sense. It is consistent with the more radical republican ideology of the *Columbiad*, but if Barlow found the *Aeneid* less congenial in 1807 than he had in 1787, why would he devote so much time and effort to making the *Columbiad* a more recognizably Virgilian epic than the *Vision* had been?

This problem has been noted before, with the most extensive discussion being that of John C. Shields. Shields notes that early American culture in general is marked by a broad pattern in which a fully conscious denial of classical influences is accompanied by a covert acceptance of that influence, which may be less than fully conscious. Cotton Mather's *Magnalia*, for example, is so saturated with borrowings from the *Aeneid* that the author's denials of this borrowing fail to convince, even though he may not have thought through with care exactly what he was doing. Edward Taylor in turn denied his affinity for the classics publicly and embraced them privately, leading Shields to conclude that his strategy was fully conscious.[102] The second part of what Shields labels the 'acceptance and denial' paradigm became more pronounced as the colonies moved through revolution to independence, so that after the Revolutionary War an affinity for the culture of Ancien Régime Europe came to look increasingly un-American. Thus Philip Freneau, one of the most important poets in early America, began his career sympathetic to the classics, but by 1795 he was railing against 'antique gibberish', and Benjamin Rush and Noah Webster began renouncing their own classical education at about the same time, in favour of an American curriculum that was more suited to the demands of a new society.[103] Barlow was revising his poem during this crucial transitional period, so one might argue that his poetry simply reflects the general trends of its age, in which the ambivalence of pre-revolutionary

[102] Shields, *American Aeneas*, pp. xxix–xxx; see Shields's more general treatment of the *Columbiad*, 58.

[103] Ibid. 83, 99, 258–9. Caroline Winterer, *The Culture of Classicism: Ancient Greece and Rome in American Intellectual Life, 1780–1910* (Baltimore, Md., and London: Johns Hopkins Univ. Press, 2002), argues that this opposition was really to how the classics were taught, with an emphasis on language instead of content, but it was opposition

classicism gives way to a clearer critique of antiquity, which the introduction to the *Columbiad* helps to articulate.

If, however, the *Columbiad* were designed merely to strengthen the critique of classicism that was coming to dominate American intellectual discourse, would it not have made sense for Barlow to have made the *Vision* less, rather than more, Virgilian as he revised it? The *Columbiad* as it stands certainly reflects the more stridently patriotic vision of the years in which it was written, but it does so in terms that seem to be more and more clearly tied to the very culture, beginning in antiquity and extending through Europe at the turn of the nineteenth century, which it was challenging. If so, this would make the *Vision* a much better poem, one in which content and form fit together better than they do in the *Columbiad*. And this in fact is what several other critics have suggested: James Woodress finds 'the youthful blemishes... more attractive than the middle-aged remodelling',[104] and Emory Elliott claims that 'critics have always felt Barlow's *Vision* to be a more interesting poem than his *Columbiad*'.[105]

I disagree—in fact, I would argue exactly the opposite point, that Barlow's revisions brought form and content more tightly together and produced a poem that is more interesting and attractive than the *Vision* because it highlights more clearly the fissures and faultlines in the intellectual milieu of its day. Between the publication of the *Vision* in 1787 and the publication of the *Columbiad* twenty years later, Barlow had gone to Europe, where he had undertaken diplomatic missions on behalf of the United States government, made a fortune in business, and participated in the political, cultural, and social events of the day, becoming an honorary citizen of post-revolutionary France. The *Vision* had been published in London

nevertheless (29–43). Not everyone agrees that the role of the classics in American culture declined in the years immediately after the Revolutionary War: see Carl J. Richard, *The Founders and the Classics: Greece, Rome, and the American Enlightenment* (Cambridge, Mass., and London: Harvard Univ. Press, 1994), esp. 1–11. To make things even more confusing, however, Lee Pearcy, *The Grammar of Our Civility: Classical Education in America* (Waco, Tex.: Baylor Univ. Press, 2006) argues that there was a good deal of ambivalence from the beginning about the place of the classics in America. I believe that the situation as I have described it helps to account for what was going on with Barlow's poem, but part of this territory is obviously contested at present.

[104] Woodress, *A Yankee's Odyssey*, 246.
[105] Emory Elliott, *Revolutionary Writers: Literature and Authority in the New Republic, 1725–1810* (New York: OUP, 1982), 114.

and Paris as well as in the US, and the *Columbiad* would be as well, suggesting that Barlow had his mind on foreign as well as domestic markets. During his time in Europe his beliefs had evolved—his republicanism became more radical and his religious beliefs passed from orthodoxy into deism (although not into atheism)—which is certainly part of the reason he undoubtedly felt dissatisfied with the *Vision*. If he had redone the *Vision* by stripping it of its classical epic trappings and creating some new American form appropriate to his new American ideology, Barlow would undoubtedly have fared better at the hands of both the politically progressive critics of his day and, I suspect, the literary historians of ours, who have traced the main movement of American literary history as away from Neoclassicism toward the emerging Romanticism of the early nineteenth century.[106]

In strengthening the poem's ties to Virgilian epic, however, Barlow actually increased its capacity to speak to audiences in Europe without, he undoubtedly hoped, losing much at home. By making the *Columbiad* into a more clearly classical epic than the *Vision* had been,[107] Barlow was able to make the argument in favour of the new American way of life in terms that should have been more persuasive than the original had been in the old world, where everyone still read the *Aeneid* in school and the appropriate form for a long poem about nationhood and values was still the epic. Barlow was back in the United States to see his revised poem through the press in the final months before publication, where the ambivalence towards the classics in general, and Virgil in particular, had grown even greater than it had been during the time when he was writing the *Vision*. His solution, to be sure, had the air of subterfuge about it: to attack his model as others were doing at the same time as he tightened the links to it. But Barlow was less than straightforward about other aspects of the *Columbiad* as well: for example, he claimed in the dedication that the work 'has cost me nothing but that

---

[106] Lawrence Buell, *New England Literary Culture: From Revolution through Renaissance* (Cambridge: CUP, 1986), 86.

[107] Conger, 'Toward', 558. As Benjamin T. Spencer notes, within the overriding concern at its beginnings to stake out a peculiarly American literature, different from those in contemporary Europe and the ancient world, no one in the United States challenged the traditional hierarchy of genres which was presided over by the epic; see *The Quest for Nationality: An American Literary Campaign* (Syracuse, NY: Syracuse Univ. Press, 1957), 39, 58.

leisurely and exhilarating labor in which I always delight' (p. iv), even though he in fact had financed publication himself, putting up $10,000 of his own money, only half of which would be recovered even if every copy sold. Nevertheless, the strategy he adopted brought him into line with the Virgilian tag that accompanied a biblical poem in the *New Haven Gazette* of 21 September 1786: 'Sicilides Musae, paulo maiora canamus' (*Ecl.* 4. 1; in the author's paraphrase, 'American Muses aim at higher subjects than those commonly sung in the Eastern continent', even while continuing to do so in Eastern terms).[108]

The one thing we must not forget, however, was that Barlow was a 'pessimist' at a time when most readers of the *Aeneid* saw the poem in more 'optimistic' terms. In criticizing Virgil for aiming to 'increase the veneration of the people for a master', Barlow made an obvious gesture both towards the prevailing interpretation of the poem in Europe and towards the growing dissatisfaction with that interpretation on the other side of the Atlantic. As we have seen, however, his own reading was considerably more nuanced, making audible the 'other voices' in Virgil's poem and using them to make his account of the settlement of the new world anything but a straightforward encomium of Aeneas's European successors. Some readers of Barlow's day, like John Quincy Adams and Brockden Brown, may well have agreed, and some other poets like Ercilla even went so far as to construct Virgilian imitations along the same lines. But the full-blown 'pessimistic' reading of the *Aeneid* was not articulated until the late twentieth century, and only after that did it achieve widespread popularity. In choosing this form to represent the American Revolution, Barlow made a decision that cost him in the end on both sides of the Atlantic: in England the *Aeneid* was generally given a pro- rather than anti-imperial interpretation, and in America the links with the classical past became even more tenuous in the years following the publication of the *Columbiad*. In this sense his poem may indeed be considered a failure. The *Columbiad*, however, tells us a good deal about how the form in which a narrative is invested determines how the past is represented.

---

[108] Michael T. Gilmore, 'Literature of the Revolutionary and Early National Periods, 4. Poetry', in Sacvan Bercovitch (ed.), *The Cambridge History of American Literature*, i. *1590–1820* (Cambridge: CUP, 1994), notes that American literature of this period was built on precisely this paradox, that it would become distinctive and surpass works written in England while remaining thoroughly indebted to English models (594–6).

3. LE PLAT'S *VIRGILE EN FRANCE*: REVOLUTION AND REPRESSION

> In an era when television and radio did not challenge the suprem-
> acy of the printed word, books aroused emotions and stirred
> thoughts with a power we can barely imagine today.... Eight-
> eenth-century Frenchmen understood enough about communi-
> cation to expect readers and readings to be diverse. But they
> believed that *livres philosophiques* could produce powerful
> responses and that *libelles* could upset the stability of the state.
>
> (Robert Darnton, *Forbidden Best-Sellers*[109])

If the *Columbiad* seems at first to be an unusual choice for an
extended analysis at the beginning of the twenty-first century,
then the subject of this final section, Victor Alexandre Chrétien Le
Plat du Temple's *Virgile en France*, may well appear downright
perverse. Subtitled *La nouvelle Énéide, poëme héroï-comique en
style franco-gothique... pour servir de'esquisse à l'histoire de nos
jours*,[110] the poem as we have it is a travesty of the first six books of
the *Aeneid* which makes the events of the poem into an allegory of the
French Revolution.

Le Plat's allegorical overlay is unusual, but there is in fact a
long series of early modern Virgilian travesties in all the major
western European languages.[111] In English, Charles Cotton began
his version of the *Aeneid* like this:

---

[109] Robert Darnton, *The Forbidden Best-Sellers of Pre-Revolutionary France* (New York and London: W. W. Norton, 1995), 217, 226.

[110] Victor Alexandre Chrétien Le Plat du Temple, *Virgile en France...*, 2 vols. (Brussels: Weissenbruch, 1807–8); references to my copy of this edn., with my trs., will be placed in the text. A brief preliminary consideration of this work appeared in Craig Kallendorf, 'The *Aeneid* Transformed: Illustration as Interpretation from the Renaissance to the Present', in Sarah Spence (ed.), *Poets and Critics Read Vergil* (New Haven and London: Yale Univ. Press, 2001), 135–7.

[111] The outline that appears in the next few paragraphs presents only the basics; much more work needs to be done on all the early modern Virgilian travesties. I shall be returning to this material at greater length in a chapter of a book on which I am now beginning work, tentatively entitled 'Tilting at Troy: Virgil's *Aeneid* and the Birth of the Novel'.

I Sing the Man (read it who list,
A *Trojan* true as ever pist)
Who from *Troy*-Town, by Wind and Weather,
To *Italy* (and God knows whither)
Was pack'd, and rack'd, and lost, and tost,
And bounc'd from Pillar unto Post.[112]

This irreverent tone may surprise a modern reader who has been conditioned to see Virgil's poem as a 'great book' of high seriousness and import, but it characterizes all these earlier burlesques. Milton's nephew John Phillips, for example, begins his parody of book 5 like this:

While *Dido* in a Bed of Fire,
A new-found way to cool desire,
Lay wrapt in smoke, half Cole, half *Dido*,
Too late repenting Crime *Libido*,
Monsieur Aeneas went his ways;
For which I con him little praise,
To leave a Lady, not ith'mire,
But which was worser, in the fire.
He Neuter-like, had no great aim,
To kindle or put out the flame.[113]

It is hard to imagine that anyone could find humour in this scene, but Phillips did, mingling verbal cleverness with an anti-French barb (Monsieur Aeneas was behaving like a Frenchman, right?) and a pointed question about the masculinity of a 'Neuter-like' hero.

Neither of these travesties is well known today, but that of Giovanni Battista Lalli was still being reprinted in the nineteenth century and has merited at least a footnote in contemporary scholarship.[114] The best-known of the group, however, is definitely the *Virgile travesti* of Paul Scarron. Beginning in 1648 Scarron began publishing his parody of the *Aeneid*, one book at a time, with the eighth book

---

[112] Charles Cotton, *Scarronides: or, Virgil Travestie. A Mock-Poem on the First and Fourth Books of Virgil's Aeneis, in English Burlesque* (Whitehaven: J. Dunn & T. Evans, 1776), 3 (my copy).

[113] John Phillips, *Maronides or Virgil Travestie: Being a new Paraphrase Upon the Fifth Book of Virgils Aeneids in Burlesque Verse* (London: Nathaniel Brooks, 1672), 1 (my copy).

[114] Giuliano Mambelli, *Gli annali delle edizioni virgiliane* (Florence: Leo S. Olschki, 1954), 327–8, lists ten edns. from the *editio princeps* in 1633 to a Sicilian edn. in 1836, with the work being most accessible in the *Virgilio Eneide travestita di Giovanni Battista Lalli*... (Florence: G. Ricci & G. Becherini, nella tipografia Ciardetti, 1822).

appearing after his death; the project was completed by Moreau de Brasei. Scarron's bibliographer lists dozens of editions through the seventeenth and eighteenth centuries, with modern editions appearing in 1858 and in 1988. Thanks to Scarron Virgilian burlesques immediately became fashionable in France, with a second book by Du Fresnoy appearing in 1649, a fourth by Furetière in the same year, and two book 6s at approximately the same time, the first by one C.M.C.P.D. again in 1649, the second by the similarly anonymous L.D.L. three years later.[115]

The best known of the German parodies is that of Alois Blumauer, which marks an important turn in the way the Virgilian burlesques were handled. Blumauer's travesty, which was popular through the eighteenth century and has been reprinted regularly through the twentieth, is much freer than those of Cotton and Phillips, using the Virgilian machinery to comment on non-Virgilian people and actions. For example, at the point in the descent to the underworld where Aeneas and the Sibyl reach the fork in the road, Aeneas asks to see lower Hell, which was instead described to him by the Sibyl in the *Aeneid* (*Aen.* 6. 562 ff.). In Blumauer's version he and the Sibyl meet Satan in a scene that has a distinctly Alice in Wonderland quality, with Satan being presented as an infernal cook in a hellish kitchen that is infused with more than a little of Dante's spirit:

> Die große Höllenküche sah
>   Der Held nicht ohne Regung.
> Viel tausend Hände waren da
>   So eben in Bewegung,
> Um für des Satans leckere
> Gefräßigkeit ein groß Soupé
>   Auf heute zu bereiten.
>
> Als Oberküchenmeister stand
>   Mit einem Herz von Eisen
> Hier Pater Kochem, und erfand
>   Und ordnete die Speisen.

[115] Bibliographical information on Scarron's burlesque may be found in Jacques-Charles Brunet, *Manuel du libraire et de l'amateur de livres...*, 6 vols. with supplement (Paris: Firmin Didot, 1860), v. 184–5, s.v. 'Scarron, Paul'; and E. Magne, *Bibliographie générale des œuvres de Scarron* (Paris: L. Giraud Badin, 1924). The poem itself may be found in Paul Scarron, *Le Virgile travesti*, ed. Jean Serroy (Paris: Garnier, 1988). See also Luigi de Nardis, 'Virgilio "deriso" in Francia nel XVII secolo', in *La fortuna di Virgilio*, 193–206.

> Er ging beständig hin und her,
> Und kommandirt' als Oberer
>   Das Küchenpersonale.
>
> Hier sott man Wucherseelen weich,
>   Dort wurden Advokaten
> Gespickt, da sah man Domherrnbäuch'
>   In großen Pfannen braten;
> Und dort stieß man zu köstlichen
>   Kraftsuppen die berühmtesten
>   Genies in einem Mörser.
>
> Hier böckelt man Prälaten ein,
>   Dort frikassirt man Fürsten,
> Da hackt man große Geister klein
>   Zu Cervellate-Würsten,
> Da hängt man Schmeichler in den Rauch,
> Und räuchert sie, dort macht man auch
>   Aus Kutscherseelen Rostbeef.

The hero saw the great kitchen of Hell and did not remain unmoved. Many thousand hands were there in motion just so, in order to prepare a grand banquet today for Satan's tasty gluttony.

Here 'Father Cook 'em' stood as supreme head chef, with a heart of iron, devising and ordering the dishes. He went about constantly here and there, and as the boss gave orders to the kitchen staff.

Here usurers were boiled soft, there lawyers were larded, and there one saw prebendary paunches frying in large pans; and there the most famous geniuses were ground in a mortar to a costly, strong broth.

Here clerics are turned to salt meat, there princes are fricasseed, there great minds are chopped into small pieces of salami, there flatterers are hung in the smoke and cured, there roast beef is made of coachmen.[116]

This is a burlesque of the *Aeneid*, but the world of salted clerics and fricasseed princes, of boiled usurers and larded lawyers, is the world of early modern Europe, not ancient Rome.

Inspired in part by Blumauer, *Virgile en France* positions itself within this tradition, developing a parody of the *Aeneid* that comments on the world of the parodist.[117] In Le Plat's poem, Troy is France, or more

---

[116] *Virgils Aeneis travestiert von A. Blumauer in neuen Gesängen von Franz Seitz...* (Leipzig: K. F. Köhler, 1841), 184–6.

[117] Ed. van Even, 'Victor-Alexandre-Chrètien Leplat', in *Biographie nationale, publiée par L'Académie Royale des Sciences, des Lettres et des Beaux-Arts de Belgique* (Brussels: Émile Bruylant, 1890–1), xi. 885.

specifically Paris, and the Greeks who sack Troy are the Jacobins who enter the city by guile, hidden in the Trojan horse of *liberté* through which the Reign of Terror is introduced. Aeneas's wanderings take him from the new world back to the old one, from Haiti to Belgium and Switzerland, then down the Dalmatian coast to Egypt, where Dido lives, and eventually to Rome. The French verses in which this story is conveyed have been described as 'grotesques et fort bizarres' ('grotesque and most strange'),[118] and the text is accompanied by lengthy notes which strain the reader's credulity even further: for example, Le Plat claims that people are divided into religious factions that parallel the political ones, so that the Spanish, Italians, and Belgians are religious monarchists, the French and Germans are the aristocrats of faith, and the Protestants represent democracy (1. 296).

It appears that readers of his own day had as much trouble figuring out what to make of this as we do now. Le Plat's scholarly note on the word *Chimaera*, for example, explains that this animal terrorizes Holland in the form of two journals, *Vaderlandsche Letter-Oeffeningen* and *Vaderlandsche Bibliotheek*, which had severely criticized the original Flemish version of the poem that had been published in 1803. But they were not the only ones, Le Plat continues, for other critics had denigrated him as an 'ape of Scarron', then insulted him with a bewildering variety of epithets: buffoon and barbarian, liar and slanderer, an author of mediocre talent and impoverished imagination, etc. (1. 178–81). One cannot help but feel bad for the author—it is, after all, difficult to imagine any writer who really deserves all this—until we realize that Le Plat has inadvertently weakened his own position: who reprints all the negative reviews of his own work in the next edition? The poem is a satire, which, Le Plat explains, is designed to instruct, to amuse, and to correct. The last goal, he continues, is often not attained (1, p. xxvi), so he sets out in *Virgile en France* to criticize the Belgians with special enthusiasm: the people are liars, the aristocracy corrupt (1. 292–6), the clergy degraded (2. 189–93), and so forth. In hindsight, then, the decision to publish the book in Brussels was not a wise one, and Le Plat should not have been surprised to find himself treated harshly at the hands of the Belgian press (2. 189–93). In response to such criticism, Le Plat proposed a sort of journalistic police that would

<hr>

[118] Brunet, *Manuel du libraire*, v. 1305.

enforce laws keeping the freedom of the press from being abused (1. 178–81). Ironically he got his wish, for after the first two volumes of his poem were published, Napoleon's agents seized all the copies they could find and tried to prevent Le Plat from finishing the work.[119]

In a sense, then, we have come full circle, ending our study with another poem like Filelfo's *Sphortias* that, initially at least, looks like a failure that was unable even to make its way into print easily. Once again, I shall argue that we can sometimes learn more from the failures of literary history than from its successes. And once again, I believe it is Le Plat's insistence on reading Virgil 'pessimistically', so to speak—his sympathetic response to, and vigorous rearticulation of, the 'other voices' in the *Aeneid*—that ultimately made *Virgile en France* a more revolutionary document than the authorities of the day felt they could tolerate.

Initially it is difficult to pin down Le Plat's attitude towards the events he is describing. Much of the force of the allegory is carried in the notes, and here the author's sympathies appear to vacillate. Early on he waxes enthusiastic about freedom of religion as a benefit of the revolution, 'qui enfanta si peu de biens parmi tant de maux' ('which has brought forth so few good things among so many evils'; 1. 66). Next Le Plat lists a group of nobles who died courageously, in accordance with their ideals: Mme la princesse de Lamballe, who returned from England to die with her queen (1. 75); Mme Elisabeth, sister of Louis XVI, who 'consomma son martyre' ('accomplished her martyrdom') as a model of fraternal love (1. 76); and Mme Roland Phelippon, who 'alla au supplice avec un courage stoïque' ('went to her punishment with a stoic bravery'; 1. 77). The condemnation of

---

[119] Van Even, 'Victor-Alexandre-Chrétien Le Plat', xi. 884–6. See also J. M. Qué-rard, *Le France littéraire, ou dictionnaire bibliographique*... (Paris: G.-P. Maisonneuve et Larose, n.d.), vii. 192. The Brussels edn. breaks off halfway through the *Aeneid*. Two later edns. contain 3rd and 4th vols. that carry the parody through to its conclusion. The later edns. only survive in institutional hands in composite sets in which some of the 1807–8 vols. are mixed with later ones, the first repr. (Offenbach: C. L. Brede, 1810) in the British Library and the second one in the Bibliothèque nationale de France (Darmstadt: Stahl, 1812); I was recently able to buy a copy of the 3rd vol. of the 1812 edn. as well. Both of the reprints were published away from the easy reach of Napoleon's agents. My story, however, is focused not on the poem Le Plat may have intended to write, but on his intervention in the history of Napoleonic France and the work done by *Virgile en France* in that time and place, so I shall restrict my discussion to the two volumes published in the Brussels *editio princeps*.

the king is presented as treasonable treachery (1. 100 ff.), with Le Plat's sympathies seeming to lie with 'le roi' ('the king', Louis XVI, in the person of Priam):

> Bravant ses ennemis, et ne voulant verser
> Le sang de sus sujets, il s'en laissa juger,
> Victime en même temps de fraternelle envie,
> Et du double poignard d'ouverte calomnie,
> On le condamne à mort: des fidèles sujets
> Il emporte au tombeau les éternels regrets.
> On étouffe sa voix sur le lieu du supplice:
> Et le bourreau l'immole ainsi qu'une genisse,
> Sur le sanglant autel de la divinité;
> Offrant aux spectateurs son chef ensanglanté.
> Tel fut le sort du roi: quand sa triste patrie,
> Ressemblant à son tronc et sans tête et sans vie,
> Répandit tout son sang; tel fut le sort des lis
> Dont la tige enfanta tant de héros chéris.[120]

(1. 135–6)

Confronting his enemies, and not wanting to shed the blood of his subjects, he let himself be judged; victim at the same time of fraternal jealousy and of the double dagger of open slander, he is condemned to death: he carries to his grave the everlasting regrets of his faithful subjects. His voice is choked off at the place of punishment, and the executioner slays him like a heifer, on the bloody altar of the god, offering to the observers his bloody head. Such was the fate of the king: when his grieving country, headless and lifeless like his trunk, poured out all its blood; such was the fate of the lilies, of which the stem brought forth so many cherished heroes.

At this sight, Aeneas recoils:

> Lorsque je vis tomber sa tête infortunée
> Sous le coup criminel de la hache sacrée,
> J'eprouvai ce frisson, ce mouvement d'horreur,
> Qui révolte l'esprit et fait frémir le coeur.

(1. 136)

When I see his unfortunate head fall under the unlawful blow of the sacred axe, I felt this chill, this impulse of horror, which shocks the spirit and makes the heart shudder.

---

[120] This is the same passage on which the royalist translator Sir John Dehnam dwelt; see above, p. 143.

It is certainly possible for readers to remind themselves that the story requires Aeneas, who is telling the story of the fall of Troy to Dido, to respond in this way and that the author's sympathies do not necessarily lie with him. We must also remember, however, that Virgilian criticism has had unusual difficulty in making such distinctions in the poem that Le Plat is rewriting,[121] and when Aeneas, and/or the author, continues to refer to the 'triste régicide' ('sad murder of the king') and finds himself 'Pleurant le sort cruel de ce prince innocent' ('weeping for the cruel fate of this innocent prince', 1. 137), we do not find the distinctions any easier to make. Indeed, when we survey the band of Trojan survivors at the end of book 2, among whom are royalists, republicans, and anarchists, we may well wonder which party, exactly, Aeneas represents and with whom Le Plat's sympathies lie.

In other places Le Plat sounds not so much like a crypto-royalist as a simple conservative, a *laudator temporis acti* who found life under the Ancien Régime preferable to life in post-revolutionary times. In a comment that concludes the notes to book 4, Le Plat rails against atheism, deism, and materialism which 'font des progrès étonnans de nos jours' ('make astonishing progress in our time', 2. 100). Near the beginning of the next book, he introduces a long critique of lawyers with a more general analysis of post-revolutionary society that makes him sound reactionary: 'Parmi les maux révolutionnaires engendrés par la liberté, l'égalité et la fraternité, la confusion des états n'est sans doute pas le moindre; parce que c'est une source permanente qui perpétue les fléaux de la societé' ('Among the revolutionary evils brought forth by liberty, equality, and fraternity, the confusion of stations is without doubt not the least, because it is a permanent source which perpetuates the calamities of society', 2. 165). One of the unfortunate results of this confusion, as we might predict, is that the republic

---

[121] See Philip Hardie, *Virgil* (Oxford: OUP, 1998), 71–9; and Don Fowler, 'Deviant Focalization in Vergil's *Aeneid*', in *Roman Constructions: Readings in Postmodern Latin* (Oxford: OUP, 2000), 49–50. To my mind, Brooks Otis's magisterial *Virgil: A Study in Civilized Poetry* (Norman, Okla., and London: Univ. of Oklahoma Press, 1995; repr. of Oxford, 1964 edn.) confused the distinctions among author, narrator, and character at the same time as it focused, rightly, on Virgil's peculiarly 'subjective' style. The work of Gian Biagio Conte, in turn, provides a powerful tool for making distinctions like this; see e.g. 'Virgil's *Aeneid*: Toward an Interpretation', in *The Rhetoric of Imitation: Genre and Poetic Memory in Virgil and Other Latin Poets*, ed. and tr. Charles Segal (Ithaca, NY, and London: Cornell Univ. Press, 1986), 141–84.

of letters has descended into anarchy, with the unprincipled and uneducated usurping the roles once occupied by men of talent (2. 179–80). In an area where, not unexpectedly, Le Plat shows special interest, the argument is followed through to its logical conclusion: 'Du temps de Louis XIV, il régnait une harmonie entr'eux qui les faisait réunir et former les sociétés les plus brillantes et les plus aimables. Il régnait parmi eux une égalité d'état et de considération qui n'existe plus aujourd'hui' ('In the time of Louis XIV there reigned a harmony among them that brought them together and formed the most brilliant and amiable associations. There ruled among them an equality of station and of respect that does not exist any more today', 2. 213–14).

So far it seems that Le Plat is on track toward a traditional reading of the *Aeneid*, one in which Virgil's support for Augustus is swept up into support for the kings and emperors of later eras. Other voices, however, intrude and complicate this perception considerably. Le Plat's retelling of the love story between Dido and Aeneas, for example, contains some significant changes which seem to have been designed to exculpate Dido and make Aeneas's behaviour look even worse than in the *Aeneid*. Dido's sister Anna, for example, is replaced by her confessor (2. 1 ff.), so that when she tries to decide how to handle the passions rising up within her, she does so not with the aid and support of a sympathetic sister but with the guidance of the church. This is part of a broader effort in *Virgile en France* to Christianize the *Aeneid*, which results in an uneasy juxtaposition of elements from pagan and Christian religion.[122] For example, Juno

---

[122] Such Christianization of the *Aeneid* and of various aspects of ancient culture associated with it was still common in Le Plat's day. For example, in the 1620s the engraver Martin Droeshout published a set of engravings entitled *XXII Sibyllarum Icones. The Prophecies of the Twelve Sybills Plainely foretelling the Incarnation, Birth, Life, Death, and comming againe to Judgment of our Lord and Saviour Jesus Christ* (London: Roger Daniell, [*c.*1620–5?]). Attention focused esp. on the Cumaean Sibyl, who accompanied Aeneas in his descent to the underworld in *Aeneid* 6. The verses in Droeshout's book that accompany the portrait of the Cumaean Sibyl make the Christian associations clear: 'A warlicke King, a sacred virgin beares, | The flow're of Bewty in his tender yeares, | She hanges the joy of all upon her breast | Discover'd by a starre shone from the East; | To whome the wisemen gold, myrrhe, incense bringe, | As to a Preist, a Prophet, and a King.' The subject retained its popularity to the end of the 17th cent., with later sets of these illustrations being printed by Christoffel van Sichem the elder and Clement de Jonghe; see *English Books: New Acquisitions*, Bernard Quaritch, Catalogue 1336 (London, 2006).

proposes that a priest be present at the scene in the cave where Aeneas and Dido are joined together (see Figure 11), and Venus agrees, knowing that under Trojan (i.e. French) law, a religious ceremony without a civil union is not binding (2. 11). This makes Aeneas responsible for deception, since he can reasonably be expected to know the laws of his own country and Dido cannot; indeed he tries to label the union as a 'Kabin', a temporary marriage contracted under her laws (2. 28), even though Dido never agreed to anything like this. These are details, but they work consistently to increase the reader's sympathy for Dido.

In book 5 the Trojan women rise up in revolt, setting the ships on fire and ultimately receiving the opportunity to stay behind and leave the men to continue the trip to their promised land. This scene can be interpreted in two ways, depending on whether one follows an 'optimistic' or a 'pessimistic' interpretation of the *Aeneid*: one can focus on Aeneas's mission and the need to sacrifice the weaker women to the heroic ideal, or one can focus on the legitimate feelings of those who are tired, afraid, and confused, more concerned with resuming normal family and civic life than with a seemingly endless journey.[123] Le Plat does the latter, producing a long note in which he explains that religion and politics have conspired throughout history to oppress women. Women and men, he writes, are both physically perfect: men are stronger and women are more beautiful, but if given a choice, women would not choose to trade places with men. Indeed, women are morally superior to men. There are, to be sure, two specifically female vices, slander and debauchery, but women fall into these vices through the fault of men, and the other vices (greed, ambition, etc.) are solely male (2. 244–5). Unfortunately, things have got worse rather than better of late, for '[l]a révolution française n'a rien enfanté en faveur des femmes: au contraire, leur condition est détériorée depuis cette époque; car les lois sont plus

---

[123] It is worth stressing once again, as I noted in the preface, that, while the labels 'optimistic' and 'pessimistic' can direct our attention to a very real and useful divergence in the path of Virgilian criticism, they highlight a difference in emphasis, not a radical distinction. In other words, responsible 'optimistic' criticism acknowledges that at least at the beginning of the *Aeneid*, Aeneas is far from perfect, while responsible 'pessimistic' criticism in turn acknowledges that the foundation of the Roman Empire brought considerable benefits to a great many people. See also the discussion of gender in Virgilian interpretation at the end of Ch. 2.

Figure 11. 'For Dido calls it marriage, | And with this name she covers up her fault' (Aen. 4.172). Le Plat, *Virgile en France...* (Brussels: Weissenbruch, 1807–8), after ii, p. viii

[handwritten margin annotations: "defends Le Plat as 'a man of his times'"]

rigides envers elles qu'auparavant' ('the French revolution has not brought forth anything for the benefit of women: on the contrary, their condition has deteriorated since that time, because the laws are more severe toward them than before', 2. 248). Some of this will undoubtedly not sit well with a modern feminist, but within the options available at the beginning of the nineteenth century, Le Plat has developed a line of argument that is notably sympathetic to those who were marginalized and oppressed in the society of his day.

This sympathy continues into a brief discussion of the Jews. This discussion appears in a note to the section of book 6 that contains the vision of the coming glories of Rome. The note veers into a long digression on how families receive their surnames, concluding with the observation that the Jews have in general retained their old custom of not adopting family names, although this is beginning to change in Germany. Political change, he continues, will precede the religious conversion of the Jews, and Le Plat is enough a man of his day to seem to suggest that this conversion is desirable. But he then quotes a Bishop Grégoire to the effect that whatever vices the Jews exhibit 'sont le résultat de leur oppression par les chrétiens' ('are the result of their oppression by the Christians', 2. 379–80), and that it is important for them and for the Christians that the Jews be fully integrated into the emerging nation-states of Europe (2. 380). Again, parts of this do not look as progressive today as they did two hundred years ago, but for a man of his times, Le Plat once again shows real sympathy for the powerless and a determination to make the powerful accountable for the results of their actions.

In other words, at several key places Le Plat responds to and strengthens the 'other voices' in the poem, the ones that remind the reader of all that has been lost in creating the Roman Empire and the kingdoms and empires that followed it. Thus although Augustus traced his roots to Aeneas, Le Plat's Aeneas in the final analysis is not an imperialist, but a republican. Notwithstanding the nostalgic glances back into the past that I have noted above, Aeneas aligns himself throughout the poem with 'les bons républicains' ('the good republicans', e.g. 1. 123, 1. 128), and when he follows Anchises' prophecy to return to his ancestral home (here interpreted as being Belgium) to set up a new government, what he establishes is clearly called a 'republic':

J'exhortais les sujets de ma nouvelle Troie,
A vivre librement comme nous dans la joie....
J'avais fait adopter mon décret organique
Et mon code nouveau dans cette république.

(1. 213)

I urged the subjects of my new Troy to live freely as we do in joy.... I have
had my integral order and my new code adopted in this republic.

This reminds us of a fundamental fact about *Virgile en France*: Le Plat's
allegory of the Trojan War makes the *Aeneid* into a story about the
French Revolution, and the outcome of the French Revolution, at least
initially, was a republic. This is much further, we recall, than either
Milton or Barlow had gone: Milton wrote a poem about a revolt in
Heaven whose Virgilian references to politics on earth remained tan-
talizingly oblique, while Barlow used the oscillation between Virgil's
support for and critique of empire to try to position his account of the
American Revolution between the old monarchies of Europe and the
new republic in America. Le Plat rewrote the source text itself to make
it describe France's passage from monarchy to republic.

    There is, however, one problem with all this: at the time *Virgile en
France* was published, France was no longer a republic, but an empire
under the control of Napoleon Bonaparte. Napoleon does not play
much of a part in the half of the poem that ended up being printed.
The few references we do find are positive enough, which might
suggest at least initially that this problem could have been manage-
able. In book 1 Le Plat recounts some of Napoleon's early military
successes, 'où il avait commencé à développer ces grands talens qui
l'ont élevé au rang suprême' ('where he had begun to cultivate his
great abilities which have raised him to the highest class', 1. 64).
Shortly afterward Le Plat describes the process by which France
passed from republic to empire:

C'est à la fin du mois de Floréal an XII, 1804, que Bonaparte, premier consul
de la république française, fut proclamé empereur des Français. Des registres
furent ouverts dans toutes les villes de la France pour recevoir les voeux des
citoyens, dont la saine majorité, convaincue du besoin et du penchant
naturel de la France vers l'état monarchique, déclara le désir de voir le
sceptre de l'empire placé dans les mains de celui qui avait le plus mérité de
la patrie, et qui pouvait le plus dignement en soutenir le poids. Toutes les

factions se turent: Carnot seul fit entendre quelques objections dans le tribunat, mais il ne se trouva personne qui joignît son avis au sien. Tous les orateurs dans le sénat, le corps législatif, prononcèrent des discours pour démontrer la nécessité de fixer les destinées de la France par la seul mode de gouvernement qui pût lui convenir. Les divers corps civils et militaires déclarèrent le même voeu dans un nombre infini d'adresses qui furent publiées à cette époque. C'est peut-être l'unique exemple que nous offre l'histoire d'un empereur élu par souscription.   (1. 65–6)

At the end of the month of Floreal, in 1804, the twelfth year of the republic, Bonaparte, first consul of the French Republic, was declared emperor of the French. The registers were open in all the cities of France to receive the votes of the citizens, of which the sound majority, convinced of the need and the natural inclination of France towards the state of monarchy, declared the wish to see the sceptre of empire placed in the hands of the one man in the country who was most deserving and who was able to bear its weight most worthily. All the political factions were silent: Carnot alone saw to it that some objections were heard at the tribunate, but he did not find anyone who accepted his advice. All the speakers in the senate, the legislature, spoke in demonstration of the need to settle the destinies of France through the only form of government which was able to suit it. The different civil and military bodies declared the same wish in an endless number of speeches which were published at this time. This is perhaps the only example history offers us of an emperor elected by subscription.

I have quoted this passage at some length because it has important implications for the reception of the poem as a whole. On the one hand, this account of how he became emperor is certainly flattering to Napoleon, who is presented as popular among the governed and legitimate in his authority. On the other hand, though, there is a suggestion here that authority rests in the people, who could also, it would seem, remove Napoleon at will. This suggestion is amplified in a note to book 5 in which Le Plat explains that the power of the governor and the liberty of the governed rest in 'droit public' ('common law'), which sets out the reciprocal obligations of both parties. These obligations prevent both despotism and anarchy, for the governor who follows them will not abuse his power and the governed will not revolt (2. 207–8). Again it seems clear that an emperor who abuses the 'droit public' must be replaced, the idea seeming to be that the free citizens of a republic can choose temporarily to transfer some of their power to an executive, but that they can also take it back again when they want. Le Plat's *Aeneid* thus remains a pro-republican poem, not the allegorical support for the establishment of the new Roman Empire on the Seine that Napoleon would undoubtedly have preferred.[124] *Virgile en France*, in other words, was a thoroughly subversive document, and Napoleon responded by seizing all the copies he could find and trying to prevent the author from finishing the work.

This might, perhaps, ascribe too much power to a book that no one today has ever heard of, but then again it might not, since the obscurity of the work is due at least in part to the suppression of the Brussels edition by the censors—not total, to be sure, but enough to make copies hard to find and to delay the completion and publication of the French version.[125] What is more, it is worth noting that the historiography of the French Revolution has traditionally granted a prominent place to the power of books and the ideas they contain to change history.[126] The crown in eighteenth-century France expended a good deal of time and effort trying to control books that it considered subversive, so that in 1764 only 40 per cent of the books published in Europe in the French language were officially licensed by the French authorities. Some of the other 60 per cent were

---

[124] i.e. the *Aeneid* could serve as support for either a republican or an imperialist in France at the turn of the 18th cent. As Jochen Hafner notes, the symbols of antiquity that saturated the French Revolution continued into the Napoleonic era: for example, Napoleon brought antique art, and art on the antique model, back to the Louvre from his Italian campaigns. See 'Revolution: II. Französische Revolution', in Manfred Landfester (ed.), *Der Neue Pauly: Enzyklopädie der Antike, Rezeptions- und Wissenschaftsgeschichte* (Stuttgart and Weimar: Verlag J. B. Metzler, 2002), xv/2, cols. 748–59.

[125] A fair number of copies seem to have escaped the police and entered circulation, so that today the Brussels edn. is available at the British Library; at Harvard, Princeton, and the Philipps Academy in Andover, Mass.; and the Bibliothèque municipale, Grenoble; Bibliothèque municipale, Versailles; Bibliothèque interuniversitaire de lettres et sciences humaines, Lyon; Bibliothèque municipale, Nantes; and Bibliothèque municipale, Chalons-en-Champagne. In addition a copy like the one I bought a couple of years ago comes on the market now and again. Ironically it therefore appears that the edn. Napoleon attempted to suppress is more common than the two reprints described in n. 119.

[126] Current discussion has taken up the question anew, debating whether the *philosophes* caused (or at least helped cause) the revolution, or whether the revolution allowed the constitution of a corpus that in hindsight was seen to have prepared and supported it; see Darnton, *The Forbidden Best-Sellers*, 169–246; and Roger Chartier, 'Do Books Make Revolutions?', in *The Cultural Origins of the French Revolution*, tr. Lydia G. Cochrane (Durham, NC, and London: Duke Univ. Press, 1991), 67–91, with accompanying bibliography.

pornographic, but a good many were the books of the *philosophes*, whose new ideas about government and society were seen as sufficiently threatening that when it was stormed on 14 July 1789, the Bastille was found to contain only seven human prisoners but every single one of the classic books of the Enlightenment, previously seized by the police and deposited there.[127] *Virgile en France* is thoroughly saturated with these same Enlightenment ideas: Voltaire and the other *philosophes* are cited freely,[128] and principles like government by social contract and the desirability of freedom of religion (both discussed above) permeate the text. The prevailing tone of the work is one of moderation and restraint, of the need for reason to prevail in all areas of life. Le Plat's two *bêtes noires* are political fanaticism, the Jacobinism that results from unrestrained popular sovereignty, and religious fanaticism, which goes hand-in-hand with it in an Enlightenment apocalypse that rewrites the Book of Revelation with considerably more power than Le Plat's carping reviewers were willing to credit (2. 265, 345–8). By the time the French version of *Virgile en France* was being printed, France was under the control of an emperor who was every bit as powerful as Louis XVI had been, and the ideas that helped topple a king could, presumably, topple an emperor as well if they were given free rein.

They were not, and therein, I suggest, lies the point. When I began my analysis of *Paradise Lost*, I noted that the traditional model postulated the *Aeneid* as Milton's source and encouraged us to look for ways in which seventeenth-century imitations of it reflected the historical events of the day. This model has proved increasingly unable to sustain the discussion in this chapter. Beginning with *Paradise Lost*, we have seen how Milton used his 'pessimistic' reading of the *Aeneid* to negotiate successfully the transition from Cromwell to Charles II, meditating on human failure while acknowledging the realities of political power within which he lived and worked. Barlow in turn used the 'other voices' in the *Aeneid*—somewhat tentatively in the *Vision*, then confidently in the *Columbiad*—to craft an epic whose efforts to control the understanding of the American Revolution

---

[127] Chartier, 'Do Books?', 70–81.
[128] e.g. Le Plat, *Virgile en France*, 56, the third note to book 1, which quotes from Voltaire's *Henriade* to describe London.

won him an audience among the generation that lived through it, even while his Virgilian allusions made him seem too conservative at home and his increasingly radical republicanism made him seem suspect abroad. The republicanism that emerged from Barlow's 'pessimistic' reading of the *Aeneid* swelled to a crescendo in *Virgile en France*, so that Le Plat lost the sense of balance that allowed Milton to navigate the treacherous waters of revolution and found his work confiscated by the agents of Napoleon, France's new Augustus. Each of these cases is different, but in each, literature is the vehicle by which writers act in the world around them. As Stephen Greenblatt puts it, 'history cannot simply be set against literary texts as either stable antithesis or stable background, and the protective isolation of those texts gives way to a sense of their interaction with other texts and hence of the permeability of their boundaries'.[129] This is indeed a new historicism, one that challenges us to re-examine fundamental definitions and to accord literature the power to make revolutions.

[129] Greenblatt, *Shakespearean Negotiations*, 95.

Conclusion

> We have been thro a poem that is one of the noblest monu-
> ments of the genius of the antients: it is a diamond, but not
> without flaws. . . . *Aeneas* asserted his claim to the *Italian*
> dominions as promised him by the gods, and fixed by fate:
> *Turnus* disputed his title very justly, for the other is a claim that
> any man may make. *Turnus* was guilty of no disobedience to the
> divine will. . . . [T]hey who read the *Aeneis* with taste and reason
> send their wishes along with *Turnus*, because he was right in his
> opposition, and because *Aeneas*'s title from heaven was not half
> so good as *Turnus*'s right of inheritance from his father *Daunus*.

(Thomas Cooke, commentary (1741) on *Aeneid* 12. 952[1])

Fifteen years ago it was assumed that the only *Aeneid* available to
early modern readers was an 'optimistic' one, with Aeneas serving as
an exemplar of virtue who established the Roman state as the political and ideological base for the institutions of that culture and the
ones that traced their origins to it. Initially, as we might have
expected, the suggestions that there could be another story to tell
were hesitant. First Lauren Scancarelli Seem identified the Possevino
passage discussed in Chapter 1 and highlighted its importance for
Virgilian criticism. Next Diana Robin tentatively proposed the possibility that Francesco Filelfo, who turns out to be a key figure in this
story, might have seen some of the same ambiguity and moral

---

[1] Publius Virgilius Maro, *Bucolica, Georgica, et Aeneis*, ed. Thomas Cooke (London:
Jacob Hodges, 1741), 454. As my argument through this book would suggest, Cooke's
commentary did not prove to be very popular: it was reprinted only once (Dublin,
1742), and both edns. are extremely rare. I have used the copy of the *editio princeps*,
from which the quotation is taken, that is in my collection, but there are only two other
copies of this book in institutional hands and one more of the reprint.

complexity in the *Aeneid* that the so-called 'Harvard' or 'pessimistic' school of late-twentieth-century readers saw. Then Joseph Sitterson, Jr. argued that Lodovico Ariosto might have seen as much pessimism in the ending of the *Aeneid* as a twentieth-century scholar of the 'Harvard school', though without explaining how a sixteenth-century reader could have arrived at such an insight. That explanation came several years later, when I provided some of the extracts discussed in Chapter 1 in which Francesco Petrarca, who effectively initiated the humanist movement in Italy, and the first generations of scholars who followed him, including Filelfo, raised real doubts about whether Aeneas achieved the goals he set for himself and about whether what he accomplished was an appropriate model for people living more than two thousand years afterwards. Two years after my article appeared, Richard Thomas published a groundbreaking book that established the existence of 'pessimistic' readings in antiquity and in modern writers who lived and worked considerably before the scholars in the post-Second World War period who are normally credited with initiating this approach to the *Aeneid*. Thomas also provided an insightful analysis that brings John Dryden's influential translation of the *Aeneid* into the discussion. This analysis complements nicely Colin Burrow's earlier observation that a good number of older English translations present an *Aeneid* of divided loyalties that cannot simply be aligned with the power of imperial Rome and its successors.[2] By this point, there was enough evidence to suggest that an original thinker of the early modern period could return to a familiar text from his school days and recover a reading that had been available in antiquity, ready to see a level of moral and ideological complexity that was neither appropriate to an educational environment nor in the best interests of those who supported it.

[2] Lauren Scancarelli Seem, 'The Limits of Chivalry: Tasso and the End of the *Aeneid*', *Comparative Literature*, 42 (1990), 116–18; Diana Robin, *Filelfo in Milan: Writings, 1451–1477* (Princeton: Princeton Univ. Press, 1991); Joseph C. Sitterson, Jr., 'Allusive and Elusive Meanings: Reading Ariosto's Virgilian Ending', *Renaissance Quarterly*, 45 (1992), 1–19; Craig Kallendorf, 'Historicizing the "Harvard School": Pessimistic Readings of the *Aeneid* in Italian Renaissance Scholarship', *Harvard Studies in Classical Philology*, 99 (1999), 391–403; Richard F. Thomas, *Virgil and the Augustan Reception* (Cambridge: CUP, 2001); and Colin Burrow, 'Virgil in English Translation', in Charles Martindale (ed.), *The Cambridge Companion to Virgil* (Cambridge: CUP, 1997), 21–37.

complexity not appropriate

children =
boys

Once the possibility had been established that a second way of reading the *Aeneid* 'against the grain', so to speak, existed alongside the more straightforward, official one, it was reasonable to ask more extensively where that reading is found and what it might mean in relation to key concerns within early modern culture. This book was designed to answer those questions. For example, in the days before copyright protection offered a writer the chance to earn a living by selling copies of his work, a writer needed a patron.[3] This was true in ancient Rome as well as in early modern Europe. A problem often emerged, however, when writers tried to balance their need for support against their desire to maintain their integrity and speak out, telling their patrons what they might not want to hear. This seems to have been a problem for Virgil, and again for Filelfo some fifteen hundred years later, so it should not surprise us to find that the *Sphortias* expresses some of the same anxieties about the author–patron relationship as the *Aeneid*. In the end, Filelfo proved less able than Virgil to maintain a balance in this area, but in its own way his failure teaches us as much as (for example) Milton's more successful Virgilian poem two centuries later.

As a school text, the *Aeneid* proved crucial in the formation of the early modern Self, for generations of schoolchildren learnt to see themselves through the eyes of Aeneas as they absorbed the values according to which they would live their lives. Yet as Stephen Greenblatt noted twenty-five years ago, Self is generally predicated against Other.[4]

---

[3] The slow development of copyright law, of course, changed the patronage system, so that a talented author in Augustan England e.g. could eventually make a living from publication royalties. Good recent information about these matters may be found in Joseph Loewenstein, *The Author's Due: Printing and the Prehistory of Copyright* (Chicago and London: Univ. of Chicago Press, 2002).

[4] A good deal of scholarly attention is currently being devoted to how a sense of selfhood developed in pre-modern times. This line of thought has been pursued with increasing intensity since the publication of Stephen Greenblatt's seminal study, *Renaissance Self-Fashioning* (Chicago and London: Univ. of Chicago Press, 1980); see esp. p. 9. A good idea of the current thinking on this issue may be gleaned from Timothy J. Reiss, *Mirages of the Selfe: Patterns of Personhood in Ancient and Early Modern Europe* (Stanford, Calif.: Stanford Univ. Press, 2003), which argues against the tendency to see the origins of a great many modern ways of thinking in the early modern period, but does so fairly and with an extensive survey of the evidence on both sides of the argument. Handwritten marginalia in early printed edns. of Virgil have contributed to this process of self-fashioning, as I have shown in 'Marginalia and the Rise of Early Modern Subjectivity', in Marianne Pade (ed.), *On Renaissance Commentaries* (Hildesheim: Olms, 2005), 111–28.

In the sixteenth and seventeenth centuries, one important Other is the indigenous inhabitant found in the new worlds encountered by the European explorers, and again, the *Aeneid* provided a model according to which the moral world of the schools could take on nuance and complexity. As we have seen, Virgil's narrative is striking in its sympathy for Dido and Turnus, for those who must fall in order for the new Roman state to rise. This is not to say that it would have been better if Rome, along with its political and spiritual descendants, had never come into being, but Ercilla, Shakespeare, and Sor Juana all used the *Aeneid* to show that the empire of the Self can only be established at great cost to the Other who falls aside along the way.

The end of the early modern period, like the end of the first century BC, was a time when revolution replaced one political system with another, and once again, the *Aeneid* provided a framework through which change could be effected and understood. The passage from the republic to the empire in ancient Rome was a tumultuous one, and the *Aeneid* captures both the sense of opportunity and the sense of loss that accompanied this tumult. It is little wonder, then, that poems written in imitation of it, in times of similar upheaval, should capture the same complexity of vision. As we have seen, *Paradise Lost* straddles the passage from the Commonwealth to the Restoration, providing a means by which Milton could negotiate the passage from one political system to another, aware of both loss and gain. Similarly, the *Columbiad* marks the movement from colony to independent state, coming to claim a position as the epic voice of a new country that was not always certain it wanted one. And *Virgile en France* struggles, in the end unsuccessfully, to hold a centrist ideology in times when extremism prevailed. In each case the *Aeneid* became a vehicle by which, in part at least, a new polity was stabilized.

Now that this story has been told, it might be useful to step back a bit from it to ask what this project might teach us more generally about how to write better literary history. Initially it is more than a little disconcerting to discover that this other Virgil, the one that complicates and challenges the one taught in the schools, has been so completely obscured for so many generations. One response, tempting perhaps if not ultimately reductive, might be simple euphoria: finally, once again, the ideology of the elite has been unmasked and

PL stabaliz the Restoration?

the arbitrary constructions of power have been revealed. The lesson for cultural historians of the future, I suppose, would then be: keep stripping away those masks. I am not sure, however, that this is a good general lesson to take from this specific example. For one thing, Virgil played a stronger role in the creation of early modern culture than any other classical author besides Cicero. A study like this one focused on the afterlife of Livy or Terence, for example, would certainly be rewarding but would undoubtedly offer less material to work with. More importantly, however, the *Aeneid* is a poem of unusual complexity, able to contain within itself multiple points of view that critique its own dominant values. Recognizing this complexity, as we have seen, helps explain why Virgilian poems like *La Araucana* and *Paradise Lost* have been interpreted in diametrically opposite ways. The *Aeneid*, however, may also have attracted a particular kind of admirer whose responses, both ideological and aesthetic, might not parallel those drawn to other classical authors.

There are, however, three suggestions for future research about which I feel more confidence that emerge from this study. The first is that modern scholars must extend the range of sources they consult as they study early modern culture. I first met Le Plat's travesty, along with a good many others, in the Rare Books and Special Collections Department of the Princeton University Library, whose holdings include the incomparable collection of early printed editions of Virgil assembled by Junius S. Morgan, the nephew of the financier J. P. Morgan.[5] Yet as the rare books curator at this library has confirmed, very few people who write on the *fortuna* of Virgil ever

---

[5] The Morgan Collection, which contains 738 books and a handful of MSS, was given to Princeton University by Junius Spencer Morgan (1867–1932, Princeton Class of 1888); it has been augmented slightly over the years, and is the largest collection of its kind in the western hemisphere. I am currently preparing a catalogue of the collection, to be published by Oak Knoll Books; in the meantime, Shirley H. Weber's 'The Vergil Collection in the Princeton University Library: A Check-List and Descriptive Catalogue' (Princeton, 1956) is available from the library, either as a photocopy of the original typescript or in electronic form. An idea of the richness of the collection and the kinds of research questions it can answer may be found in two articles I prepared while working there: 'The *Aeneid* Transformed: Illustration as Interpretation from the Renaissance to the Present', in Sarah Spence (ed.), *Poets and Critics Read Vergil* (New Haven and London: Yale Univ. Press, 2001), 121–48; and 'The Virgilian Title Page as Interpretive Frame, or, Through the Looking Glass', *Princeton University Library Chronicle*, 64 (2002), 15–50.

come to use the editions and commentaries to be found there, the books on which an understanding of the *Aeneid* in this period must be based. Fortunately there are some indications that this situation may be changing. The explosion of interest in the history of the book, for example, is directing attention towards the physical attributes of books that were until recently seen as possessing primarily antiquarian interest, so that these same volumes are now being re-examined with an eye on who owned them, what comments these early owners left in their books, and how the illustrations in early editions help us understand how their texts were envisioned through the ages.[6] Trends in textual studies also offer grounds for hope in that, for some textual scholars at least, emphasis is shifting away from modern critical editions based on reconstructed authorial intention to earlier editions that reflect the production of texts as the result of a series of negotiations that actually took place within a social network of

---

[6] The study that launched book history as a field was Lucien Febvre and Henri-Jean Martin's *L'Apparition du livre* (1958), which has been translated into English as *The Coming of the Book: The Impact of Printing 1450–1800*, tr. David Gerard (London and New York: Verso, 1990); a now-classic orientation to *histoire du livre* may be found in Robert Darnton, 'What Is the History of Books?', *Daedalus*, 111/3 (1982), 65–83, repr. in Cathy N. Davidson (ed.), *Reading in America: Literary and Social History* (Baltimore, Md.: Johns Hopkins Univ. Press, 1989), 27–52. Some recent works that suggest how book history can illuminate some of the issues raised in the present study include Lisa A. Jardine and Anthony Grafton, ' "Studied for Action": How Gabriel Harvey Read his Livy', *Past and Present*, 129 (1990), 30–78; Evelyn B. Tribble, *Margins and Marginality: The Printed Page in Early Modern England* (Charlottesville, Va., and London: Univ. Press of Virginia, 1993); William H. Sherman, *John Dee: The Politics of Reading and Writing in the English Renaissance* (Amherst, Mass.: Univ. of Mass. Press, 1995); Anthony Grafton, *Commerce with the Classics: Ancient Books and Renaissance Readers* (Ann Arbor: Univ. of Mich. Press, 1997); Craig Kallendorf, 'In Search of a Patron: Anguillara's Vernacular Virgil and the Print Culture of Renaissance Italy', *The Papers of the Bibliographical Society of America*, 91 (1997), 294–325; Steven Zwicker, 'Reading the Margins: Politics and the Habits of Appropriation', in Kevin Sharpe and Steven N. Zwicker (eds.), *Refiguring Revolutions: Aesthetics and Politics from the English Revolution to the Romantic Revolution* (Berkeley–Los Angeles: Univ. of California Press, 1998), 101–15; Kevin Sharpe, *Reading Revolutions: The Politics of Reading in Early Modern England* (New Haven: Yale Univ. Press, 2000); and H. T. Jackson, *Marginalia: Readers Writing in Books* (New Haven and London: Yale Univ. Press, 2001). Irving A. Leonard, *Books of the Brave: Being an Account of Books and of Men in the Spanish Conquest and Settlement of the Sixteenth Century New World* (Berkeley–Los Angeles and Oxford: Univ. of California Press, 1949), predates Febvre and Martin's book, but as the introduction to the 1992 repr. by Rolena Adorno suggests Leonard's study is surprisingly relevant to the current critical environment.

authors, editors, and ultimately readers.[7] If these trends continue, we may well be able to recover more of the perspectives that can be found only in the books of eras past.

It also, I believe, makes sense to extend this work to manuscript material, both works that were reproduced in handwritten form and handwritten marginal comments in early printed books. This can be difficult, since there are more copies of most texts that made their way into print than of those that did not. In some cases, as we have seen with the *Sphortias*, not being printed is a sign of failure. Even here, however, the case can be instructive, for as we have seen, Filelfo would have played a very different role in the story told here had his poem been more successful. In other cases, not being printed can reflect a change in taste (i.e. a text that was popular in an earlier period was not judged commercially viable after the invention of printing) or a conscious preference for circulation by manuscript, which in general can be more effectively controlled than circulation in printed format.[8] In a surprising number of cases, however, key data are available only in manuscript, and restricting one's research to books for which modern printed editions exist is to risk telling part, but not all, of a story.

As someone who has done this kind of work myself for many years, I am aware that what I am advocating is not always easy. Let me give an example, one which happens to be relevant to this account of the other Virgil. In November of 2003, I was approached by a prominent rare book dealer in Italy who had for sale a copy of the 1487–8 Florentine edition of Virgil. This is an important, although not especially rare, book, in that it happens to be the first edition of the

[7] The seminal work here is Jerome J. McGann, *A Critique of Modern Textual Criticism* (Chicago: University of Chicago Press, 1983), with support from D. F. McKenzie, *Bibliography and the Sociology of Texts* (London: British Library, 1986). This approach has aroused a great deal of impassioned discussion among bibliographers and textual critics, but has proved difficult to implement in the preparation of edns. in traditional print form. The principles involved are, however, compatible with presentation in computerized format; see e.g. the Cervantes Project of Eduardo Urbina, at http://www.csdl.tamu.edu/cervantes/english/texts.html.

[8] Fundamental work in this area has been done by Margaret J. M. Ezell, who has shown first that women writers, then writers who lived outside big cities, preferred to circulate their works in MS form long after the invention of the printing press. See *The Patriarch's Wife: Literary Evidence and the History of the Family* (Chapel Hill, NC, and London: Univ. of North Carolina Press, 1987), esp. chap. 3, 'Women Writers: Patterns of Manuscript Circulation and Publication', pp. 62–100; and *Social Authorship and the Advent of Print* (Baltimore, Md., and London: Johns Hopkins Univ. Press, 1999).

popular commentary of Cristoforo Landino,[9] and the dealer's copy also contains a handwritten commentary throughout by one Andrea Tordi, an otherwise unknown individual from the area around Florence. The dealer asked me if I would look over the commentary and write something about it, which we could then use to help sell the book. I am interested in commentaries like these, so I spent a week in December going through several hundred pages of Tordi's marginalia on the *Aeneid*. Here and there I found some remarks of some interest, but most of what I read was exactly what I expected, ranging from synonyms for difficult words in the text to grammatical, historical, and mythological explanations of problem areas in the poem. Finally, towards the end of his commentary, Tordi departed from his usual practice and glossed *Aen*. 12. 748, a line in which Aeneas presses the downed Turnus as a hunting dog pursues a wounded stag, by quoting another text that struck him as relevant. The lines he quoted in his gloss were *Orlando furioso*, 2. 9. 7–8, which clearly allude to Virgil even though modern editors of Ariosto seem to have missed the reference.[10] Then in response to the last line of the poem, 'uitaque cum gemitu fugit indignata sub umbras' ('and with a groan, his spirit

[9] The book, which is dated 18 Mar. 1487 (1488 in modern style), is no. 6061 in W. A. Copinger, *Supplement to Hain's Repertorium bibliographicum*, 2 vols. and addenda, part 2 (London: H. Sotheran & Co., 1898–1902); no. 10211 in T. M. Guarnaschelli, E. Valenziani, *et al.*, *Indice generale degli incunaboli delle biblioteche d'Italia*, 6 vols. (Rome: La libreria dello stato, 1943–81); and no. 55 in Giuliano Mambelli, *Gli annali delle edizioni virgiliane* (Florence: Leo Olschki, 1954); it is also recorded in Martin Davies and John Goldfinch, *Vergil: A Census of Printed Editions 1469–1500* (London: Bibliographical Society, 1992), 64 (no. 68), which lists thirty-nine other known copies. Roberto Ridolfi, 'Lo "stampatore del Vergilius, C. 6061" e l'edizione principe di Omero', in *La stampa in Firenze nel secolo XV* (Florence: Leo S. Olschki, 1958), 95–111, assigns this book to an anonymous 'printer of Vergilius', an attribution that is accepted in Dennis Rhodes, *Gli annali tipografici fiorentini del XV secolo* (Florence: Leo S. Olschki, 1988), 120 (no. 773), with illustration no. 30. The copy discussed here is now in the Special Collections Division of the Princeton University Library. On Landino's commentary and its importance, see Craig Kallendorf, *In Praise of Aeneas: Virgil and Epideictic Rhetoric in the Early Italian Renaissance* (Hanover, NH, and London: Univ. Press of New England, 1989), 129–65, with bibliography, 206–16.

[10] Tordi wrote 'e donde l'uno cede laltro vitare [?] immantinente il piede, l'Ariosto' (fo. 67ᵛ), which was intended as a quotation of 'e donde l'uno cede, | l'altro aver posto immantinente il piede' ('and where the one gives way, | the other presses home without delay', *Orlando furioso*, 2. 9. 7–8), which in turn imitates 'trepidique pedem pede feruidus urget' ('he presses on | against his trembling enemy, foot to foot', *Aen*. 12. 748). I am grateful to Albert Ascoli for helping me identify this quotation. Tordi's commentary is discussed at length in Craig Kallendorf, 'Cristoforo Landino, Andrea

fled indignantly to the shades', *Aen.* 12. 952), Tordi suddenly delivered a scathing critique of Aeneas that removes him decisively from the moral world of the schools, writing that Turnus's spirit was indignant 'quia illi mortem deprecante, et victo, ac supplici, ac coniuge spoliato ab Aenea, not esset parcitum: quod victis concedi solet...' ('since he had not spared that man begging to be released from death—something which is customarily granted to the conquered—even though he had been conquered, was a suppliant, and had been deprived of his wife by Aeneas', fo. 70^r; see Figure 12). Thus we see that Tordi saw the same things in the *Aeneid* that Petrarca and Filelfo did, and that he had the *Orlando furioso* in mind as a relevant imitation at this point in his reading. One could argue, I suppose, that this is not much of a reward for the forty hours of reading it took me to get this far in Tordi's commentary, but I would disagree. In these marginalia we have clear evidence of one more reader who went beyond the simplistic reading of the *Aeneid* from his school days, along with some of the support that Sitterson did not have when he claimed that Ariosto read the *Aeneid* through a 'pessimistic' lens.

I also believe this study shows us that we need to become more sophisticated in the way we analyze the relationship between two works of literature. This relationship was traditionally referred to under the rubric 'influence studies' and has long been a standard subject in traditional literary scholarship. As long ago as the 1950s, however, Claudio Guillén argued that influence is an essentially psychological matter that affects the process of literary creativity but not the product, effectively linking it to the intentions of the author.[11] Discussions in this area took a decisive turn in the opposite direction in the 1960s, when Julia Kristeva introduced the term

Tordi, and the Reading Practices of Renaissance Humanism', in Elisabeth Leeker and Joachim Leeker (eds.), *Text, Interpretation, Vergleich: Festschrift für Manfred Lentzen* (Berlin: Erich Schmidt Verlag, 2005), 345–58.

[11] Claudio Guillen, 'The Aesthetics of Influence Studies in Comparative Literature', in W. P. Friederich (ed.), *Comparative Literature: Proceedings of the Second Congress of the ICLA* (Chapel Hill, NC: Univ. of North Carolina Press, 1959), i. 175–93; expanded somewhat in *Literature as System: Essays Toward the Theory of Literary History* (Princeton: Princeton Univ. Press, 1970), 17–52. See also the critique of this essay in Ulrich Weisstein, *Comparative Literature and Literary Theory: Survey and Introduction*, tr. William Riggan (Bloomington and London: Indiana Univ. Press, 1973), 40–7. The effort to locate influence in psychological process ended up in Harold Bloom's *The Anxiety of Influence* (New York: OUP, 1973).

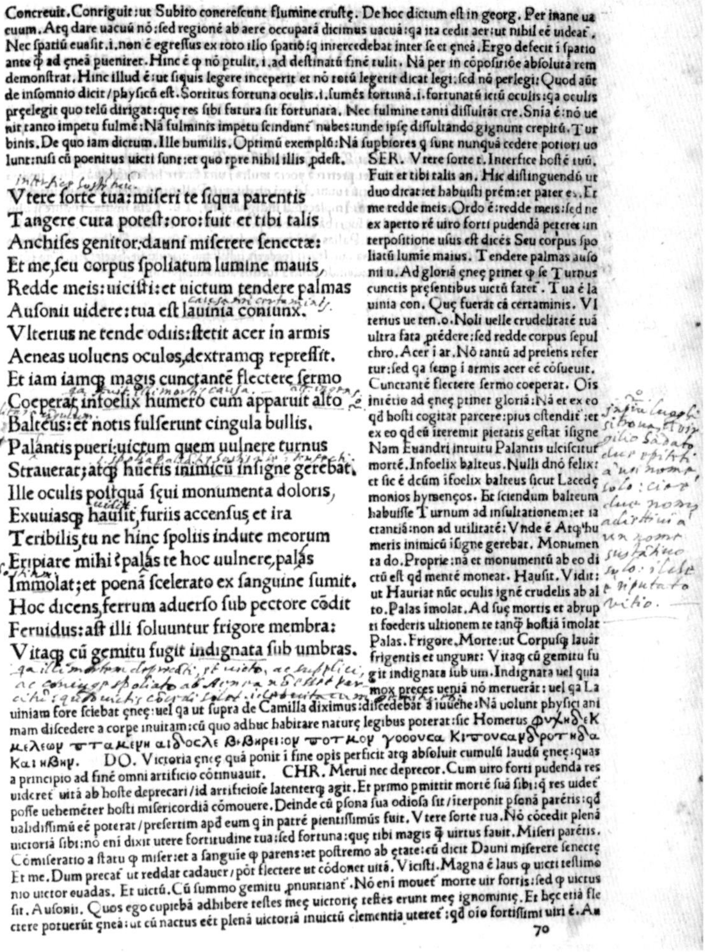
Vtere forte tua: miseri te siqua parentis
Tangere cura potest: oro: fuit et tibi talis
Anchises genitor: dauni miserere senectæ:
Et me, seu corpus spoliatum lumine mauis,
Redde meis: uicisti: et uictum tendere palmas
Ausonii uidere: tua est lauinia coniunx.
Vlterius ne tende odiis: stetit acer in armis
Aeneas uoluens oculos, dextramq; repressit.
Et iam iamq; magis cunctantẽ flectere sermo
Coeperat, infoelix humero cum apparuit alto
Balteus: et notis fulserunt cingula bullis.
Palantis pueri: uictum quem uulnere turnus
Strauerat: atq; humeris inimicũ insigne gerebat.
Ille oculis postquã sæui monumenta doloris,
Exuuiasq; hausit, furiis accensus, et ira
Terribilis, tu ne hinc spoliis indute meorum
Eripiare mihi? palas te hoc uulnere, palas
Immolat: et poenã scelerato ex sanguine sumit.
Hoc dicens, ferrum aduerso sub pectore cõdit
Feruidus: ast illi soluuntur frigore membra:
Vitaq; cũ gemitu fugit indignata sub umbras.

Figure 12. Andrea Tordi's gloss on *Aen.* 12. 748. Virgil, *Opera* (Florence: 'Printer of Vergilius', 1487–8), 70 (Princeton University Library)

'intertextuality' to highlight the relationship between two texts without reference to authorial subjectivity. Structuralist critics helped fill out the implications of this new approach,[12] but among classicists,

[12] Graham Allen, *Intertextuality*, The New Critical Idiom (London and New York: Routledge, 2000).

authorial subjectivity returned through the back door in the work of Gian Biagio Conte, who recognized a reconstructed author writing for an implied reader whose literary experience allowed for the recognition of intertextual references.[13]

More recent work is beginning to acknowledge Martindale's assertion that 'meaning is always constructed at the point of reception'[14] and to privilege the role of the reader in defining the meaning of allusions. A number of poststructuralist responses to intertextuality have focused attention on a reader who in some way or other does more than passively recognize a reference embedded in a text. As early as 1966, Earl Wasserman suggested that allusion 'ought to be defined broadly enough to include a creative act by the reader'; that is, as Joseph Pucci puts it, the reader 'constitutes the allusion' and 'makes meaning'. The reader of an allusion 'configures on his own terms the interpretive outcomes of this connection.... [T]he language of the allusion makes possible but does not determine the creation, function, or conceivable interpretations of the allusion.'[15]

The consequences of this approach depend on something that has been noticed but not adequately explored, the fact that there are two readers operating in allusion: the critic who notices the allusion and the author who wrote it. The alluding author begins the process by reading an earlier text, then working out an interpretation of that text. As he or she begins writing, the new text unfolds in dialogue with the old one, in such a way that the potential meaning of one or more words resonates against their original usage in another text,

---

[13] Gian Biagio Conte, *The Rhetoric of Imitation: Genre and Poetic Memory in Virgil and Other Latin Poets*, ed. and tr. Charles Segal (Ithaca, NY, and London: Cornell Univ. Press, 1986), 23–99.

[14] Charles Martindale, *Redeeming the Text: Latin Poetry and the Hermeneutics of Interpretation* (Cambridge: CUP, 1993), 3. See also Stephen Hinds, *Allusion and Intertext: Dynamics of Appropriation in Roman Poetry* (Cambridge: CUP, 1998), 47–51.

[15] The first quotation is from Earl Wasserman, 'The Limits of Allusion in "The Rape of the Lock"', *Journal of English and Germanic Philology*, 65 (1966), 443–4, qtd. in Joseph Pucci, *The Full-Knowing Reader: Allusion and the Power of the Reader in the Western Literary Tradition* (New Haven and London: Yale Univ. Press, 1998), 22; the following quotations are from the same book, pp. 43 and 36, respectively. See also Don Fowler, 'On the Shoulders of Giants: Intertextuality and Classical Studies', in *Roman Constructions: Readings in Postmodern Latin* (Oxford: OUP, 2000), 115–37; and Lowell Edmunds, *Intertextuality and the Reading of Roman Poetry* (Baltimore, Md., and London: Johns Hopkins Univ. Press, 2001), both of which contain extensive bibliography.

where they meant something that is seen as relevant again. The critic, the second reader, works backwards and recreates this process as he or she is able to understand it, reading the second text and coming to a preliminary idea about what it means, then noticing a relationship to an earlier text that the author could have known, then going back and forth between the two to reconstruct the author's reading of the first text on the basis of the allusions and what they appear to reveal. Schematically the process might be represented like this:

text^1 (T^1)—[reading of author (R-A)]—text^2 (T^2)— reading of critic (R-C)

I have placed R-A in brackets to indicate that it is normally a reconstruction of a reading that is not available in the same way as R-C is. The critic will have his or her own reading of T^1 that may be independent of T^2, and certainly was so before the allusion was noticed, but the recreation of R-A also generates a reading of T^1 through the filter of T^2.

To help explain this model, which is the one that has structured this study, I would suggest four axioms:

1. The active agent in recognizing and interpreting allusion produces R-C and, by extension, R-A, and has to work within the hermeneutic possibilities for T^1 and T^2 as he or she understands them. In other words, R-C is always the result of a critic who is situated, in time and place, as a member of an interpretive community that fosters some hermeneutic options for given texts and discourages, even blocks off, others. The common interpretations of T^1 will foreground some lines and scenes in the mind of the reader-critic, who will be more likely to recognize and attribute meaning to them in T^2 than the lines and scenes from T^1 that are neglected by comparison within his or her interpretive community.[16] Certainty at any stage is therefore impossible, and some allusions identified in R-C must be considered possible allusions only, subject to re-evaluation by different interpretive communities. The situatedness of R-C nevertheless explains at least in part why this study has appeared at this time, for the widespread (although by no means universal) acceptance of the 'pessimistic' approach to the *Aeneid* at the beginning

[16] Pucci, *Full-Knowing Reader*, 44.

of the twenty-first century has emphasized the importance of certain key scenes from the *Aeneid* to me and helped me in turn to recognize imitations of these scenes in the later works written in dialogue with Virgil.

2. R-A is not the product of Iser's implied reader, the appropriate and sympathetic receiver of the cues embedded in T[1] by its author,[17] but is instead a construct that emerges from the recognition of fragments of T[1] in T[2] and the effort of the reader-critic to interpret their significance in T[2] in relation to their original significance in T[1]. Often, especially with older works, this construct is all there is. The recreated reader-author, however, can merge with the author as actual reader if relevant external evidence like criticism of T[1] or a copy of T[1] annotated by the reader-author can be found.[18] In cases like this, the reader-author's actual reading of T[1] provides a check on the constructed R-A, supplementing and, if necessary, correcting the work of the critic.

3. Some allusions will remain local, a fragment of one text embedded in another that serves primarily to enrich verbal texture, but the most richly rewarding allusive contact will be systematic, one of a number of references that contribute substantially to meaning.[19] Classicists have tended to focus on local allusions,[20] but Joseph Farrell uses the relationship between Homer and Virgil to suggest that more attention should be paid to systematic allusions in cases when 'a totalizing relationship' has been created.[21] References that enter an allusive system have the added advantage of the system as a guide to their interpretation—that is, the understanding of any given allusion from T[1] in T[2] can be checked at least in part against the understanding of other allusions from T[1] in R-A for plausibility and coherence. This axiom, as we have seen, proves especially useful in

---

[17] Wolfgang Iser, *The Act of Reading: A Theory of Aesthetic Response* (Baltimore, Md.: Johns Hopkins Univ. Press, 1978), 37–8.

[18] As an example of how this process works, see Hilaire Kallendorf and Craig Kallendorf, 'Conversations with the Dead: Quevedo and Statius, Annotation and Imitation', *Journal of the Warburg and Courtauld Institutes*, 63 (2000), 131–68.

[19] U. J. Hebel, 'Towards a Descriptive Poetics of Allusion', in Heinrich Plett (ed.), *Intertextuality* (Berlin and New York: De Gruyter, 1991), 135–46.

[20] Hinds, *Allusion and Intertext*, 101.

[21] See Edmunds, *Intertextuality*, 154.

trying to provide a larger direction to the mass of references that link
La Araucana and *Paradise Lost* to the *Aeneid*.

4. In allusion meaning flows both chronologically backwards as
well as chronologically forwards.[22] In other words, R-C is created
when the critic reads backwards, first reading T², then T¹ through it.
However R-A is recreated in a reciprocal process by which T¹ and the
critic's provisional understanding of it are pulled forward into T² and
the critic's provisional understanding of it, with both matrices of
meaning being adjusted and readjusted as the critic moves between
the two texts to recreate R-A. Quoting Pope, Wolfgang E. H. Rudat
refers to this as a ' "mutual commerce" between alluding and allusive
contexts, an intense interaction that seems to go both ways'.[23] As we
have seen, this mutual commerce is especially important to the
relationship between the *Aeneid* and *Paradise Lost*, where Aeneas's
failures take on added resonance against the Christian concept of sin,
while Adam and Eve's story becomes even more poignant when we
see it as a rewriting of Aeneas and Dido's.

For writers working in the classical tradition, allusion is an important aesthetic and literary technique. It is also necessary, however, to add a
full accounting of the double reception—that of the modern scholar
and that of the early modern writer—to any list of parallel passages
from a classical text and a later imitation of it in order to capture the
complexity of allusion and its potential for unlocking meaning.

Finally, I would suggest that considerably more work needs to be
done on the relationship between what is done in the schools and
what is produced as 'high culture' by the graduates of those schools.
The model provided by the *Aeneid* and its early modern progeny
suggests that adoption as a school text can become a proverbial two-
edged sword. On the one hand, the fact that every educated person
knew the *Aeneid* for hundreds of years provided opportunities that

[22] Craig Kallendorf, 'Philology, the Reader, and the *Nachleben* of Classical Texts',
Modern Philology, 92 (1994), 137–56; Fowler, 'On the Shoulders', 130.

[23] W. E. H. Rudat, 'Milton's Dido and Aeneas: The Fall in *Paradise Lost* and the
Virgilian Tradition', *Classical and Modern Literature*, 2 (1981), 46. In a stimulating
essay that reached me only after I had finished writing this section, David Quint
makes the same point: 'We can study his [i.e. Milton's] Virgilian imitations not only
to understand *Paradise Lost*, but for the way that they shed light retrospectively on the
Aeneid itself' ('The Virgilian Coordinates of *Paradise Lost*', *Materiali e discussioni per
l'analisi dei testi classici*, 52 (2004), 177).

were fully exploited by writers like Le Plat, who parodied Virgil with the confidence that their work would be understood and appreciated in ways that are simply not possible today. On the other hand, though, the *Aeneid* was such a ubiquitous part of early modern culture that, as late as the 1970s, readers of Shakespeare's *The Tempest* simply failed to see it as the central subtext that it is now widely recognized to be. In other cases, I believe that having left school with a clear interpretation of the *Aeneid* actually impeded the abilities of many readers to recognize a Virgilian imitation that was rooted in an interpretation fundamentally different from what they had been taught, when such an interpretation was worked out by someone like Sor Juana or Joel Barlow who had reason to challenge the traditional understanding of the poem and the imaginative abilities to proceed in unexpected directions. Until we know more, though, about what went on in the early modern schoolroom, we will not be able to recover how those experiences helped shape the literature of the period.

I have saved this final point for last intentionally, because it suggests that the end of a work of scholarship does not necessarily bring closure. I believe that what has been worked out in the preceding chapters offers new insight into early modern culture and, ultimately, into Virgil's poetry as well. But if, as Charles Martindale suggests, the chain of receptions never ends,[24] then new readers will bring new experiences to these texts, see new things there, and write new books and articles about them. But that, I suppose, is the open-ended joy of literary studies in our postmodern age.

[24] Martindale, *Redeeming the Text*, 7–8.

Appendix 1
Manuscripts of Filelfo's *Sphortias*

Since there is considerable confusion about precisely how many manuscripts of the *Sphortias* survive, it is worth sorting this out here. Basic sources, none of which cites all the manuscripts, are: G. Benaducci, 'Contributo alla bibliografia di Francesco Filelfo', in G. Benaducci (ed.), *Atti e memorie della Reale deputazione di storia patria per le provincie delle Marche*, 5 (1901), 461–535; Aristide Calderini, 'I codici milanesi delle opere di Francesco Filelfo', *Archivio storico lombardo*, 42 (1915), 335–411; and Diana Robin, *Filelfo in Milan, Writings 1451–1477* (Princeton: Princeton University Press, 1991), 195–6. The manuscripts, with their current shelf marks and basic bibliography on them, are:

1. Florence, Biblioteca Laurenziana, Plut. 33, 33, 15th cent., containing the first four books of the poem; see A. M. Bandinus, *Catalogus codicum Latinorum Bibliothecae Mediceae Laurentianae*, 5 vols. (Florence: Praesidibus Adventibus, 1774–8), ii, cols. 129–30; Benaducci, 'Contributo', 500 (no. 1); and Calderini, 'I codici', 401 (no. 99).

2. Milan, Biblioteca Ambrosiana, H97 sup., 15th cent., containing eight books with some marginal annotations; see Benaducci, 'Contributo', 500 (no. 1); and Calderini, 'I codici', 343–4 (no. 19).

3. Milan, Biblioteca Ambrosiana, R12 sup., 15th cent., containing eight books; see Benaducci, 'Contributo', 500 (no. 1); and Calderini, 'I codici', 343 (no. 18).

4. Milan, Biblioteca Trivulziana, 731 (C 72), 15th cent., containing eight books with marginal annotations and Filelfo's arms; see Giulio Porro, *Catalogo dei codici manoscritti della Trivulziana*, Biblioteca storica italiana pubblicata per cura della Reale deputazione di storia patria, 2 (Turin: Fratelli Bocca, 1884), 345–6; Calderini, 'I codici', 378–9 (no. 43); Franco Catalano, 'La nuova signoria: Francesco Sforza', in *Storia di Milano*, vii. *L'età sforzesca dal 1450 al 1500* (Milan: Fondazione Treccani degli Alfieri, 1956), 32 (illustration); Caterina Santoro, *I codici miniati della Biblioteca Trivulziana* (Milan: Comune di Milano, 1958), 31 (no. 32); eadem, *I tesori della Trivulziana: La storia del libro dal secolo VIII al secolo XVIII* (Milan: Biblioteca Trivulziana, 1962), 10 (pl. 9); eadem, *I codici medioevali della Biblioteca Trivulziana* (Milan: Biblioteca Trivulziana, 1965), 170–1 (no. 278); L. Firpo

(ed.), *Francesco Filelfo educatore e il 'Codice Sforza' della Biblioteca reale di Torino* (Turin: Unione tipografico-Editrice torinese, 1967), 85 (illus.); Élisabeth Pellegrin, *La Bibliothèque des Visconti et des Sforza, ducs de Milan, supplement...* (Florence: Leo S. Olschki, and Paris: F. de Nobele, 1969), 41 (no. 174); and Albinia C. de la Mare, 'Script and Manuscripts in Milan under the Sforzas', in *Milano nell'età di Ludovico il Moro*, Atti del convegno internazionale, 28 febbraio–4 marzo 1983, 2 vols. (Milan: Comune di Milano, 1983), 405 (pl.) and 407 n. 49.

5. Paris, Bibliothèque nationale de France, Ms. lat. 8125, 15th cent., written by Fabricius Elphistheus with the arms of Filelfo and of Alfonso of Calabria, the Aragonese prince of Naples; see *Catalogus codicum manuscriptorum Bibliothecae Regiae*, pt. 3 (Paris: Typographia regia, 1744), iv: 430; Giuseppe Mazzatinti, *La biblioteca dei re d'Aragona in Napoli* (Rocca S. Casciano: L. Capelli, 1897), 26 (no. 38); Calderini, 'I codici', 402 (no. 99); T. De Marinis, *Le biblioteca napoletana dei re d'Aragona* (Milan: Hoepli, 1947), 2: 74 and pl. 101; C. Samaran and R. Marichal (eds.), *Catalogue des manuscrits en écriture latine portant des indications de date, de lieu ou de copiste*, 4 vols. (Paris: Centre national de la recherche scientifique, 1959–81), iii/1 (texte), p. 616; and Pellegrin, *La bibliothèque... supplement*, 41 (no. 174).

6. Paris, Bibliothèque nationale de France, Ms. lat. 8126, 15th cent., containing eight books with marginal annotations, copied by Paganus Raudensis and containing the arms of Filelfo and Francesco Sforza; see *Catalogus... Bibliothecae Regiae*, pt. 3, iv. 430; Léopold Delisle, *Le Cabinet des manuscrits de la Bibliothèque impériale*, 3 vols. (Paris: Imprimerie impériale, 1868–81), i. 127 and 132–3; Benaducci, 'Contributo', 500 (no. 1); Calderini, 'I codici', 402 (no. 99); Elisabeth Pellegrin, *La Bibliothèque des Visconti et des Sforza ducs de Milan au XVe siècles*, Publications de l'Institut de recherche et d'histoire des textes, 5 (Paris: Centre national de la recherche scientifique, 1955), 336 (C. 40); Samaran and Marichal (eds.), *Catalogue des manuscrits*, iii/1 (texte), p. 15 and iii/2 (planches), pl. CLXVIII; Pellegrin, *La Bibliothèque... supplement*, 41 and pl. 129; and de la Mare, 'Script and Manuscripts', 402 n. 24.

7. Rome, Biblioteca Casanatense, 415 (C.III.9), 15th cent., containing fragments of books 1–11 with marginal annotations; see Benaducci, 'Contributo', 500 (no. 1); G. Giri, 'Il codice autografo della Sforziade di Francesco Filelfo', in G. Benaducci (ed.), *Atti e memorie*, 420–57; D. Fava, *Mostra di codici autografi in onore di Girolamo Tiraboschi nel II centenario della nascita* (Modena: Società Tipografica Modenese, 1932), 52 (no. 82); and Ministero della pubblica istruzione, *Indici e cataloghi*, NS ii. *Catalogo dei manoscritti della Biblioteca Casanatense* (Rome: Ministero della pubblica istruzione, 1958), v. 37.

8. Vatican City, Biblioteca Apostolica Vaticana, Vat. lat. 2921, containing four books; see Benaducci, 'Contributo', 500 (no. 1).

9. Venice, Biblioteca Nazionale Marciana, Lat. XIV, 262 (4719), a miscellany of the 15th–16th cents. that includes extracts from book 4; see Benaducci, 'Contributo', 500 (no. 1).

Of these manuscripts, nos. 1, 2, 4, and 7 have been considered autographs by one or more of those who have looked at them. Paris, Bibliothèque nationale de France, Ms. lat. 8128, identified by De la Mare, 'Script and Manuscripts', 407 n. 49, as a copy of the *Sphortias*, perhaps in Filelfo's hand, does not in fact contain this poem.

Appendix 2
Filelfo's Virgilian Studies

The manuscript containing Filelfo's lecture notes (see at Ch. 1 n. 58) is Vatican City, Biblioteca Apostolica Vaticana, Chigi H.IV.99, with the notes on fos. 133^r–8^r; a full description of the manuscript may be found in E. Pellegrin *et al.*, *Les Manuscrits classiques latins de la Bibliothèque Vaticane,* i. *Fondo archivio San Pietro à Ottoboni* (Paris: Éditions du Centre national de la recherche scientifique, 1975), i. 268–9.

Several other manuscripts that shed some light on Filelfo's Virgilian studies have survived. First, Vatican City, Biblioteca Apostolica Vaticana, Barb. lat. 134 (IX 3), a 15th-century manuscript of the *Eclogues*, contains glosses attributed to Filelfo (Benadduci, 'Contributo', 500 (no. 11); Calderini, 'I codici milanesi', 398 (no. 68); and Bianchi, 'Note', 333 n. 28). Next, a copy of Servius (now the property of a private owner) shows that Filelfo's interest in Virgil and Virgilian scholarship extended well past Francesco Sforza's death. Copied for Gian Galeazzo Sforza when he was Duke of Milan (1476–81) from Petrarca's Servius (now Milan, Biblioteca Ambrosiana, S.P. Arm. 10, scaf. 27), or at least corrected from it, this manuscript is in the hand of Filelfo himself or someone whose hand is modelled on his; see de la Mare, 'Scripts and Manuscripts', 407; descriptions of the manuscript are in the Sotheby's sale catalogue, *Catalogue of T. E. Marston Sale* (London, 1961), lot 195 and pl. 25; Elisabeth Pellegrin, *La Bibliothèque des Visconti et des Sforza*, Supplément (Florence: Leo S. Olschki, 1969), 50–1; and the Sotheby's sale catalogue, *Western Manuscripts and Miniatures* (London, Tuesday 23 June 1998), 75–81 (lot 57). Finally, Vatican City, Bibliotheca Apostolica Vaticana, Vat. lat. 3251 is a copy of Virgil with the commentary of Servius that Filelfo had owned. It contains a few verses from Greek authors added in his hand; see Pierre de Nolhac, *La Bibliothèque de Fulvio Orsini* (Paris: F. Vieweg, 1887), 195. (I am grateful to Peter K. Marshall and Virginia Brown for some of this information.) Unfortunately, therefore, we do not have a true commentary by Filelfo on the whole of the *Aeneid*.

Such commentaries are lacking for many other ancient authors as well, which has led Aristide Calderini, 'Ricerche intorno alla bibliotheca e alla cultura greca di Francesco Filelfo', *Studi italiani di filologia classica*, 20 (1913), to claim that Filelfo's learning was surprisingly shallow, that he owned many books he never read, or never read completely through, or never drew from in his own writings (418), a claim that Garin picks up and expands on ('L'opera', 549). This claim is curiously at odds with Filelfo's reputation in his own day, in that his contemporaries often disliked him personally but generally respected his learning; the tension between the two perspectives emerges in Symonds's comment that Filelfo's works were 'ridiculously over-valued then, and now perhaps too readily depreciated' (*Revival*, 209). It would probably be fairer to note that different humanists worked in different ways, and that the evidence presented in Chapter 1 makes it clear that Filelfo read the *Aeneid* very carefully indeed, even if modern scholars are unable to retrieve a commentary like, say, the one in the famous Ambrosian Virgil (Milan, Biblioteca Ambrosiana, A 79 inf.), published in a facsimile edn. by J. Galbiati, *Francisci Petrarcae Vergilianus codex... in lucem editus* (Milan: U. Hoepli, 1930), with discussion by G. Ravesi in *Vedere i classici*, exhibition catalogue (Vatican City: Biblioteca Apostolica Vaticana, 1996), 257–9 (no. 46), with bibliography; and *Codex: i tesori della Biblioteca Ambrosiana* (Milan: Rizzoli, 2000), 134–5 (no. 77), which Petrarca worked on for thirty-six years (A. Petrucci, *La scrittura di Francesco Petrarca* (Vatican City: Biblioteca Apostolica Vaticana, 1967), 39–51).

Select Bibliography

Adam, Rudolf Georg, 'Francesco Filelfo at the Court of Milan (1439–1481): A Contribution to the Study of Humanism in Northern Italy', Ph.D. thesis (University of Oxford, 1974).

Adorno, Rolena, 'Literary Production and Suppression: Reading and Writing about Amerindians in Colonial Spanish America', *Dispositio*, 11/28–9 (1985), 1–25.

Allen, Graham, *Intertextuality: The New Critical Idiom* (London and New York: Routledge, 2000).

Armitage, David, Armand Himy, and Quentin Skinner (eds.), *Milton and Republicanism* (Cambridge: Cambridge University Press, 1995).

Barker, Arthur, 'Structural Pattern in *Paradise Lost*', *Philological Quarterly*, 28 (1949), 17–30.

Barlow, Joel, *The Vision of Columbus: A Poem in Nine Books* (Hartford, Conn.: Hudson & Goodwin, 1787).

—— *The Columbiad, a Poem* (Philadelphia: Fry & Kammerer, for C. and A. Conrad & Co., Philadelphia, and Conrad, Lucas, & Co., Baltimore, Md., 1807).

Bentley, Richard, *Milton's Paradise Lost* (London: Jacob Tonson, 1732).

Bianchi, Rossella, 'Note de Francesco Filelfo al "De natura deorum," al "De oratore," e all' "Eneide" negli appunti di un notaio senese', in *Francesco Filelfo nel quinto centenario*, 325–68.

Blessington, Francis C., *'Paradise Lost' and the Classical Epic* (Boston: Routledge & Kegan Paul, 1979).

Bottari, Guglielmo, 'La "Sphortias"', in *Francesco Filelfo nel quinto centenario*, 459–93.

Bowra, C. M., *From Virgil to Milton* (London: Macmillan, 1948).

Boys, John, *Aeneas, His Descent into Hell...* (London: Printed for the Author, 1661).

—— *Aeneas, His Errours, or his Voyage from Troy into Italy...* (London: Printed by T. M. for Henry Broome, 1661).

Brotton, J., '"This Tunis, sir, was Carthage": Contesting Colonialism in *The Tempest*', in Ania Loomba and Martin Orkin (eds.), *Post-Colonial Shakespeares* (London and New York: Routledge, 1998), 23–42.

Buell, Lawrence, *New England Literary Culture: From Revolution through Renaissance*, Cambridge Studies in American Literature and Culture (Cambridge: Cambridge University Press, 1986).

Burrow, Colin, 'Virgil in English Translation', in Martindale (ed.), *The Cambridge Companion to Virgil*, 21–37.

—— 'Virgils: From Dante to Milton', in Martindale (ed.), *The Cambridge Companion to Virgil*, 79–90.

Carnicelli, D. D., 'The Widow and the Phoenix: Dido, Carthage, and Tunis in *The Tempest*', *Harvard Library Bulletin*, 27 (1979), 389–443.

Certeau, Michel de, *The Practice of Everyday Life*, tr. Steven Rendall (Berkeley–Los Angeles, Calif., and London: University of California Press, 1984).

—— *Heterologies: Discourses on the Other*, tr. Brian Massumi, Theory and History of Literature, 17 (Minneapolis: University of Minnesota Press, 1986).

Chartier, Roger, *The Cultural Origins of the French Revolution*, tr. Lydia G. Cochrane (Durham, NC, and London: Duke University Press, 1991).

—— *On the Edge of the Cliff: History, Language, and Practices*, tr. Lydia G. Cochrane (Baltimore, Md., and London: Johns Hopkins University Press, 1997).

Clark, Elizabeth A., *History, Theory, Text: Historians and the Linguistic Turn* (Cambridge, Mass.: Harvard University Press, 2004).

Clarke, M. L., *Classical Education in Britain 1500–1900* (Cambridge: Cambridge University Press, 1959).

Cohen, Walter, 'The Discourse of Empire in the Renaissance', in Marina S. Brownlee and Hans Ulrich Gumbrecht (eds.), *Cultural Authority in Golden Age Spain*, Parallex Series (Baltimore, Md. and London: Johns Hopkins University Press, 1995), 260–83.

—— 'The Literature of the Empire in the Renaissance', *Modern Philology*, 102 (2004), 1–34.

Connolly, Joy, 'Border Wars: Literature, Politics, and the Public', *Transactions of the American Philological Association*, 135 (2005), 103–34.

Conte, Gian Biagio, *The Rhetoric of Imitation: Genre and Poetic Memory in Virgil and Other Latin Poets*, ed. and trans. Charles Segal (Ithaca, N.Y. and London: Cornell University Press, 1986).

Cristóbal, Vicente, 'De la *Eneida* a la *Araucana*', *Cuadernos de filología clásica, estudios latinos*, 9 (1995), 67–101.

de la Cruz Juana Inés, *Obras completas*, 4 vols. (Mexico: Fondo de Cultura Economica, 1951–7).

Darnton, Robert, *The Forbidden Best-Sellers of Pre-Revolutionary France* (New York, N.Y. and London: W. W. Norton, 1995).

Davies, Stevie, *Images of Kingship in Paradise Lost: Milton's Politics and Christian Liberty* (Columbia, Mo.: University of Missouri Press, 1983).

Davis, Elizabeth B., *Myth and Identity in the Epic of Imperial Spain* (Columbia, Mo. and London: University of Missouri Press, 2000).

Desmond, Marilyn, *Reading Dido: Gender, Textuality, and the Medieval Aeneid*, Medieval Cultures, 8 (Minneapolis: University of Minnesota Press, 1994).

Eckmann, Sonja, 'Das Aeneis-Supplement der Pier Candido Decembrio: Die pessimistische "Stimme" der Aeneis?', *Neulateinisches Jahrbuch*, 4 (2002), 55–88.

Edmunds, Lowell, *Intertextuality and the Reading of Roman Poetry* (Baltimore, Md., and London: Johns Hopkins University Press, 2001).

Elliott, Emory, *Revolutionary Writers: Literature and Authority in the New Republic, 1725–1810* (New York: Oxford University Press, 1982).

Ercilla, Alonso de, *The Araucaniad*, tr. Charles Maxwell Lancaster and Paul Thomas Manchester (Nashville, Tenn.: Vanderbilt University Press, 1945).

—— *La Araucana*, ed. Isaías Lerner (Madrid: Cátedra, 1993).

Erskine-Hill, Howard, *Poetry and the Realm of Politics: Shakespeare to Dryden* (Oxford: Clarendon Press, 1996).

Foucault, Michel, 'Discourse on Language', appendix in *The Archaeology of Knowledge*, tr. A. M. Sheridan Smith (New York: Harper & Row, 1972), 215–37.

—— *Power/Knowledge: Selected Interviews and Other Writings 1972–1977*, ed. Colin Gordon, tr. Colin Gordon, Leo Marshall, John Mepham, and Kate Soper (New York: Pantheon Books, 1980).

—— *Discipline and Punish: The Birth of the Prison*, tr. Alan Sheridan (New York: Random House/Vintage Books, 1991).

—— *Power*, ed. James D. Faubion, tr. Robert Hurley *et al.*, Essential Works of Foucault, 1954–1984, 3 (New York: New Press, 2000).

Fowler, Don, 'Deviant Focalization in Vergil's *Aeneid*', in *Roman Constructions: Readings in Postmodern Latin* (Oxford: Oxford University Press, 2000), 40–63.

Francisco Filelfo nel quinto centenario della morte, Atti del XVII Convegno di Studi Maceratesi (Tolentino, 27–30 settembre 1981) (Padua: Antenore, 1986).

Fuchs, Barbara, *Mimesis and Empire: The New World, Islam, and European Identities* (Cambridge: Cambridge University Press, 2001).

Galinsky, Karl, *Augustan Culture: An Interpretive Introduction* (Princeton: Princeton University Press, 1996).

Garin, Eugenio, 'L'opera di Francesco Filelfo', in *Storia di Milano*, vii. *L'età sforzesca dal 1450 al 1500* (Milan: Fondazione Treccani degli Alfieri, 1956), 541–61.

Giustiniani, Vito R., 'Il Filelfo, l'interpretazione allegorica di Virgilio e la tripartizione platonica dell'anima', in *Umanesimo e Rinascimento, studi offerti a Paul Oskar Kristeller*, Biblioteca de 'Lettere italiane', Studi e testi, 24 (Florence: Leo S. Olschki, 1980), 333–44.

Graff, Gerald, and James Phelan (eds.), *William Shakespeare The Tempest: A Case Study in Critical Controversy* (Boston and New York: Bedford/St. Martin's, 2000).

Grafton, Anthony, with April Shelford and Nancy Siraisi, *New Worlds, Ancient Texts: The Power of Tradition and the Shock of Discovery* (Cambridge, Mass., and London: Harvard University Press, 1992).

Greenblatt, Stephen, *Shakespearean Negotiations: The Circulation of Social Energy in Renaissance England* (Berkeley–Los Angeles: University of California Press, 1988).

—— 'Learning to Curse: Aspects of Linguistic Colonialism in the Sixteenth Century', in *Learning to Curse: Essays in Early Modern Culture* (New York and London: Routledge, 1990), 16–39.

—— *Marvelous Possessions: The Wonder of the New World* (Chicago: University of Chicago Press, 1991).

—— (ed.), *New World Encounters.* A Representations Book (Berkeley–Los Angeles and London: University of California Press, 1993).

—— and Catherine Gallagher, *Practicing New Historicism* (Chicago and London: University of Chicago Press, 2000).

Greene, Roland, *Unrequited Conquests: Love and Empire in the Colonial Americas* (Chicago: University of Chicago Press, 1999).

Haase, Wolfgang, and Meyer Reinhold (eds.), *The Classical Tradition and the Americas*, i. *European Images of the Americas and the Classical Tradition* (Berlin and New York: Walter de Gruyter, 1994).

Hale, John K., '*Paradise Lost*: Twelve Books or Ten?', *Philological Quarterly*, 74 (1995), 131–49.

Hamilton, Donna B., *Virgil and The Tempest: The Politics of Imitation* (Columbus, Ohio: Ohio State University Press, 1990).

Harding, Davis, *The Club of Hercules: Studies in the Classical Background of Paradise Lost* (Urbana, Ill.: University of Illinois Press, 1962).

Harrison, S. J., 'Some Views of the *Aeneid* in the Twentieth Century', in S. J. Harrison (ed.), *Oxford Readings in Vergil's Aeneid* (Oxford: Clarendon Press, 1990), 1–20.

Hill, Christopher, *Milton and the English Revolution* (London: Faber & Faber, 1977).

Hinds, Stephen, *Allusion and Intertext: Dynamics of Appropriation in Roman Poetry* (Cambridge: Cambridge University Press, 1998).

Howard, Leon, *The Connecticut Wits* (Chicago: University of Chicago Press, 1943).

Hulme, Peter, *Colonial Encounters: Europe and the Native Caribbean, 1492–1797* (New York and London: Methuen, 1986).

—— and William H. Sherman (eds.), *'The Tempest' and Its Travels* (Philadelphia: University of Pennsylvania Press, 2000).

Hume, P. (ed.), *The Poetical Works of John Milton* (London: Jacob Tonson, 1695).

Ianziti, Gary, *Humanistic Historiography under the Sforzas: Politics and Propaganda in Fifteenth-Century Milan* (Oxford: Clarendon Press, 1988).

James, Heather, *Shakespeare's Troy: Drama, Politics, and the Translation of Empire*, Cambridge Studies in Renaissance Literature and Culture, 22 (Cambridge: Cambridge University Press, 1997).

Kallendorf, Craig, *In Praise of Aeneas: Virgil and Epideictic Rhetoric in the Early Italian Renaissance* (Hanover, NH, and London: University Press of New England, 1989); Spanish trans.: *Elogio de Eneas: Virgilio y la Retórica Epideíctica en el Temprano Renacimiento Italiano*, tr. Susana Cella (Santiago, Chile: RIL Editores, 2005).

—— 'Historicizing the "Harvard School": Pessimistic Readings of the *Aeneid* in Italian Renaissance Scholarship', *Harvard Studies in Classical Philology*, 99 (1999), 391–403.

—— 'The *Aeneid* Transformed: Illustration as Interpretation from the Renaissance to the Present', in Sarah Spence (ed.), *Poets and Critics Read Virgil* (New Haven and London: Yale University Press, 2001), 121–48.

—— 'Enea nel "Nuovo Mondo": il *Columbeis* di Stella e il pessimismo virgiliano', *Studi umanistici piceni*, 23 (2003), 241–51.

—— 'Cristoforo Landino, Andrea Tordi, and the Reading Practices of Renaissance Humanism', in Elizabeth Leeker and Joachim Leeker (eds.), *Text, Interpretation, Vergleich: Festschrift für Manfred Lentzen* (Berlin: Erich Schmidt Verlag, 2005), 345–58.

Kinney, Arthur F., and Dan S. Collins (eds.), *Renaissance Historicism: Selections from English Literary Renaissance* (Amherst, Mass.: University of Massachusetts Press, 1987).

Kott, Jan, 'The *Aeneid* and *The Tempest*', *Arion*, ns 3 (1976), 424–51.

Le Plat du Temple, Victor Alexandre Chrétien, *Virgile en France...*, 2 vols. (Brussels: Weissenbruch, 1807–8).

Lida de Malkiel, María Rosa, *Dido en la literatura española: Su retrato y defensa* (London: Tamesis, 1974).

Lupher, David A., *Romans in a New World: Classical Models in Sixteenth-Century Spanish America* (Ann Arbor: University of Michigan Press, 2003).

Lyne, R. O. A. M., *Further Voices in Vergil's Aeneid* (Oxford: Oxford University Press, 1987).

McManamon, James Edmond, 'Echoes of Virgil and Lucan in the *Araucana*', Ph.D. thesis (Illinois, 1955).

McWilliams, John P., Jr., *The American Epic: Transforming a Genre 1770–1860* (Cambridge: Cambridge University Press, 1989).

Mambelli, Giuliano, *Gli annali delle edizioni virgiliane*, Biblioteca di bibliografia italiana, 27 (Florence: Leo S. Olschki, 1954).

Martindale, Charles, *Redeeming the Text: Latin Poetry and the Hermeneutics of Reception*, Roman Literature and Its Contexts (Cambridge: Cambridge University Press, 1993).

—— (ed.), *The Cambridge Companion to Virgil* (Cambridge: Cambridge University Press, 1997).

—— *John Milton and the Transformation of Ancient Epic*, 2nd edn. (London: Duckworth, 2002).

—— and Richard Thomas (eds.), *Classics and the Uses of Reception* (Oxford: Blackwell, 2006).

Mignolo, Walter, 'The Darker Side of the Renaissance: Colonization and the Discontinuity of the Classical Tradition', *Renaissance Quarterly*, 45 (1992), 808–28.

—— *The Darker Side of the Renaissance: Literacy, Territoriality, and Colonization* (Ann Arbor: University of Michigan Press, 1995).

Milton, John, *Complete Poems and Major Prose*, ed. Merritt Y. Hughes (Indianapolis: Odyssey Press, 1957).

Newton, Thomas, *Paradise Lost. A poem in twelve books…*, 2 vols. (London: For J. and R. Tonson & S. Draper…, 1750).

Nicolopulos, James, *The Poetics of Empire in the Indies: Prophecy and Imitation in La Araucana and Os Lusiadas* (University Park, Penn.: Pennsylvania State University Press, 2000).

Norbrook, David, *Writing the English Republic: Poetry, Rhetoric and Politics 1627–1660* (Cambridge: Cambridge University Press, 1999).

Nosworthy, J. M., 'The Narrative Sources of *The Tempest*', *Review of English Studies*, 24 (1948), 281–94.

Novara, A., 'Un poema latino del quattrocento: *La Sforziade* di Francesco Filelfo', *Rivista ligura di scienze, lettere ed arti*, 28 (1906), 3–27.

O'Gorman, Edmundo, *The Invention of America: An Enquiry into the Historical Nature of the New World and the Meaning of Its History* (Bloomington, Ind.: Indiana University Press, 1961).

Pastor Bodmer, Beatriz, *The Armature of Conquest: Spanish Accounts of the Discovery of America, 1492–1589*, tr. Lydia Longstreth Hunt (Stanford, Calif.: Stanford University Press, 1992).

Patterson, Annabel, *Censorship and Interpretation: The Conditions of Writing and Reading in Early Modern England*, rev. edn. (Madison: University of Wisconsin Press, 1984).

—— *Pastoral and Ideology: Virgil to Valéry* (Berkeley–Los Angeles: University of California Press, 1987).

Paz, Octavio, *Sor Juana Inés de la Cruz o las trampas de la fe* (Barcelona: Seix Barral, 1982).

Pearcy, Lee, *The Grammar of Our Civility: Classical Education in America* (Waco, Tex.: Baylor University Press, 2006).

Pitcher, John, 'A Theatre of the Future: *The Aeneid* and *The Tempest*', *Essays in Criticism*, 34 (1984), 193–215.

Porter, William, *Reading the Classics and Paradise Lost* (Lincoln, Neb., and London: University of Nebraska Press, 1993).

Pucci, Joseph, *The Full-Knowing Reader: Allusion and the Power of the Reader in the Western Literary Tradition* (New Haven and London: Yale University Press, 1998).

Putnam, Michael C. J., *The Poetry of the Aeneid: Four Studies in Imaginative Unity and Design* (Cambridge, Mass.: Harvard University Press, 1965).

Quint, David, *Epic and Empire: Politics and Generic Form from Virgil to Milton* (Princeton: Princeton University Press, 1993).

—— 'The Virgilian Coordinates of *Paradise Lost*', *Materiali e discussioni per l'analisi dei testi classici*, 52 (2004), 177–97.

Radzinowicz, Mary Ann, 'The Politics of *Paradise Lost*', in Kevin Sharpe and Steven N. Zwicker (eds.), *Politics of Discourse: The Literature and History of Seventeenth-Century England* (Berkeley–Los Angeles and London: University of California Press, 1987), 204–29.

Reinhard, Wolfgang (ed.), *Humanismus und Neue Welt*, Deutsche Forschungsgemeinschaft, Kommission für Humanismusforschung, 15 (Weinheim: VCH Verlagsgesellschaft, 1987).

Reinhold, Meyer, *Classica Americana: The Greek and Roman Heritage in the United States* (Detroit: Wayne State University Press, 1984).

Richard, Carl J., *The Founders and the Classics: Greece, Rome, and the American Enlightenment* (Cambridge, Mass., and London: Harvard University Press, 1994).

Robin, Diana, *Filelfo in Milan: Writings 1451–1477* (Princeton: Princeton University Press, 1991).

Rosmini, Carlo De', *Vita di Francesco Filelfo da Tolentino*, 3 vols. (Milan: Muigi Mussi, 1808).

Ryan, Michael T., 'Assimilating New Worlds in the Sixteenth and Seventeenth Centuries', *Comparative Studies in Society and History*, 23 (1981), 519–38.

Said, Edward, *Orientalism* (New York: Vintage Books/Random House, 1979).

—— *Culture and Imperialism* (New York: Vintage Books/Random House, 1994).

Schmidgall, Gary, *Shakespeare and the Courtly Aesthetic* (Berkeley–Los Angeles and London: University of California Press, 1981).

Seem, Lauren Scancarelli, 'The Limits of Chivalry: Tasso and the End of the *Aeneid*', *Comparative Literature*, 42 (1990), 116–25.

Shakespeare, William, *The Tempest*, ed. Frank Kermode, The Arden Shakespeare (London: Methuen, 1954).

Shields, John C., *The American Aeneas: Classical Origins of the American Self* (Knoxville, Tenn.: University of Tennessee Press, 2001).

Sitterson, Joseph C., Jr., 'Allusive and Elusive Meanings: Reading Ariosto's Vergilian Ending', *Renaissance Quarterly*, 45 (1992), 1–20.

Skura, Meredith Ann, 'Discourse and the Individual: The Case of Colonialism in *The Tempest*', *Shakespeare Quarterly*, 40 (1989), 42–69.

Smith, Nigel, *Literature and Revolution in England, 1640–1680* (New Haven and London: Yale University Press, 1994).

Stray, Christopher, *Classics Transformed: Schools, Universities, and Society in England, 1830–1960* (Oxford: Clarendon Press, 1998).

Stubbs, H. W., 'Vergil's Harpies: A Study in *Aeneid* III (with an Addendum on Lycophron, *Alexandra* 1250–2)', *Vergilius*, 44 (1998), 3–12.

Thomas, Richard, *Virgil and the Augustan Reception* (Cambridge: Cambridge University Press, 2001).

Todd, Charles Burr, *Life and Letters of Joel Barlow, LL.D.* (New York: Da Capo Press, 1970; repr. of New York and London, 1886 edn.).

Todd, Henry J., *The Poetical Works of John Milton. With notes of various authors . . .*, 2nd edn., 7 vols. (London: J. Johnson *et al.*, 1809).

Todorov, Tzvetan, *The Conquest of America: The Question of the Other*, tr. Richard Howard (New York: Harper Collins, 1984).

Tudeau-Clayton, Margaret, *Jonson, Shakespeare and Early Modern Virgil* (Cambridge: Cambridge University Press, 1998).

Veeser, H. Aram (ed.), *The New Historicism* (New York: Routledge, 1989).

Vegio, Maffeo, *Short Epics*, ed. and tr. Michael C. J. Putnam, with James Hankins, I Tatti Renaissance Library, 15 (Cambridge, Mass.: Harvard University Press, 2004).

Venuti, Lawrence, 'The Destruction of Troy: Translation and Royalist Cultural Politics in the Interregnum', *Journal of Medieval and Renaissance Studies*, 23 (1993), 197–219.

Verbart, A., *Fellowship in Paradise Lost: Vergil, Milton, Wordsworth*, Costerus New Series, 97 (Amsterdam and Atlanta, Ga.: Rodopi, 1995).

Waquet, Françoise, *Latin or the Empire of a Sign: From the Sixteenth to the Twentieth Centuries*, tr. John Howe (London and New York: Verso, 2001).

Waswo, Richard, *The Founding Legend of Western Civilization: From Virgil to Vietnam* (Hanover, NH, and London: University Press of New England, for Wesleyan University Press, 1997).

White, Hayden, *Tropics of Discourse: Essays in Cultural Criticism* (Baltimore, Md.: Johns Hopkins University Press, 1978).

Wilson, Hugh, 'The Publication of *Paradise Lost*, the Occasion of the First Edition: Censorship and Resistance', *Milton Studies*, 37 (1999), 18–41.

Wilson-Okamura, David Scott, 'Virgilian Models of Colonization in Shakespeare's *Tempest*', *ELH* 70 (2003), 709–37.

Wiltenburg, Robert, 'The "Aeneid" in "The Tempest"', *Shakespeare Survey*, 39 (1987), 159–68.

Winterer, Caroline, *The Culture of Classicism: Ancient Greece and Rome in American Intellectual Life, 1780–1910* (Baltimore, Md., and London: Johns Hopkins University Press, 2002).

Woodress, James, *A Yankee's Odyssey: The Life of Joel Barlow* (Philadelphia and New York: J. B. Lippincott, 1958).

Zabus, Chantal, *Tempests after Shakespeare* (New York and Houndmills: Palgrave, 2002).

Index

Index Locorum